SOUTHERN ILLINOIS UNIVERSITY PRESS
Carbondale and Edwardsville

Textual Carnivals

The Politics of Composition

Susan Miller

Edited by Dan Gunter
Designed by D.E. Perkins
Production supervised by Natalia Nadraga

Paperback edition, 1993
96 95 94 93   4 3 2 1

Library of Congress Cataloging-in-Publication Data

Miller, Susan, 1942–
    Textual carnivals: the politics of composition / Susan Miller.
      p.   cm.
    Includes bibliographical references.
    1. English language—Rhetoric—Study and teaching—Political
aspects— United States. 2. English philology—Studying and teaching
(Higher)—Political aspects—United States. 3. English language—
Composition and exercises—Study and teaching—Political aspects—
United States.   I. Title.
PE1405.U6M55   1991
808'.042—dc20   90-34244
                                                              CIP

ISBN 0-8093-1922-5 (pbk.)

The paper used in this publication meets the minimum requirements of
American National Standard for Information Sciences Permanence
of Paper for Printed Library Materials, ANSI Z39.48-1984. ∞

For

my mother, Margretta Boose Miller Bowers,
who promised herself that I would never be afraid of anything,
and for friends in Utah who help me contain her hope

Contents

Preface

This book began to write itself as I composed *Rescuing the Subject*, a slightly earlier study of relations among historically described writers, their discrete writing technologies, historical rhetoric, and the "composition" I have taken as my topic now. As I attempted to theorize that history and its consequences for student writers in what was at bottom a call to acknowledge a cognitive sociology of the text, I began to hear another language altogether. It translated that writing into a narration of what it is like to be a scholar devoted to written texts that no established discourse endows with cultural or literary privilege. This narrative bounced my authorial "self"—the words I was writing at the time—off tracks left by my ambivalent experiences as a composition teacher and administrator in four academic settings. Patterns in that past experience, and questions about it that I have asked and attempted to answer here, began to take a smiling shape, winking at the self-contained "serious" writing that I was completing at the time.

This study is, then, language for that particular wink. It does not represent anything so simple as a change of mind about what we now take to be the academically respectable and still morally correct seriousness of composition studies, although it may appear to. But it does turn everything I have learned about composition, especially about its relation to history, on its head. It acknowledges the consequential politics around American writing as an important constituent of cultural maintenance, and it attempts to overcome what I take to be increasing distraction from the actual results of that politics for American students at all levels and for their teachers. Writing it has slowly reminded me why I first left an already validated academic field for what was then a decidedly nonserious world of composition teaching and study. I have encountered and renovated my naive motives for that departure with a more fully informed belief—that those of us who are "in" composition are uniquely placed across the border separating textual and "real" worlds, where we might become more powerful critics of the intellectual politics that encloses each.

This belief, which in various early forms sustained me and many contemporaries in conversion to composition studies, was first a product of classist, often gendered, enclosures around us as writers and teachers of writing. Then without the theoretical languages for articulating our goals that I have used here, we (or at least I) only knew that we were often uncomfortable with views that our colleagues took to be the most basic common sense. Their easy separation of literary from student authorship, their assurance about the meaning in a separate literary language, and their attitudes toward unentitled students and their teachers placed us in roles that our graduate study had neglected to model. We were imagined as self-sacrificing saints, and simultaneously as transgressive irritants, and we inevitably responded (as Renate Lacmann explains in "Bakhtin and Carnival" [145]) as nonidentical to ourselves, as "ex-centric." Nonetheless, the slow successes of our contrary puzzlement about professional common sense—especially those of Dave Bartholomae, Rick Coe, Joe Comprone, Erika Lindemann, and Jim Raymond, whose insights and support have meant so much to me and many others—allowed us to elaborate our own, at first private, tradition.

Now, what began as my failure to understand common sense in light of purposeful curiosity about its roots and implications has become an alternative content and method, a different style of intellectual inquiry. I hope others will find my version of this inquiry useful, especially as a way to fit their own professional observations of the trials and successes of treasured students and colleagues into the cool categories that comprise textual studies—to "history," "literature," "rhetoric," "composing," and even "writing program administration."

As you will see, placing experience and perceptions of it against those established categories involves taking a number of risks. I am, therefore, more than politely grateful to the colleagues who encouraged me to write, who helped me to continue despite frustration with what I discovered by writing, and who have approved these results. I owe a great deal of gratitude to the 1987 University of Utah Research Committee, which provided a two-quarter research fellowship on the basis of a proposal that outlined this critique of institutional dispositions toward composition studies. I am equally grateful to Norman Council, my colleague and dean at the University of Utah, who calmly (as always) granted my request to take this leave while I was directing Utah's new University Writing Program. Neither of us could have imagined the results.

In addition, I would like to thank Laurel Brown, Katherine Fitzgerald, Karen Lawrence, and Richard Price at the University of Utah; George Gadda, Carol Hartzog, and Mike Rose at UCLA; and Sara Garnes at Ohio State University. Each made important supportive and substantial contributions in the early stages of writing. I am also indebted to Kip Thorne for his hospitality in Pasadena while conducting research, and to my colleague in Family and Consumer Studies, John Brownlee, who contributed his expertise as a psychologist to the survey techniques I employed and spent many hours explaining his clinical observations of the psychology of marginalization. Nicole Hoffman, Marianne Barnett, Dean Rehberger and Michael Rudick intervened at exactly the right times with editorial advice, comments, questions, and theoretical suggestions. But my greatest substantial debt must be paid to the 129 colleagues across the country who have trusted me with their answers to a lengthy, self-revealing survey. Their thoughtful honesty honors them and defines the pride of our profession.

My reviewers—Lisa Ede, Bill Irmscher, Lynn Bloom, John Trimbur, Donald Morton, and Winifred Horner (who read from a sickbed, yet with clear eyes)—have been wonderful in every critical and supportive sense. As before, without Kenney Withers's editorial energy and personal encouragement and the patience of his excellent colleagues at Southern Illinois University Press, this book would not be in your hands.

Textual Carnivals

Introduction
The Political Carnival of Composition

This study is blatantly a fiction, which is to say that I have come to understand the politics of writing by learning that power is, at its roots, telling our own stories. Without "good" stories to rely on, no minority or marginalized majority has a chance to change its status, or, more importantly, to identify and question the "bad" tales that create it. In this case, the required new narrative portrays teachers and students of writing in American higher education, who have for some time been the subjects of a marginalizing and negative—but nonetheless widely believed—myth.

I hope to substitute a new narrative for that denigrating tale by rereading this myth against a characterization of composition as a "carnival," a metaphoric representation much like the one that Bakhtin and others have used to understand relations between high and low discourses. Both actual and imagined carnivals offer, as Peter Stallybrass and Allon White explain in *The Politics and Poetics of Transgression*, historically enclosed, ad hoc, and transient sites for examining "the low." In most theorizations, the carnival represents a licensed suspension and inversion of a dominant culture. Here, however, it figures this relation from the peculiar situation of a transitional site within an institution, from a simultaneously low and culturally privileged position that creates the blurred identities and mixed perceptions that I detail. The textual carnival is precisely *textual*—a foundation for established discourse— yet is equally a debased intrusion of the unregulated "real" into that discourse. This figure powerfully connects "debased" and "established," "marginal" and "central" structures that define and constrain the nature, and the consequences, of unauthorized and officially untheorized writing.

These pairs—"debased and established," "marginal and

1

central"—immediately call to mind discussions of a politics of composition that are already well underway. The uneasy relationship between "composition" and "literature" now receives explicit attention in English studies and some notice in more public settings. These terms of professional difference guide, but do not limit, explorations of tension in this study.

In the ongoing discussion, "composition" and "literature" are both hypostatized agents. They take actions as identifiable groups of people who want to control, or to further the interests of, other identifiable people. "Composition" and "literature" stand in, that is, for communities who are imagined to be operating in the same institutional settings, but not in the same ways or at the same levels of power. In this conversation, both look at and act on each other across a boundary that most on either side see dividing "high" from "low." But neither group has fully explored their original and continuing mutual dependency, the ways that the position of one is actually required by the socially constructed status and larger cultural implications of the other.

This dependency focuses my interest in how both composition and literature are agents in one ideological action whose force equally controls academic and public views of written language. Each term will, therefore, be treated as a professional "field" and as an instance in a broader (and deeply political) educational history. With help from traditional (Big) history, contemporary theory, and examples from documented and reported practices, I hope to offer some corrected views of their usual separations and new interpretations of the connections between them.

Consequently, I have addressed a history of education in written language and the structures of teaching and learning, of intellectual politics, and of institutional habits that this history has established. Chapters 1 and 2 address both the received "story" of language instruction and the historical "plot" that formed images of composition courses in America. Chapter 3 treats composition as a "subject," in the person of its students and the content of its research and theory. Chapter 4 examines the stigma of composition teaching, and chapter 5 addresses institutional operations in budgets, supervision, and reward systems that maintain and clarify these configurations. Throughout, I have had help from diverse factual sources, particularly from early catalogue descriptions of English departments (chapter 2) and reports by colleagues who have invested their professional lives in composition instruction and its leadership (see Appendix: Survey). The new story told here results from many voices, so separate perspectives have been acknowledged by interlacing the text with excerpts from this survey, to elaborate (at times, to counter) my interpretive telling. My goal is to provide a space for reflecting on commonly unified structures of belief, the superstructural tradition that specific political interactions in English studies are instances *of*.

Both the old and a new version of this professional account have been unacknowledged as ways to understand a larger cultural significance of writing. To make explicit the particular ideological requirements that connect "composition" to "literature," I have also placed both terms in the context of the broad shift in humanistic inquiry that is now underway. Telling a "good" story about composition involves bringing information about its past and about its current students, teachers, research, and institutional structures into a symbolic domain, the space traditionally reserved for more "important" topics. We need to marshal the interpretive energy to "read" composition as though the politics in question are equal to the workings of social interests that we have already recognized in a broader discourse. A corrective good story about composition, like new feminist versions of women, depends on including characters and their ordinary daily actions in the symbolic domain that traditionally marginalizes them, denying their significance in symbolic as well as factual "reality." A revised account requires that we endow agency and dignity on its protagonists by making them "relevant" to contexts we already find greater than the sum of their parts. The "text" of composition achieves clarity only through a continuing oscillation between facts and what I am calling "fiction," a lens of symbolic interpretation that portrays composition more consequentially than reportage alone.

In this symbolic domain, composition is an institutionalized place for a specific but broadly constitutive social ambivalence in our cultural systems. This ambivalence is partially, but only partially, explained in specific differences between composition and literature. But composition is also an emblem for the "low" in a more comprehensive social and political hegemony, the cultural system that in large measure sustains itself by enclosing productions of consequential discourse in well-established and accepted systems of permission and denial.

Taken separately, composition is thereby at least potentially what Stallybrass and White call an "underground self with the upper hand" (5), as my conclusion suggests. It effectively organizes a cultural approach to otherwise disorganized, disjunctive aims and powerful results that might be realized in written language, just as the historic carnival organized consequential social, private, and economic activities, placing their illegitimacy in regard to "established" values in the playful and ad hoc setting of a fair. Like the carnival, composition teaching and its professionals' research represent a marvelous labor of "transcoding, displacement, and partition involved in the elaborate networks of *super-* and *sub-*" (Stallybrass and White 4). This labor allows an academic activity to domesticate otherwise "illegitimate" writing, not only by organizing academic values around it, but also by making this writing an emblem of related values throughout society. Processes of translation, relocation, and division into categories of high and low discourse serve the entire field of language study known as "English," but they also serve a much broader network of institutional and cultural purposes that English was established in the late nineteenth century to serve.

I must of course have an answer to the expected charge that these assertions result from the storyteller's conventional need to create a new and total reality. But a great deal of evidence directs us to relate our experiences with composition to larger structures that maintain cultural hegemony. Although neither radical literary and gender theorists nor sociologists, political scientists, or certain economists have made this specific connection, grounds for a broader political interpretation of composition do not rely on my, or on anyone else's, imagination.

The teaching of writing, at least according to publishers of textbooks for writing courses, engages about four million freshman-level students each year. If we consider how many additional students take upper-level writing and graduate courses in rhetoric and composition theory, adding another million to this figure is probably not an exaggeration. If we divide this expanded number by twenty-four, the mean class size reported in the Association of Departments of English "1983–84 Sample" (Huber 45), we can estimate that at least 165,000 teaching assignments are made each year in classes relevant to postsecondary writing, not counting classes offered in government or professional settings. Estimating an average course load in writing courses among two- to four-year institutions would be foolish, but it is probably safe to guess that at least 25,000 individuals are engaged in college-level composition teaching each academic year. Were the number half this, it would still represent an impressive investment of academic resources, but the number is undoubtedly higher.

If we also consider that, at an average price of ten to fifteen dollars, composition textbooks require at least a $40 million expenditure for students, and that wages for composition teaching involve at least $50 million (if we assume a low figure for average pay of $2,000 per course), we could safely estimate (adding administrative costs) that $100 million is spent each year in America on something we might think of as teaching students to write at the college level. Were high-school and extra-academic statistics included, the numbers would be staggering. Whatever else composition is, it is a major national industry when measured monetarily.

Considering how small writing classes are in comparison to the average college course, writing instruction also represents a major temporal investment. The labor-intensive character of taking, or of teaching, a writing course is well documented on the pulse, if not in the statistics, of the four to five million individuals involved each year as writing teachers and students.

This magnitude, if nothing else, invites us to account for the origins of composition in English studies, for its substantial establishment in this century as a "subject," for its theories of teaching and place in institutions, and for emerging alternatives to its traditions. I am not, however, about to argue that so great an investment should have "better" or more measurable results, nor will I assume that its size will persuade readers of its broad social importance. The first argument begs almost every question about dislocations and enclosures of consequential discourse in the theoretically "universal" American educational system. Using these or even less casually derived numbers to argue about the extent of approved "good writing" diverts us from a proper skepticism about such a universal discourse ideal and its source in purposes for mass education. And this argument keeps composition in a simultaneously submissive and self-serving relation to its surroundings, the "place" that already implies its supposed failures. The second argument has only rarely, if ever, gained assent about the significance, or the mismanagement, of any prevalent social practice. The point of quantification is simply that this great investment of thought, time, and money can readily be assumed to have a cultural politics of its own, one with consequential and instructive results.

For instance, composition helps define "levels" of writing, authorship, and status that are necessary for vernacular literary study to maintain its traditional place in the center of mass education. It also in this regard supports a comprehensive social desire to maintain the cultural ideal of "social place." But as a carnivalesque site within consequential discourse hierarchies, composition additionally embodies a contrary impulse, giving both its faculties and its students what Bakhtin called "temporary liberation from the prevailing truth of the established order" (109). It inadvertently defines alternatives to superior, "artistic" study, thereby blurring its own and its participants' particular purposes and identities in its now established modern "theme park." If it is nothing else, composition is an alternative to reading, and only reading, texts that constitute the quasi-religious ideal of a textual canon. This ordinariness offers respite from—and a supremely important constituent of—the fiction of the written artifact that is universally significant and perfectly composed or executed.

But in addition, composition instruction offers the culture at large an emblem for the repugnant "body" of writing by individuals. It is an institutionalized way of discriminating between those who will or will not occupy a space for contributing to (and for changing) powerful discourse traditions well outside canonical ideals. Acting from its own traditions, it can repress and commonly assimilate the majority of American writers who obtain credentials in higher education, indoctrinating them into openly middle-class values of propriety, politeness, and cooperation. By taking as one of its goals the "conventional," composition assures that these values will maintain their continuing, if disguised or displaced, status.

To interpret these social functions, we must allow that language *learning* is the crucial locus for power, or for disenfranchisement, in any culture. It unites the "actual" and systems of control, theorized horizontal and vertical planes on which social practices and discursive formations meet (see Hall 50–53). But accepting this statement as an invitation to elaborate on usually mundane images of composition requires some willingness to modify common disciplinary interpretations of its history and practices in favor of exploring their relation to the workings of hegemony. We need, that is, to place composition against "a superstructure—laws, institutions, culture, beliefs, values, customs" that controls a "whole way of life including culture and ideas far more subtle and effective than naked force supported by ideological institutions, which effectively enlists almost everyone in the 'party' of the ruling class, sets limits to debate and consciousness, and in general serves as a means of preserving and reproducing class structure" (Ohmann, *Politics* 8).

Richard Ohmann's acute analysis of the writing "student," and of the disinterested world in which composition textbooks imagine that student to produce discourse, have significantly contributed to the tenor of this study, as have many of his insights about the relative status of composition teaching. But his work and many parallel polemics about composition nonetheless argue for a more traditional radicalism than my emphasis on how composition is an element in, and an active symbol of, hegemonic cultural maintenance. Earlier critics have maintained the dialectical oppositions of a doctrinaire Marxism by pitting one stratum against another, by calling for change in the higher as a solution to the problem of the lower, and by at least implicitly retaining the traditional split between the Cartesian "subject" and "object." They often value a student "creativity" and "originality" whose possibility or force would be decisively questioned in contemporary theory. They speak of "good writing" versus "bad writing," "hierarchy versus community," "literature versus composition" or "society versus individual," pairs that continue the totalizing habits that have characterized processes of language education.

These habits have been particularized by the work of a number of educational and literary social critics, like Raymond Williams and Michael Apple, who recognize hegemony as the "truly total" deep structure of values that constitutes the distinct "common senses" that characterize separate societies (Apple 115). We participate, as agents and as objects, in the inequalities of domination, repression, and privileging that maintain particular cultural settings—in this case, the carnivalesque setting for "unimportant" writing. Williams highlights a hegemonic process he calls "the *selective tradition*," which is "always passed off as 'the tradition,' the significant past" (205). This process of selection leads us to emphasize some, but not other, meanings and practices, claiming for them neutral "prominence" and "continuity." It is obviously the process of selecting canonical literary texts and methods of teaching them, or (as I argue in chapter 1) in composition of choosing a certain historiography to explain the field. The selective tradition has identified some but not other features of textual production that particular historical methods authorize us to include within or to exclude from our research and teaching.

We might, for example, explore a particularly relevant example of hegemonic selection. Apple and others have pointed out that current "process-oriented" curricula teach students methods for inquiry while they appear to deemphasize content and thereby effectively depoliticize the content of education. As I will elaborate in chapter 3, they require students to see language, and all reality, as a social construction, without also teaching them how "to inquire as to *why* a particular form of social collectivity exists, *how* it is maintained, and *who* benefits from it" (Apple 115).

Students of literature may be taught that Stanley Fish's or any other concept of "interpretive community" defines the range of "valid" interpretations of a text. Students of composition may learn that their particular writing classroom and major field of study create separable and different "standard" writing practices. But neither literature nor composition students will in all probability also be taught the agendas of these communities for including and excluding particular alternative interpretations or standards. As Robert Scholes said of Fish in *Textual Power*, attacking his limited view of interpretive communities, he "has never made clear what an interpretive community is, how its constituency might be determined, or what could be the source of its awesome power" (153).

Similarly, those composition theorists who are now describing social constructions of textual standards and practices with the ostensibly neutral attitude of the early Foucault are usually not accounting for what is at stake in the entitlements of these groups, neither among themselves nor in pedagogical treatments for students (e.g., Bruffee). In some classrooms, student peer groups establish criteria for evaluating writing. In many cross-curricular programs, introductory composition curricula emphasize the differences among argumentative patterns in separate disciplines. But the biases and sources of power of these newly highlighted agencies of judgment usually go by the board. Analyzed by the reasoning of Apple and Williams, current process-oriented teaching and research tend to reduce our understanding of powerful, politically active structures, not to increase it. For all their novelty and superiority over rote learning, these "new" constructions of theory and practice continue our roles as agents of hegemonic selection. They encourage us to believe that we oppose established norms while instead crafting new systems that inadvertently maintain them.

Two previous approaches to composition and to its broad social implications that have supported this study have also, therefore, stimulated its skepticism about common explanations of the relation of English, and specifically of composition, to their surroundings. The first, the most frequent approach to political issues in English studies, links "tradition" and "reform," as in the titles of Arthur Applebee's *Tradition and Reform in the Teaching of English: A History* and the 1986 NCTE yearbook, *Consensus and Dissent: Teaching English Past, Present, and Future* (edited by Marjorie Farmer). While issues raised in these books will receive elaborate attention later, for now we need to be aware that the form of their arguments is fully implicated in hegemonic selection. This form opposes "the" tradition to the possibility of reforming it. By this bipolar opposition, in the implication of "reform" as "change," we semantically imply that language study willingly engages in critical self-scrutiny, is always openhanded with its harshest critics, and is always willing to try fresh, maverick ideas.

But by its polarity, the pair of tradition and reform imitates the logocentric structure that encompasses all of us as participants in cultural hegemony. A pair proposes one term, "tradition," as a given without which the other, "reform," is inconceivable. Such "reforms" in fact re-form tradition by sustaining its root metaphors and masking what was at stake in its basic structure (Culler 93–94). In composition theory, the same analysis might be applied to the pair "product" and "process." These matched, semantically opposed but formally mutual terms sustain what is in fact a single paradigm for the field. Both terms result in giving priority to either fixed or unfixed "meanings," the issue at stake in the majority of literary studies. Process and product are, then, a politically diversionary pair, for they work together to help us avoid confronting the social and institutional consequences that a piece of writing may or may not have.

A second example of a critique that reveals hegemonic processes, and that further engages in "blaming the victim" for actions that it was in fact established to take, is Albert Kitzhaber's 1963 report of the Dartmouth Study of Student Writing, *Themes, Theories, and Therapy: The Teaching of Writing in College.* This locus classicus for many common complaints about the transgressions of composition attacked the course, "freshman English," the "administrative adjustments and precautions that indicate little confidence in the expertness of those who teach it," and the lack of rigor and scholarship in the textbooks used for the course (10).

Kitzhaber found that the course is confused in its goals. (*The* is a significant limitation here, indicating a major agenda in composition.) Some courses that he surveyed aimed to give students minimal skills, some to introduce them to literature, some to inculcate "accuracy," some to promote "significant ideas," some to motivate, some to acquaint students with the history and structure of the English language. Where more than one course constituted the "course" of freshman English, Kitzhaber found little by way of progression. The second course appeared either to be totally unrelated to the first or to be the same course taught again, perhaps requiring a longer paper.

Kitzhaber also characterized teachers of writing as graduate students and junior instructors whose status pleases administrations in need of cheap labor, pleases senior professors needing graduate students, and pleases graduate students who need work. "Some of these teachers are enthusiastic, experienced, expert; more are bored or resentful, lack previous teaching experience, are ill-informed on what they are supposed to teach . . . and are teaching with little supervision or guidance" (14). The teaching of composition also suffered, he said, from "the lack of status that the freshman course has long suffered from" (14). It is often viewed as subcollegiate, thought of as practical, a "how-to," and denied intellectual rigor. It is used to winnow entrants to open-admissions colleges, and "the best minds in the profession have rarely concerned themselves [with it]. . . . Few first-rate men have taken the trouble to write textbooks for Freshman English" (14–15). Reasoning that the number of textbooks regularly produced for freshman English is so great because their preparation requires little effort, Kitzhaber also noted how alike they are and that "fads and novelties affect choice of these books as much as they do choice of women's hats" (17).

While it is still common to hear these complaints about composition, Kitzhaber's introductory critique certainly would require revision were it being published today. But an obvious, updating revision would only be cosmetic. It might include "change," for instance, that appears in Carol Hartzog's documentation of the recent trend to revise writing curricula in her *Composition in the Academy*, and it might indicate, as does the "1983–84 Sample" of the Association of Departments of English that numerous graduate programs now include degrees and courses in rhetoric and composition to remedy the ignorance of the young teachers about whom Kitzhaber complained. But these additions would be signs of Kitzhaber's own call for the kind of reform he wanted, to promote Dartmouth's or another school's superior courses.

Certainly his objections to composition practices have been made again, if with different explanations, in recent arguments like Maxine Hairston's article "The Winds of Change." They have been documented anew in Richard Larson's emerging Ford-sponsored survey of practices in composition programs. It would be "politically" wiser to revise the language of "first-rate men" and "women's hats," but not politically different to do so without also making other interpretations of the evidence he selected and questioning that selection itself.

To make this political difference, we would have to infer from Kitzhaber's description something other than a call for a "new" (or, I would argue, for a re-formed) course. We would instead need to explain how and why composition was, and in significant measure still is, established to be as he says it is. His description calls the carnival to mind as we know it both from experience and from theory. "Composition" contains diverse, in fact disparate, activities. Its participants, its students, and most of its teachers are uncredentialed or "illegitimate" denizens of the best-established and most legitimate institution. Composition appears to be cacophonous, anarchic, and trivial, but it nonetheless produces predictable and sustaining economic and social benefits. In a strong sense, it is like the Old Testament God and the Lacanian woman—always in a state of becoming, of reinventing itself to compensate for its perceived lack of fixed goals and methods. But it is nonetheless in many ways a ritualistic performance that does not change except by substituting new rituals and codes for old ones.

These need not necessarily be criticisms, or at least not a priori criticisms. Our first concern should be to explain the sources of these carnivalesque qualities in the historical realization of cultural ideals that I sketch in the first part of this study. We must deal, that is, with the uses of composition as it is. We can admit that collegiate instruction in writing is negatively marginal to its institutions and often to the interests of those who provide it. But we then would logically ask how our accepted social and theoretical values have worked together to create this condition, preventing writing from becoming a recognized "canon" of abilities whose mastery can be recognized. Composition instruction and research have continued under many of the conditions Kitzhaber described, so it is reasonable to assume that these academic activities and the modern contexts that commonly support them reveal something at stake in maintaining their problematic situations.

Kitzhaber's work demonstrates that it is possible to adopt a zealous spirit of reform, to admit that adverse conditions exist, and still to avoid political analysis by covering over the contexts that produce problematic particularities. But if we are to contemplate more than personal or local causes for the stunning regularity in descriptions of prejudice against student writing and those who implement instruction in it, or of incidents that appear to pit "composition" against "literature," we must go beyond, or before, examples to identify and explain patterns that reproduce them.

To further this explanation, I have relied on a number of theories that address the problematics of marginalization, from both cultural and textual studies. I may appear to have eclectically adopted these touchstones for explanation, juxtaposing critical and experiential approaches in cultural studies, feminist theory and history, leftist criticism, sociology, psychology, and poststructuralism. All of these frames for understanding have avowed legitimate methodological and philosophical interests in their separations, and none of them, I would freely concede, is used here as a consistent text against which a politics of composition is read. But each in some measure addresses the workings of alienation, isolation, and self-consciousness that must be at the heart of a political reading of composition and of its results for recognizing "levels" of discourse. Composition is a cultural practice whose illegitimacy is so important for maintaining quasi-religious values around writing that validated forms of social, cultural, and textual inquiry studiously ignore the emblem and active intervention that it might offer their own concerns. But this ignorance need not be mutual.

The basic problem with my proposal for this new perspective on composition, as with any political analysis, is that it inevitably defines itself polemically. Perspectives that conflict with our commonly impersonal, expository stance toward re-

> The remaining comment about prejudice offers an interesting twist on the denigration of composition specialists perceived as the "rude proletariat." To what appears to be a theoretical contrary, this respondent said his department's "greatest tension is from the hot shot Marxist theorists. . . . They are new, have little time for day-to-day work of the department, carry all the prejudices of their corrupt elders, and speak to graduate students about composition and teaching in tones that say 'if you put your fingers in that shit, they will never come clean again.' They have no way of speaking about what we do." (Appendix, p. 247)

search and teaching, our "objectivity," quickly take on high moral seriousness, a certain coarse, evangelical tone. Unfortunately, we often look on the importance and credibility of political subjects as inversely proportionate to their scope and implied urgency. As Janet Batsleer and her coauthors put it in *Rewriting English* (another revisionist view of our discipline), the "well-behaved pluralist joins the club, and subscribes to the rules. The tough-talking activist doesn't get past the bouncer, and can safely be ignored" (26). Barbara Herrnstein Smith has offered another form of this caveat. She notes that even institutionalized theory, as this study certainly is, may verge on being "self-excommunicating" (22). It may, that is, be taken as irreparably transgressive, a "*satanic*" statement rather than a contribution within "the lingering conception of the academy as a quasi-religious institution" (10).

As *Rewriting English* furthers this characterization of the politics that determines whether new critiques will be either important or forgotten, it points out that "literary ideologies" have monopolized "discursive legitimacy" inside the wide orbit that also contains composition and commentaries on it. These literary ideologies have a "remarkable capacity to absorb, transform and neutralize political impulses, including their own" (27). One path of this capacity, as many readers might verify, is taken through our profession's persistent self-abnegation, which in composition means that most teachers have little time to consider the symbolic cultural implications of their work. Their assigned self-sacrificial role includes "dedication," which names ordinary engagement in and even desires to invent new forms of the most time-consuming sorts of trivial labor.

Composition teachers consequently are often effectively isolated from intellectual worlds in which unstructured time for self-reflection is mandatory, just as they are persuaded that neutral "objective" or "transcendent" research and instruction take precedence over criticism that disputes traditional values. In a magnificent tautology, the practices that take our time are *already* validated, even and especially in their temporal demands, on the basis of apparent "need" for them. Political issues in composition are, therefore, often contained by isolated discussions of administrative turf and particular if prominent disruptions of composition programs. More comprehensive critiques may raise anxieties about the role of the teacher, so they are hidden, if uncomfortably so, in an ideology that holds us to our lasts. (See chapter 4.)

This capacity of literary ideologies to absorb political theories must also prepare me to take as my greatest lesson from Ohmann and Kitzhaber that few in either literature or composition, and even fewer in what I take to be obviously related fields, are intimately acquainted with what they have said. Kitzhaber's dissertation, for instance, must still be read in its original form and cited as "unpublished," with all that implies about how far beyond the bouncer it got.

Nonetheless, there are good reasons to overcome prejudices against a political subject of composition. The field of composition cannot be, as it has not been, unaffected by the current crisis in English studies that British social critics are ahead of us in documenting in books like *Rewriting English* (Batsleer et al.) and its predecessor, *Re-reading English* (edited by Peter Widdowson). Gerald Graff's *Professing Literature* similarly makes it clear that composition is implicated as a field in critiques of social and intellectual power relations, for we are incrementally experiencing signs that new theories result, as he says, "when consensus breaks down" (253). Taken together, the token conference slot for a political subject; recent critiques of the enclosure of literary studies like those by Robert Scholes, Edward Said, Frank Lentricchia, Michael Ryan

(*Marxism and Deconstruction*); the work of increasing numbers of feminist social critics like Gayatri Spivak (*In Other Worlds*); and the summations of metacritics like William Cain (*The Crisis in Criticism*)—all these will impel composition professionals to account for the political event their work constitutes daily, or will make their silence its own loud commentary.

Part I

Where the Carnival Has Been

1 The Story of Composition

The field of composition has had, we can all agree, a difficult time getting "established," for reasons that go beyond the usual problems of new academic enterprises and into social agendas for the regulation of public language. The first part of this interpretation of those difficulties describes a brief history of those social agendas, but it is not intended to be History. Instead, this chapter and the next tell about the absence of attention to textual production in the usual "story" of English, and about a less exposed "plot" that organizes roles and tensions that create the concerns of students and teachers of composition and institutional structures to deal with them.

Historical forces against legitimizing composition, like particular historiographies that have been chosen in the field to overcome these forces, have operated in a social context that first legitimized the field of "English" as a whole. The origins and purposes of organized English studies consequently need review with "composition"—as an institutional project and as public writing—in an imagined position of agency. Like the attention to gender and to other social problematics that has inverted standard, or "big," political and social histories, attention to various ways of institutionalizing writing can invert typical accounts of the entrenched investment in "literature" that we usually take for granted. At the very least, placing composition in the center of our history reveals the nature of its essential attachment to literary studies.

To achieve this perspective, we need first to look at reasons that our most common images of native English literary history usually do not raise the specter of "writing" at all, even in American English studies, where the "unauthorized" writing of a broader pool of students has been organized as an obvious curricular project. Both English and American ways of legitimizing literary study can then be placed against a slightly different tradition, the standard history of rhetoric and its supposed continuity with composition instruction.

Invisible Writing

George Gordon, an early literature professor at Oxford, put the case for education in specifically vernacular literature succinctly in his inaugural address: "England is sick, and . . . English literature must save it. The Churches (as I understand) having failed, and social remedies being slow, English literature has now a triple function, still, I suppose, to delight and instruct us, but also, and above all, to save our souls and heal the State" (quoted in Eagleton, *Theory* 23).

Gordon's statement, as Terry Eagleton argues in *Literary Theory: An Introduction*, reveals that a particular social agenda had everything to do with the nineteenth-century establishment of native literary education. English literature, perfectly ready for a formerly religious task of curing cultural alienation, was placed to become, quite precisely, the "poor man's classics." As Eagleton interprets Gordon's intent, "literature would rehearse the masses in the habits of pluralistic thought and feeling, persuading them to acknowledge that more than one viewpoint than theirs existed—namely, that of their masters. It would communicate to them the moral riches of bourgeois civilization, impress upon them a reverence for middle-class achievements, and, since reading is an essentially solitary, contemplative activity, curb in them any disruptive tendency to collective political action" (25).

While Eagleton's interpretation may seem doctrinaire, it has support from a number of parallel historical events. For instance, this missionary purpose for literary studies reveals why Scottish and lower-class "red brick" universities were the first to appoint professors of specifically vernacular subjects, including rhetorically based vernacular composition: their students would "need" literary and composition indoctrination along the lines Eagleton describes more than their counterparts at elitist institutions. But it is equally verifiable that soon after these earliest appointments, the study of vernacular literature was taking on the classics in a universal professional struggle for prominence. Oxford, Cambridge, and eastern American schools became sites where the original "need" at red brick institutions was now applied to the elite. Later, as Eagleton and others have often pointed out, F. R. Leavis and his followers entrenched social gains for English after the disruption of World War I. They did so by giving "English" a past, the "great tradition" whose recognition allowed them to claim that native belles lettres has a history parallel to ancient counterparts.

The New Critics additionally used analyses of texts themselves, in a move that appears to have fortified the sense of spiritual isolation that would, in Eagleton's view, divorce literary study from commercialism and social activism. But whatever its motives, this atheoretical theory eliminated the literary reader's need to know history, philology, and Latin, thereby further universalizing the possibilities Gordon had described for relating the study of vernacular literature to the "souls" of students. In America, this universalism was overtly described after the World War II, when American literary curricula became almost exclusively New Critical in orientation. Placing literature against religious attitudes and their exclusive definitions of "superior texts" led to statements like "the Decline of the West was felt to be avertible by close reading" (quoted in Eagleton, *Theory* 34).

This statement hardly expresses the egalitarianism often cited as the motive for establishing New Critical hegemony over literary texts. Even scattered characterizations of vernacular literary study suggest that from its establishment as a professional and, more important, as a culturally *central* academic pursuit, vernacular literary study has been identified with quasi-religious social functions. In only a slightly strenuous act of imagination, then, we can infer from this identification that it would be likely that a new field of "English" would ignore, or would thoroughly appropriate, practices in language education and in textual production as it set about to describe itself. An official history of English would preferably exclude the "low," along with any mention of anxieties about potential textual failure or even what we might call textual rehearsals. Instead, timelessness, perfection, and spirituality, the common topics of religious persuasion, would constitute the subtext of the "great tradition" (as they have), and foster a Hegelian approach to historical literary scholarship. When actual language, its learning, or its chancy production and publicity must come up, they would be linked to the duty to "civilize" the audience for literature, so the audience might appreciate it. This obligation would, for instance, justify the "lower," elementary work of learning and teaching vernacular grammar, syntax, pronunciation, and even spelling. These tasks of lower learning would be valued only for leading to reading closely and appreciating the "best"—that is, the most ambiguous yet still correct—examples of English.

The extent to which this possibility for explaining "English" has in fact controlled its received history has been overwhelming, as a number of choices about telling this story demonstrate. Anyone who has studied literature is aware that information about textual imperfections, conditions of publishing and even of originating literary "works," and historical changes in the social status of writing and written products has rarely contributed to "reading" a literary work. Such omissions are overshadowed by a number of overt choices to reform or gloss over historical conditions for reading and writing. These conditions and the attitudes that accompanied them nonetheless point toward an alternative, decidedly non-universal vision of literary culture and its professionalization.

Even setting aside what has amounted to a back-formation that rereads literature as the ultimate purpose, not the servant, of the earliest elementary language instruction and training in rhetoric, education in language or in literary examples was not always associated with the blood lust for moral perfection that has characterized literary attitudes to "low" work. To take an early example, Quintilian's *Institutes* can be cited as a source of lengthy discussions of barbarisms and solecisms, but domineering applications of these terms in English instruction came much later. His treatment of "writing" is a manual for impeccable transcription, not for prose composition (I.v). His standards for the excellence of Latin style, "correctness, lucidity and elegance" (I.v.1), were set by very different motives than the pointed linguistic exclusiveness that was invoked later in support of associating good writing with theological proprieties. "Language," he said, "is based on reason, antiquity, authority and usage" (I.vi.1). Far ahead of, or behind, later assumptions about the relation of grammar to morality, Quintilian's barbarians were only foreign speakers and authors whose usage it was sometimes appropriate to adopt.

Associating a sanctifying public morality with reading and correctness did have precedents in classical education, but the absoluteness of the connection could not take hold as a massive educational agenda until the rise of inexpensive publishing and two-edged social "reforms" gave educational practices their distinct modern quality, the universality that characterizes religion. Progress toward this universality, still a custom more honored in the breach than in its observance, has always been halting and slow, not a powerfully active great traditional force. It is clear that well into the Victorian era "it would be a mistake to imagine that reading had any but the most incidental place in the life of the masses" (Altick 29). By 1600 there had been 360 grammar (classical) schools in England, and "as yet little sign of the social exclusiveness that later was to reserve grammar-school and university education largely for children of noble or gentle birth" (17). Allowances have to be made for the unlikely scenario that rural farmers spared their children for literacy lessons, as they must for the equally prohibitive cost of books, but Tudor and Stuart English people had quite democratically participated in vernacular education.

Protestantism, however, which from Luther's *Theses* to the present has relied on at least the appearance of democratic literacy, actually restricted reading from early in its growth. Although Henry VIII had authorized distribution of the Bible in 1540, its reading was denied to women in 1543. This pattern of expansion and repression of the literate public endured: books and political pamphlets became necessities for conducting the new Protestant religion and Calvinist economy, but strong reactions to successful dissent resulted in denunciations of frivolous or "demoralizing" reading material. Secular courtesy books themselves discouraged reading plays and romances, and jestbooks and other light literature were justified only on medicinal grounds, as cures for melancholy. Sermons denounced, and were juiced up to substitute for, drama.

Despite and because of Protestantism, the English literacy

rate was scarcely higher in 1780 than it had been during Eliza-beth's reign. The Civil War virtually destroyed endowed pri-mary schooling, and new versions of these places where the lowborn might learn to read and spell were slow to form because the restored monarchy wished to prevent another success on the part of commoners. As Richard Altick put it, "The upper class urgently needed to shore up its own posi-tion" (31). One obvious way to do this, of course, is to prevent masses of people from reading (and, of course, from writing).

But such prevention constructs a dilemma that could plausi-bly be said to have created the character of native and many nonnative speakers' education in English ever since. It may be, as Soame Jenyns had said in the *Free Inquiry into the Nature and Origins of Evil*, that it flies in the face of divine intention "to encourage the poor man to read and think, and thus to become more conscious of his misery" (quoted in Altick 33). But it is also impossible to teach the masses their "place," in all its senses, unless they are brought to schools to learn it. Literacy, as Brian Doyle stresses in "The History and Politics of Literacy," "is a two-edged sword" (*Re-reading* 29). Without it, masses of people are unlikely to learn the passive virtues Eagleton described, or to become properly ineffectual in rela-tion to their political contexts.

The solution to this problem, at least *a* solution that appears to have gained great favor, was to found schools like those Sunday schools and other public schools initiated in the nine-teenth century, where learning to read, spell, and possibly to write were made as unattractive as possible, both for stu-dents and for their teachers. It follows, of course, that pub-licly acceptable versions of the proper business of education will exclude—overlook and demean—questionable agendas within this unattractive pursuit. But in the schools them-selves, as Altick goes on to document in grim detail, vernacu-lar language can be taught by "reading and repetition," with all of the mindless punitive apparatus that can be brought into play without doing permanent harm (and sometimes with it) to the student's physical well-being.

It also helps to make teaching these "elementary" subjects the province of what Altick calls "the acme of incompetence. . . . Teachers were, in Macaulay's words, the 'refuse of other callings—discarded servants, or ruined tradesmen; who cannot do a sum of three; who would not be able to write a common letter' " (150). It is a wonder, then, as well as a sign of the actual power of reading, that the English reading public, estimated at about 80,000 at the beginning of the nineteenth century, ever became the people who checked out 370,605,000 books from public libraries in 1957 (364).

Some additional wonderment about this growth of a literate public belongs to the intense and repressive nationalism that was necessarily promoted to accomplish British colonizations. The English empire required appropriating not only the politics but, if the two are distinguished, the language of half the globe, including America. Chauvinistic and antagonistic attitudes toward the native language have naturally come up in England's entire history, marked as it has been by invasions in all directions. But from the time that Henry V had established Chancery English, a written English of the law whose influence has been comparable to a later Henry's Protestantism, we can identify continuing significant contributions to standardized national language and standardized discursive practices (Richardson). "Cultural union" also became the goal of educational practices, so much so that David Hume spoke Scots but wrote in metropolitan English, in the interest of constructing abstract models for standards of "taste" (Doyle 21). It did not take long for the restored monarchy to recognize the virtues of such abstract models in creating political "loyalty" to an equally abstract "England" and to its native linguistic products, even though "English rhetoric" and "belles lettres" resulted from a decidedly Scottish Enlightenment.

In the eighteenth century, this national loyalizing agenda for spreading standard English was largely given over to women, who were thought to have "natural" affinities for the personal, domestic qualities of their native language rather than for scientific or classical subjects. As Doyle says in "The Hidden History of English Studies," "the dominant conception of woman as homemaker and the notion of women as potentially and acceptably employed in professions were absorbed into a quasi-professional and at the same time quasi-maternal composite function whereby women educated the children of the national 'corporate body' " (23). Introduced to universities, English texts provided training for these feminine mentors of children in, at first, a "woman's subject." The "pink sunsets" approach assured that studying, or teaching, native language would not contaminate the "hard" sciences of Latin, Greek, and mathematics. As we will see, this gender bias has had an enormous part in defining the politics of composition.

Eighteenth-century English colonialism also entailed missionary cultivation of the world's masses by placing them in the medium of English. By at least 1791 in Sierra Leone, and even more clearly in the further colonizations of the nineteenth century, linguistic salvation was highly valued. In 1867, for instance, the minutes of the Ceylon Committee affirm that "English should be to the natives of Ceylon what Latin is to the natives of Great Britain." In Africa as well, English was to be the natives' Latin, the resuscitated Roman breath of dominance (Batsleer et al. 23). Typical moralistic analogies with Roman conquest are even more frightening if we recall that Latin was then and well into this century the learned language of any upper-class education. Colonizations begin, and remain, at home. An attitude much different from the relative diffidence in Quintilian's openhanded criteria for stylistic choice, as from the spirit of Tudor and Stuart open schooling, formed upper-class attitudes toward increased numbers of both the foreign and the local (human) subjects of vernacular language instruction. These attitudes not only entrenched the lower class's "national character," but also shored up its subsidiary status.

Given these historical attitudes, the English language increasingly became the institutionalized masculine locus of nationalistic power. Coleridge and Henry James both decried the multiplication of "uneducated" (lower-class, especially female) readers, distinguishing them from the middle- and upper-class male, classically educated readers who have in new versions become the "professional" members of the "Criticism, Inc. or Criticism, Ltd." that John Crowe Ransom was still promoting in 1968 (quoted in Batsleer et al. 17). It is rare to acknowledge the singularity of this crucial nineteenth-century institutional turn toward English, specifically toward national English *literature*. It meant, for instance, turning away from science as a possible alternative to this centralizing focus for the "public," whose images of educational and other national achievements would remain embedded in the quasi-religious spirit of literary texts.

We can understand, given this context, why any matter related to teaching or research in reading and composition would be excluded from smoothly superior accounts from within a dominant literary establishment. Its particular mission, development, and character are devoted to displacing the inevitably ordinary circumstances around the texts it chooses to call extraordinary. To colonize and save the isolated souls of its passively constituted individual and "expressive"—but never socially forward—human subjects, literary study logically must be dissociated from textual production. The history of "literature" must by definition be told as a history of *authorship* and of the authorized voice, whose origins, successes, and privileges are not bound to the material circumstances of either readers or writers.

All of this is to say that attention to actual writing practices or to their educational settings highlights the "low," the ad hoc qualities of the carnivalesque. Such attention suggests fissures, hesitations, conflicting purposes, and the multiple origins of ideas, as against a mythologically cool, organized space of univocal "statement." In a traditional version of textual history, people characterized as "authors" are almost always imagined as in control of language. Authors are treated, at least in introductory views of them designed for the poor men with new classics, as though they have been purposefully engaged in self-conscious artistic and public documentation of their "thought."

This is not to claim that scholars hide or remain unaware of the facts of textual history: their work makes this critique possible. But the religious associations endowed to literary texts have, as I have pointed out, created processes of selection and priorities that control the scope of historical scholarship. In addition, some excellent factual reasons can explain why historians have described only the traditional author and have omitted details of actual writing to validate this author's autonomy within intellectual worlds. Given the evidence in the dates of various later technologies of writing alone, it would have been almost impossible for pre-twentieth-century authors to have engaged in anything like "the [written] composing process" that many composition specialists now assume occurred, or should have been taught, in any age.

As Elizabeth Larsen has summarized in "A History of the Composing Process," composing technologies until the twentieth century largely included only memory and mental composition, the warrants for claims that history *is* the product of a World Mind. Drafting, revision, and multiple copies of various starts made before an author/writer graphically recorded a text were not, as they now can be, the "sources" of literary or any other writing (Larsen, "History"; "Technology"). Earlier phenomenologies of "writing" support the persisting view that written words contain actually disembodied thought. A text was not a generative way to think *in* language itself. The entirely portable ballpoint pen, was not, after all, invented until 1942.

But these facts, which have now been highlighted in composition studies but not in literary traditions, are not the primary reason that historians legitimize a "pure" literary history in the ways they traditionally have. Given the social history of a very broadly defined "literacy" that lies behind the establishment of literary studies, what has been at stake in excluding from its history the educational and material circumstances for creating visible texts has had much more to do with spiritual regulation, a process of assuring a well-behaved, cooperative body politic. As we will see, this agenda appears to be the subtext that was most influential in establishing composition as an instructional program, even in American higher education.

American Writing

At first blush it appears that British literary "English" agendas might have been spared Americans, especially in relation to written composition. A country founded on documents that unite various linguistic communities depending on each other absolutely, at least at the outset, might have made democratically written English and education in its production one of its most important and privileged undertakings. We now, after all, anthologize Ben Franklin's recommendations to a large colonial readership about improving style by "translating" from great English authors to our own style and back again. But British English was also the Roman Latin of the American colonies, as much as it was of Africa or India, when most book collections still contained only imported volumes. The New England "Errand," the Puritan's revolutionary mandate to colonize America for Calvinism and for American versions of correct spelling, became defunct after the English Restoration. But this errand was readily transmogrified into a journey toward the frontier, which substituted for revolution an ever-inviting boundary to which civilization and the parts of speech could be transported.

This is not to gloss over the distinct character of American literacy (much more common in colonial New England by virtue of its Puritan agendas than in England at the same time), nor to claim that American reasons for prissiness about correct language are identical to those in England. Both the texture of American politics and the root metaphors of vision, space, freedom, and individualism that shaped distinctly American social attitudes must be accounted for. We can find evidence of elitism and teaching practices designed to discourage reading and writing in histories of the linguistic and literary nature of American national character, but some significant differences between British and native education warrant explanation. Composition became the thriving college-level pursuit it is now only in America because of distinct educational and popular practices.

Arthur Applebee (1–13) recounts a history of the teaching of English in America that requires us to sort out three traditions to understand this American distinction. He identifies "ethical," "classical," and "nonacademic" educational traditions—the moralistic, puritanical readers and spellers of elementary education, the classical pedagogy of "discipline" that was called into play to exercise the mental "faculties" in eighteenth- and early nineteenth-century rhetorical strains, and the nonacademic social institutions that thrived in an early American printed culture.

As others have pointed out, we have more thorough accounts of instruction in reading than in writing because reading leads to acceptance of literary values more clearly than writing does. Early American colonists and citizens, those who learned to read under religious rather than literary programs, were themselves latterly constituted barbarians. They were taught "to read" by being subjected to a moral, "ethical" connection between the written word and religiosity, the connection that gave credence to later substitutions of literary for religious values in their national curricula. As Stephen Tchudi shows in "A Documentary History of the Teaching of English," American language instruction was limited to lessons in reading and spelling, as most elementary vernacular instruction had always been in England. Elementary schooling focused on judging the child according to mastery of correct spelling. As *The New England Primer* (c. 1690) had it, "Thy Life to mend/This book attend" (Tchudi 4–5). Lindley Murray's infamous *English Grammar, Adapted to the Different Classes of Learners* (1795) taught parsing to "discipline the mind" and to help students write "with propriety" (Tchudi 5).

Placing the beginning of institutionalized English studies in 1890, Applebee shows how literature had over time become the valued content of American language education, so that "by 1900 the question would have shifted from whether to teach grammar, rhetoric, literary history, spelling, and composition, to *how* to teach English" (21). Literary training in character might be contaminated by the same chaff of immorality that had always been feared: in 1893 a class of high-school boys was commended for refusing to read an unexpurgated edition of *Hamlet*. But Arnold's ideals of "culture" (versus anarchy) and his vision of unequal but harmoniously coexisting classes were well-established precedents for the rise of Leavis and the New Critics' great tradition, as they were for American New Criticism. At various times, each of these ideas was perceived as a way to save war-torn American souls. In the nineteenth century, the supposedly unique disruptiveness of the Civil War and industrialization could be neutralized, many claimed, by turning to a "true perspective" offered by Emerson, Irving, Hawthorne, and others (24). And this perspective could be formalized, as it was when the 1892 report of the national Committee of Ten established college entrance exams with "uniform lists" of preparatory readings. Influen-

tial anthologies interacted with these lists to establish literature, in a literary canon, as the true equipment of America's
educated.

Before these developments, language education had still
emphasized the ancient and continuing use of literature to
learn and to demonstrate knowledge of correct grammar and
rhetorical principles. Harvard's 1874–75 entrance exam, for
instance, exemplifies this earlier view: "*English Composition.*
Each candidate will be required to write a short English composition, correct in spelling, punctuation, grammar, and expression, the subject to be taken from such works of standard
authors as shall be announced from time to time" (quoted in
Applebee 30). This assignment produced the damning evidence used in the Harvard Board of Overseers' Report establishing composition as a remedial subject. It indicates how
relatively short the time was between an instrumental view of
literature to teach grammar and syntax, as it had been in
classical language practices, and its privileged status as the
ground of all "meaning."

It was controversial to combine composition and literature
symbiotically as the Harvard exam did. Soon after the examination began, the largely successful campaign to separate the
two pedagogical arenas was begun, on the grounds that composition needed to receive its own proper attention and was
not receiving it within literary teaching. But nationalistic, abstract ideals of literary study soon dominated as both the goal
of and the justification for writing instruction. The schools
taught writing about literature, if writing at all. Applebee (68)
quotes one teacher who summarized this political ideology of
literature (and dismissal of composition) on all American levels: "The first great aim in the literature course is a training
for citizenship by a study of our national ideals embodied in
the writings of American authors, our race ideals as set forth
by the great writers of Anglo-Saxon origin, our universal ideals
as we find them in any great work of literary art."

This narrative so far suggests that Puritan and later influences allowed composition, in something like the form its
current professionals mean the word, to hold its own throughout American educational history, demeaned as that status
was. But the evidence of "composition" in the Harvard assign-

ment tells us that interest in writing at the time did not go beyond checking newly admitted lower-class students to see how clean behind the ears their grammar and mechanics were. As Michael Halloran points out in "Rhetoric in the American College Curriculum: The Decline of Public Discourse," Latin had been more strictly enforced as Harvard's learned and social language than at Oxford and Cambridge throughout the seventeenth century; English language disputation was introduced only in the 1750s at Harvard and Yale (250). In the universities, the requirements in "composition" had been rudimentary at least until written language began to compete with oral rhetoric and debate for attention. In the schools, as late as 1859, a Vermont child was expelled because, with the encouragement of his (?) parents, he had refused to write compositions. The parents, no doubt with the child's happy cooperation, protested that instruction in speaking and thinking logically on one's feet, not in writing, was the proper subject of education. But the court upheld the expulsion, "ruling that English composition was an allowable mode of teaching and interpreting other branches of knowledge" (Heath 35). There are reports of similar cases in many states in the last half of the nineteenth century, an indication that American writing was not thought of as the proper business of the schools until at least this century. As we will see, the nature of this proper business remains uncertain.

It is consequently in what Applebee calls the "extracurriculum," in nonacademic American traditions, that we find writing in a distinctly American place. There it was thought of as necessary equipment for citizenship. The mandate for composition—and ironically the source of its finally demeaned status—evolved over the time between the *New England Primer* and the second half of the nineteenth century, taking shape in nonacademic traditions of popular writing that were used to share knowledge and to maintain distant ties.

In an excellent study, Shirley Brice Heath has documented ways that writing was located in the everyday life of American eighteenth-century colonials and nineteenth-century citizens. Citing Kenneth Lockridge's *Literacy in Colonial New England* (a study that has not gone without correction), she agrees that New England went from about 50 percent male literacy to almost universal male literacy between the middle of the seventeenth and the end of the eighteenth century. Lockridge also claims that rural farmers were about 85 percent literate by 1790 (Heath 28).

This popular literacy was a social responsibility. The new Americans needed capacities not only for independent experimentation, invention, and enterprise to feed and house themselves, but ways to share useful information about these matters with neighbors across large distances of unsettled space. Articles, pamphlets, and broadsides "advertised" ordinary information about farming, mechanical necessities, and health in forms that were later adapted for business and technical writing courses at land grant universities. Reports, "process" descriptions, and letters were addressed quite personally from one usually anonymous successful manager of a problem ("a businessman," "a farmer") to others who were conceived of as individuals, not as a "readership." Periodicals published numerous such missives, often addressed to "Mr. Editor," an indication that these publications were clearing houses or bulletin boards transmitting this written conversation.

It is difficult to understand empathetically how important it was in this period that writers either take, or not take, personal responsibility for their writing. This issue became increasingly prominent after Alexander Hamilton's troublesome libel suit, which legally established the idea that a text may be analyzed to determine its writer's intent (and accountability). When a writer was willing to be named as "author" of a piece of writing, the reading public was anxious to know every detail of that person's life. Heath claims that "by the 1830's, when individuals were increasingly called on to identify themselves in periodicals, they were asked to do so because of the growing nationalistic confidence in American writing" (30).

But as this confidence took hold, an antidote was ready to hand. Editors began to substitute "fillers" for individual submissions and to lay down rules for the form, liveliness, and importance of submissions. Locally knowledgeable citizens were accused of merely wanting to see their names in print, contributing to a "flood of stupidity" (quoted in Heath 31). At the same time as Harvard's first appointment of a

Boylston Professor of Rhetoric, "rhetoric," in the form of directions to imagine an "audience" rather than a correspondent and to follow standard formats, was introduced to the public realm. (This direction may account for some of the American public's continuing knee-jerk repugnance for the word.) Despite the continued energy of personal letter writing, which has always been a way for women to acquire the complex literacy denied them through formal education, writing began to be thoroughly appropriated as a formal school subject, the sort of instruction the Vermont parents opposed.

Public writing consequently took on "authorized" as well as illegitimate aspects in a distinctly literate country whose printed "voice" Ben Franklin had helped disseminate to the "common man." In this American setting, despite its geographical and social differences from England and its rebellion against monarchy, anxieties about wanton entries into public debate and knowledge-making became institutionalized by mechanisms that in effect censored the country's written forums. As we shall see, this censorship showed up in textbooks as well, where the range of writing that might be taught was reconceptualized and limited.

As is obvious to all of us who read standard histories of English-language education in America, these forces against populist participation in public writing, which might well constitute a standard "prehistory" of composition, are usually overlooked. Our image of our past does not, that is, interpret American nonacademic writing as a possible positive or negative influence on institutionalized writing instruction and research. So far as most of us are concerned—and "concerned" here is meant as active worry—composition began in America only in 1850, in schools, with the kind of instruction to which those Vermont parents took great exception.

It is possible, of course, to answer that formal histories are by definition unconcerned with "undiscoursed" events in American literacy. But that caution is possible only from traditional historiographic methods that give priority to institutionalized practices, defining them as the ongoing traditions or "mind" of a particular time. It is reasonable to infer from this oversight, especially as it is manifest in prominent histories of rhetoric in America, that educators think of writing through the national, race, and universal ideals that were sought when an American agenda established "English" as a literary discipline. A developing and finally overwhelming social program took literary texts and literary meaning as both its agents and its goals. It gathered existing religious aims in elementary instruction and practical aims in populist writing into the English of the schools. That English, whose predominant images cooperated with developing middle-class values, encompasses popular images of what it means to write well. It stresses upward mobility, imitation of a largely hidden American upper class, and stringent mores, as against improprieties imagined to be shunned by that upper class. The history of English in America has been depoliticized by imagining this particular scholastic brand of writing. Abstractions like "the curriculum," "progressive education," and "rhetoric" hide many considerations of nationalistic, colonizing, and pointedly political programs.

Our Side of the Story: Neoclassical Continuity

So far I have been suggesting two primary points about a social prehistory of composition. First, actual writing is not usually included in the literary history constructed over the last 150 years, for reasons other than the scope of evidence available for such studies. Second, the political and social agendas that have placed native belletristic literature rather than classical languages and literature, science, history, or philosophy in the "center" of education have worked against language instruction devoted to writing and in favor of minimal, or complex but ideologically limited, acquisitions of reading. In making these points, however, I have not denied that composition studies has a story of its own. In fact, the growing specialization of composition history appears to elevate composition above these surroundings, in problematic attempts to turn the low, excluded carnival of writing into a legitimate theater of the text.

The issue here is one of strategic choices. Given the traditional low status of composition and of its underclass faculties, how can the field achieve a respectable past, either as an elaboration of standard historical accounts of English or as a critique of them? What should the stance of composition be toward itself and toward traditional histories of rhetoric or literature that ignore it and thereby perpetuate its ad hoc and transient position as the traveling sideshow stationed beside "great" texts? The alternative to exclusion that has begun many a discipline is to look for one's own story, to accept exclusion as a matter of the range of other histories, and to find evidence for unique buried roots that sprout new plants in a garden of language-related histories. This alternative effectively separates our images of the history of composition from its embedment in the literary and educational history I have been outlining. The issue then immediately becomes whether the independent growth of composition is a weed (as American popular writing became) or cultivated and nourishing new fruit.

Composition historians have naturally, but with unacknowledged ambivalent results, made the latter choice by looking for beginnings in a buried ancient past that will explain the field's distinctness and argue for its value. In one self-crafted version of this history, the neoclassical account, composition is the logical, inevitable, and rediscovered progeny of ancient rhetoric. This approach relies on old historiographic methods, as is appropriate in accounts that aim to establish legitimacy, if disappointing from an already marginalized field. This story of composition provides catalogues of the greats, human and documentary, to create an impression that what goes on in current writing instruction and research is either the result of, or a needed reaction to, well-established precedents. In this approach, the dominant theme is continuity and union. Historical discontinuities and fragmentations are seen not only as unfortunate, but as the results of practices that lie on a spectrum bounded by inadvertent idiocy and overt maliciousness.

Composition's neoclassical accounts overtly require that the words "rhetoric" and "composition" represent the same idea, so that this branch of history can establish a legitimate past and identify the new field of composition as a revived child of a father who acknowledges it. Versions of composition that take this stance have relied, appropriately, on a few chronological accounts. For instance, Edward P. J. Corbett's invaluable introductory survey of rhetoric from Aristotle to the twentieth century in *Classical Rhetoric for the Modern Student* tells a history of rhetorical theory based on prominent rhetoricians, the textbooks whose printings can be documented from records of publishing, and revivals of interest in rhetorical scholarship. This combined data is probably the source for both the negative and positive neoclassical approaches to composition history that dominate the field.

Students and followers of Corbett have, however, chosen a curious and telling metaphoric construction of his data. They place their project of neoclassical retrieval in an agonistic—in fact antagonistic—relation to the past. Influential studies have chosen militaristic language like that adopted by Wilbur Samuel Howell in *Eighteenth-Century British Logic and Rhetoric*. Howell calls the seventeenth century an intellectual "revolution," a not uncommon figure in old histories. But Howell's language has further defined an entire interpretive stance. He calls John Locke a "hero" in the revolution and supplies the master tropes of increasing "limits," "restrictions," "separations," and finally of vivid "chasms" between logic, the parts of a whole art of discourse, and the rhetoric taught in later academic contexts. "Under auspices like these [i.e., those of the nineteenth-century elocutionists] rhetoric became anathema to the scholarly community and sacred only to the anti-intellectuals within and outside the academic system. The chasm which yawned between the elocutionists . . . and the traditional or the new rhetoricians of the eighteenth century . . . was very wide" (712). Whately accuses, Campbell "attacks" (708), "Demosthenes outranks Cicero" (656), and "Campbell took the modern side" (602). Writing in charming imitation of the great classical orators, whose lost "vehemence" Blair lamented, Howell dramatically renders a model for many historians of composition, who advocate the point (which Howell actually questions) that classical rhetoric should have remained essentially unchanged from Aristotle, Cicero, and Quintilian on. For instance:

> Only rhetorical pronunciation had remained free of *attack* during the period which Ramus had started by making delivery the second division of his *bifurcated* rhetoric and his *opponents* had ended by returning delivery to its former place in the

scheme [of rhetoric]. . . . The elocutionists in seeking to elevate the fifth part of rhetoric . . . were responding to the criticism against the traditional system . . . to *preserve* only what
the system itself had saved from successful *assault.* In other
words, the basic justification of their school could have been
that the previous *immunity* of *pronuntiatio* to *attack* entitled it to
be regarded as having continuing validity. (153; my emphases)

I quote this passage at length because its animations have
been used in so many neoclassical efforts to establish a direct
link between a whole rhetoric and a continuing composition.
Neoclassicists see classical rhetoric first as a whole, unified
system and second as a victim of "decline" into the sorry state
from which composition studies should rescue it, while at the
same time being rescued by it. The crisis of this plot is usually
at precisely the point that Howell and others highlight, Renaissance Ramism and the rise of elocution.

One important implication of Howell's description, and of
his language, is that they establish Hegelian terms of interpretation. Lawrence W. Rosenfield, in "An Autopsy of the Rhetorical Tradition," argues:

As Western thought became ever more schizoid in its efforts
to fragment self and social consciousness, it was no accident
that rhetoric, lying at a strategically important juncture linking
the two, should suffer exceptional damage in its attempts to
maintain its integrity. *Like a duchy located in an area of convergence
between two enemies engaged in a maniacal civil war, it has been
sacked by both sides for their own purposes until its resources are
almost depleted. So long as the warfare continues, there is little hope
for restoration.* (73; my emphasis)

These images and the philosophic position that permits an
animated and personified "Western Thought" are common
in many treatments of rhetoric and composition. W. Ross
Winterowd refers to how "off and on again during its long
history, rhetoric has undergone the *debasement* of being *reduced*
to style" (261; my emphasis). Ronald Reid's review of the
Boylston Professorship of Rhetoric uses the language of "decline," "survival," and "attack." Similarly, in their introduction to *Essays on Classical Rhetoric and Modern Discourse,* Robert
Connors, Lisa Ede, and Andrea Lunsford discuss the eigh-

teenth-century "triumph of the belles-lettres movement" (4) and how "rhetoric, which had rediscovered its classical roots and flowered briefly in the eighteenth century . . . had withered by the end of the nineteenth" (5). Oral rhetoricians, they say, had to establish their own departments or be "ignored to death" (6). They take current "attacks" to be a sign of classical rhetoric's vitality (11) and close with a discussion of "challenges," "gaps," and possible "bridges" between theory and practice, various disciplines, and methods. Classical rhetoric is for them a synthesizing pursuit, capable of unifying and retrieving historical losses.

Like essays in James Murphy's *The Rhetorical Tradition and Modern Writing*, where Murphy proposes classical rhetoric as writing's salvation, other essays in *Classical Rhetoric and Modern Discourse* translate theory and practice in ancient oral rhetoric into useful models for writing instruction. But aside from theoretical arguments against their Hegelian premises, not against the practice of such reawakening, the language and logic of these accounts of "rhetoric" and their many counterparts raise two problematic issues even for those without objections to their philosophical assumptions. First, the logic of this "rhetorical" history of composition imposes unity and transferability on supposedly halcyon ancient days of instruction in public speaking that was designed for a discrete ruling elite. And second, the language in these accounts is a lament against fragmentations of rhetoric that might well be interpreted differently. That is, a series of multiply caused discontinuities in rhetoric has responded to continuing new print and writing technologies and to exigencies for new writers and readers in novel discourse situations.

This is not to say that no theory is needed to interpret composition's teaching, research, and place among other kinds of language instruction or that a unified modern version of classical rhetoric would necessarily be a poor choice. But alternative explanations of the relation of rhetoric to modern discourse are ignored, explanations which would in fact better reinforce the new study of writing that composition scholars want to promote. This new study would have a mandate to replace oral rhetoric with analyses of specifically written discourse—and with explanations of the inevitably democratic

and pluralistic new discourses that result from print technology. But neoclassical historians do not account for this technology or for new ways of publishing and reading that have
inevitably recentered "rhetoric" in a series of actual changes
in its doctrines. They avoid, as most history has until recently,
politically and socially determined educational institutionalizations of language theory and practice during a concurrent
evolution of rhetorical theory.

Many other sources from outside this immediate circle of
composition historians criticize their interpretations of the history of rhetoric and consequently suggest a different history
of composition. Walter Ong, for instance, has pointed out
that classical rhetoric was itself a combative, disciplined, male
pursuit and has accounted for its disappearance with curious
sociobiologic developmental arguments. He associates oral
rhetoric with Freudian infantile orality and its disappearance
with the admission of delicate females to the schools (Ong,
"Rhetoric and Consciousness," *Rhetoric, Romance, and Technology; Fighting for Life*). He notes "the ego dominance fostered
by rhetoric" (*Rhetoric, Romance, and Technology* 15), thereby
providing a somewhat less Hegelian and more likely political
reason that classical rhetoric would not be taught in "democratic" and nationalistic education.

Even the site of the twentieth-century American revival of
academic rhetoric (identified by Corbett in *Classical Rhetoric for
the Modern Student* [627] and again in his 1985 article "The
Cornell School of Rhetoric") provided an alternative view.
Hoyt Hudson's 1923 article "The Field of Rhetoric," which
Corbett cites as "maybe the most influential" of Hudson's four
seminal articles on the field, gives us a good sense of actual
twentieth-century re-visions of rhetoric and its imagined relations to composition, literature, and English departments.

By his argument, composition is the modern version of
"oratory." Most modern persuasion is, he says, conducted in
print, but the rules of persuasion are the same as in ancient
days (172). Composition, he says, "has now two distinct
branches, writing and oratory" (172). Hudson was devoted to
the idea that both persuasive writing and oratory should be
conducted by the same principles, but he was equally devoted

to a position that would decisively divorce, not unite, composition and rhetoric. He used the theory/practice distinction that Ede and Lunsford denounce. Distancing rhetoric from the collegiate teaching of writing, Hudson insisted that rhetoric is an analytical, not a practical, art.

For Hudson, rhetoric is not a unified theory of generating any kind of writing, but an evolving set of principles applied in a distinct class of literary works that induce belief and action and are available for study. English departments, if they are to "absorb" rhetoric, should be "aware of the distinction between rhetoric and other forms of literature," which are fine, not useful, arts. He also offers a precedent for Cy Knoblauch and Lil Brannon's highly controversial interpretation of classical rhetoric in *Rhetorical Traditions and the Teaching of Writing*. Medieval and Renaissance speeches, he argues, used "conventional themes" and "old" subject matter, so that defining rhetoric as display in such times "[was] quite warranted. In any period when subject-matter was conventionalized, the consideration of invention would be neglected." In "all times the tendency is present—the tendency to depend upon tradition or convention for material and devote oneself wholly to style and writing and delivery in speaking; so that rhetoric becomes a study of how to vary a phrase, how to turn a compliment, write certain kinds of letters and formal addresses" (179). Rhetoric is the whole art, he says, only in "times of stress."

This openhanded explanation, so unlike the combative life-and-death agonistic interpretations that neoclassical composition historians have imposed on the complexity of changing rhetorical study, comfortably distinguishes composition from rhetoric. It explains narrowing and widening eras of history by embedding them in social and political contexts for discourse production. Hudson—who had just come through the divorce of speech from English departments—argued for placing rhetoric within literary studies so long as its socially consequential interests remained vivid. He was writing, of course, before the ascendancy of Leavisite New Criticism, with its hope for literary salvation in the West through close reading and its equation of attention to textual motives and results with mortal sin. But his reasoning implies that in assigning no inven-

tion, early composition instruction supported conventionality, which its original (and continuing) purpose has in fact
been to support.

Others who write more recently, like Michael Halloran,
imitate Hudson's emphasis on the public, persuasive nature
and mission of the study of rhetoric and the loss of this mission, but not the diminution of the field. Halloran shares
the view that ancient rhetoric was not theoretically unified
("Rhetoric in the American College Curriculum"). He has also
pointed out "the futility of trying to resurrect the classical
ideal" of mastering all knowledge to become a universally
effective maker of public discourse ("End of Rhetoric" 624).
He notes that "it is no longer valid to assume that speaker and
audience live in the same world and to study the techniques
by which the speaker moves his audience to act or think in
a particular way" (625), mainly because the "audience" is
unknowable. "Deprived of a given world, the modern author
is likewise deprived of a given rhetoric" (630).

The issue remains, of course, *why* the classical historians of
composition have not chosen Hudson's or Halloran's stance,
or even Ong's, but instead take on their subject with what
popular humor calls "an attitude." Some reasons have already
been established: they have compelling motives for wanting
to theorize a field they see as suffering from unconsidered
practices. They have wanted to create the legitimacy of their
field and of its professional pursuits on the grounds Quintilian
mentioned, authority and the ancients. They have been interested in showing how the interest that dominates in their
surroundings, literary study, is or at least was part of rhetoric,
not the reverse. Rhetoric is not irrelevant to literature, but by
their logic literature might well be irrelevant to it. Rhetoric,
not literature, offers salvation.

These historians also imply that to a world of initiated and
potential insiders the fate of classical rhetoric holds the secret
of the demeaned status of composition. If so ancient and
powerful a study could be chopped to bits and require the
engineering of Hannibal to restore its goals, composition need
not blame itself for the position it holds. Those in that lower
position may investigate techniques and practices unknown

to the literary outsiders created by this argument, in a strategy of drawing a larger perimeter around one's enemies.

But this attitude also reveals a remarkable tendency in composition studies to entrench its own ineffectuality. No historical lesson has been taken from the success of Leavis and the New Critics. It offers the present time nothing so attractive as reading the text of circumstances around the first composition teaching itself, without reference to esoteric, hermetic—in this case functionally lost—information. Awakened in the dead of the night, few even within the classical school could automatically cite an example of (or perhaps even pronounce) *homoioteleuton;* few would want to try. The point is that the advocated result of this strain of composition history, reestablishing classical rhetoric, ends up excluding its earliest pedagogy, most colleagues, and all new students of writing. It echoes the call for "rhetoric" in popular American publications that required formality in place of the conversational tone used in early American popular writing.

In almost every neoclassical account of the history of composition, incidental issues are mentioned whose thorough investigation would at least partially destabilize the arguments in which they are embedded. New departments of English, the beginnings of land grant universities, the division of "knowledge" into effective scholarly disciplines (which is usually treated as another sign of "fragmentation"), the rise of literary studies, and the workload (often over 100 students per class) of teachers of discourse in the nineteenth century—all are mentioned with varying emphases as the background in which classical rhetorical approaches to writing fell. Any of these conditions, as shown by this review of the context in which the rise of literary studies became possible, would provide evidence to contradict the argument that an attack on rhetoric was the motive for changing the conduct of discourse education. And any of these background matters would also oppose the idea that a Roman elitist educational practice, which promoted a way to totalize discourse production into a nondemocratic politics, can now usefully guide writing instruction.

It is consequently difficult to overlook how this strain of

composition history represents unconscious but willing participation in Raymond Williams's "selective tradition." This approach to rhetoric and composition enacts the hegemonic practice of highlighting, on the ground of "importance" and continuity, a past that would reproduce the repressive structures that the present pretends to replace. To argue that classical rhetoric is, or should have been, the progenitor of modern composition is to argue for an educational system based on an absolutely firm belief about the few who may "speak" consequentially and the many who will be excluded both from making and from understanding complex discourse. To make these arguments for the purpose of equating composition with prominent academic interests is also to approve of their privileges, the fabric of hegemonic common sense. In this case, the unspoken result from that common sense is at least partially that those with no claim on or need for a "great" tradition will nonetheless be excluded from one.

As each section of this chapter has indicated, the tendency to exclude the majority from easy converse with language ideals while containing them in organized spiritual longing for these ideals has deeply felt and well-executed purposes. Composition history, our own story about the past, can easily enough be engaged in these purposes unless it chooses another method: to stress the actual historical discontinuity with earlier curricula that composition courses embody.

2 Rereading for the Plot
Putting Writing in Its Place

The stories of English sketched in chapter 1 imply that composition had no distinct beginning apart from ancient discourse theory and practice, and certainly not a distinct origin that can be tied to an equally distinct professional study of vernacular literature. By making writing invisible in our histories, and equally by displaying it as a remnant of a continuous rhetorical tradition, we have participated in an almost absolute separation of high from low that the pair "literature" and "composition" so easily implies. Even naturalistic historians of composition perpetuate this separation. James Berlin, Robert Connors, Sharon Crowley, John Trimbur, and William B. Woods, who share what Connors calls an "openly propagandistic agenda . . . as reformers" (quoted in North 97), have in varying degrees overlooked the connection between a cultural history of composition and a cultural history of literary studies. They have pointed out the linguistic social anxieties that characterized the late nineteenth century, the resulting (and manufactured) "literacy crisis" of the time, the introduction to Harvard of "remedial" teaching, and the obsession in it with mechanical marking of errors. But they have predominantly linked these social facts to their reeducation of teachers in new agendas for composition pedagogy, not to the precise academic situation in which composition courses first appeared. (See, e.g., Berlin; Connors, "Rise and Fall," "Mechanical Correctness," "Static Abstractions"; Crowley; Woods.)

Consequently, neither neoclassical nor naturalistic composition history has directly answered some obvious questions that reveal both a distinct origin for the "composition" we know and the larger cultural agenda that entitles it. For instance, both approaches avoid mentioning a general distribution of literacy and overlook the politics of that distribution, which Harvey Graff has explored in detail (e.g., *The Legacies of Literacy*). They do not address the social passivity of a literacy fostered by education in reading, the social prejudices and moralism that met students, not teachers, in early composition courses, or ways that emerging, nationally dominant vernacular literary education pulled public writing into its agendas. Most important, neither traditional histories of English studies nor more recent neoclassical and naturalistic composition histories address the primary tension between separatist and integrationist impulses that we experience now and can document in early reactions to the literary nature of the "English composition" portion of Harvard's entrance examination. Neither, that is, suggests why composition is so tenaciously claimed to be part of English, despite traditional silence about it in literary history, criticism, and theory.

One reply to this and similar questions is that the people involved in English from its beginnings contain in one body two pursuits that they intellectually, professionally, and socially compartmentalize. This human union will be considered fully later (chapters 4 and 5), but for now it must be seen as a result from the genealogy of composition, not as its cause. English studies as we know them have much to do with a constitutive ambivalence toward writing, a duality we recognize, if partially, in received histories of the discipline by noting how one professor, Francis James Child at Harvard, claimed his specialization in literature as a rejection of work with rhetoric and student writing. Discrete composition instruction has not unambiguously been a natural if compartmentalized occupation of the literary professor, so conflicts about this "natural" union deserve some explicit attention.

Most obviously, if we engage the logic of the carnival, writing (in every sense) is tied to literature as its necessarily covered-over "Other." Both are institutionalized as part of one professional study. And further, the two have always been one, like the two sides of the paper that Saussure used to explain how cutting through *langue* also tears *parole*, in his metaphor for the relation of a paradigmatic system of language to its diachronic, temporal, ordinary utterances. But composition's part in making up the American version of English that it helps to define has not been so clear that we avoid raising

Teaching Composition and Literature

Fifteen respondents identified problems between factions in literature and composition that result when composition is taught by everyone or by some literature specialists. Five mentioned that the high work load and relatively great amount of time required to teach composition are too demanding for those in literature; 4 additional people generalized that composition teaching is "barely tolerable" for literature professionals. Two others simply said that "most people don't like to teach writing" or that it is "onerous." Two mentioned that literature specialists "really teach literature" when they teach composition; 1 mentioned that the freshman curriculum is perceived as "intellectually threadbare" and not central to the mission of English; the remaining person in this group reported that his department chair had said that "composition should be taught in context" and that the composition specialists (unfortunately) manufacture artificial contexts for it. (See Appendix, p. 244)

questions about why and how composition and literature remain supralogically entwined.

The Originating Unity of Literature and Composition

While it would be a mistake to think of English departments in America as ex nihilo creations, their significant establishment may be attributed to specific points in nineteenth-century educational history. I say "educational" history, but other conditions provided a parallel, but often difficult to connect, set of social circumstances at the founding of the "new university" and the formation of its ambivalent dispositions toward vernacular language. This ambivalence is visible in both theory and practice that are inextricably bound up in social circumstances, as many composition historians have claimed. But common explanations of composition's moments of inception are usually undertheorized. These moments cannot, that is, be fully explained either by a list of cultural events taking place when they did or by close descriptions of teaching practices—neither those we have abandoned nor those that some relentlessly pursue despite their apparent failures.

This need for an additional perspective on "facts" becomes clearest in common disagreements about whether composition or literature was the driving force that made departments of English possible. It is often argued that there is no real reason that literary studies should be the home of writing instruction (e.g., Blair, "Only One of the Voices"), but it is equally common to claim that literary study needed the justification of practical interests to ensure institutional support for a new discipline that had not too long before been thought of only as "pink sunsets" or gentlemanly dilettantism (see, e.g., Berlin, *Rhetoric and Reality* 20; G. Graff 37). In their separate descriptions of Where English Departments Came From, William Riley Parker, James Berlin, and especially Wallace Douglas and Richard Ohmann agree that social conditions that transformed universities in the late nineteenth century must be accounted for in either argument. Western expansion, post–Civil War dislocations and unease, industrialization, "the impact of science" (Parker 347), and the 1862 Morrill Act establishing land grant universities all placed American higher education in a new aspect toward its constituencies.

This new positioning of higher education had much to do with how college enrollments fell significantly after the Civil War, at least partially because the needs of graduates appeared irrelevant to a classically unified course of study leading only to a few elitist and gentlemanly professions. Established eastern institutions were naturally responsive to these new pressures, both to maintain themselves as a growth industry in keeping with new commercial standards for success and to maintain educational leadership in a period when the geographic distribution of the population and the number of universities rapidly expanded. As Gerald Graff emphasizes in *Professing Literature* (19–36), the classical "college," the forerunner of a new university, had been unembarrassed by its focus on "well bred men" who needed literary, not vocational, preparation for their roles in society. "The college spoke for the ruling class, [but] it was a ruling class that felt curiously displaced from the rising sources of power and influence" (21). When the old college collapsed in favor of the new university, its presidents, men like Porter at Yale and McCosh at Princeton, recognized that their agenda for social cohesiveness in this class depended on unity within each graduating class. They resisted innovations like the elective system and Johns Hopkins's radical plan to ignore the four-year, classical curriculum altogether (27).

The "moral tone" that college presidents and their faculties instilled had a great deal to do with language learning. It influenced the displaced, transcoded version of classical instruction in Greek and Latin literature, the template from which composition instruction would be drawn. For instance, the Hegelian "human spirit" that modern education was intended to transmit from the ancients was intimately bound up in Hegel's belief that "the mechanical elements in the learning of language" have spiritual value. As Graff says, "grammar for Hegel . . . was the alphabet of the Spirit itself" (29). It represented the religious thread from Puritan reading lessons that is continually wound through the language curriculum, even though this grander vision of grammar has had little to do with reductive experiences of learning and teaching it as "discipline" for the (mental) faculties.

The new university arose within this entire social and moral collegiate context. The old colleges were obviously faltering in their emphasis on Greek and Latin grammar as "literature" and were increasingly giving an ineffectual upper class the status of patrons, not producers, of consequential American writing. But their curricula had also been oratorical, if not fully "rhetorical." Students had learned English as their forebears had learned Greek or Latin (G. Graff 38), using textbooks that might provide "82 pages of philological notes to 102 pages of Shakespeare's play" (39). Their courses in forensics and oratorical training, which included "theme writing," suggest that continuity from rhetoric can, or should, be found in the composition courses that followed hard on. But the connection was a curricular designation, not a theoretical continuity from a unified ancient discourse art, however truncated it had become. The students in the early nineteenth century at Yale, for instance, read their often-noted themes aloud once a week, and prizes were given to the best class orator, as they were to the class poet (G. Graff 43–44). Orality, not literacy, was at issue in the college curriculum devoted to vernacular language development.

Graff remarks that "the establishment of the course called Harvard Composition shows how the study of English literature could evolve from oratory and elocution" (44). But this interpretation, which emphasizes continuity from the colleges to the quite different new universities, is misleading. It diverts us from the essence of this particular change: Harvard prototypically transformed its 1865 requirement to read English aloud to a very different *written* "composition" in 1873. This significant difference takes meaning from an entire context of philosophical, moral, social, and "class" changes that Graff and others describe. All of these elements need consideration in an explanation of "where composition comes from." They had placed Harvard's president, Charles William Eliot, in a position to lead toward the new university whose presidency he assumed in 1869. All of them contributed to his specific designation of "English," as both literature *and* composition, as this new university's great "central" project.

Wallace Douglas, in "Rhetoric for the Meritocracy," perceptively analyzes Eliot's new vision, which was outlined in his inaugural address. Douglas points out that "the basis of Eliot's educational reform was his recognition of deficiency in the values and attitudes of the American people" (127). Douglas quotes Eliot to explain this deficiency: "We do not apply to mental activities the principle of division of labor. . . . The American people have held the vulgar conceit that a Yankee can turn his hand to anything. . . . They insensibly carry [the conceit] into high places, where it is preposterous and criminal" (127). This was to say, Douglas infers, that Eliot saw "something gone wrong with the stratification or licensing system of the society" (127). Eliot opposed the notion that "just anyone" could accomplish tasks previously thought to belong to an elite, but at the same time he wanted to expand the range of students and subjects Harvard would address. Douglas explains that Eliot "had in mind only an increasing professionalization of the gentlemanly . . . professions," for which "special training" and perhaps even "knowledge and experience" might be argued to be necessary. But Eliot nonetheless had a dilemma, the paradox of elitism against populism or of the classics against "relevant" studies.

Douglas suggests that Eliot's answer to this new problem was to redefine the possible qualities of the college-produced elite. Harvard would be, Eliot said, open to "students in all conditions of life," and the university would support poor students of "capacity and character." But in a brilliant move Eliot added that "the recipient [of this largess on the part of Harvard] must be of promising ability and best character" (quoted in Douglas 128).

The catch was that there were, in Eliot's view, two possible sorts of recipients, those who were from "refined" homes and those who were not. The first group, the already elect, needed no test of their worthiness. They would be provided, in Douglas's words, "a kind of moral superstructure, a set of driving principles" (129)—the content and discourse models of their native literature. But while both the predestined and those on trial might turn out to be true sons of Harvard, those without the character of the elite—we might say those not always already in the text of *certification* that Harvard had previously instrumentalized—needed a test.

Given the often-cited facts about appointments and the curricula that established "English" after Eliot's inauguration, it is unnecessary to argue about whether composition or literature justified the new department of English that Eliot explicitly named as central in this program of principles and a test. Both literature and composition were to replace the classics; both were explicitly thought of as utilitarian means toward a well-educated populace. While it may appear to us in view of the more recent tensions between literary and composition studies to be the sheerest idiocy to think so, it then seemed that composition and literature, together, logically contained the elements that a properly evolving national culture would require. They together, not singly, would combat the "conceit" that anyone might turn a hand (and its writing) to anything. As "English," literature and composition seemed visibly to provide both principles and a test. They could allow those who were already certified to forge ahead, while making those who were not stay longer at a border checkpoint. In this way, English could perhaps instill in the nonelect the necessary refinements of taste, in the form of correct grammar and spelling, two historically important signs of cultured propriety that Harvard's way of teaching composition was going to provide.

This is a strong claim, and it might be judged farfetched were it not so clear that the dual curriculum in English after its establishment at Harvard between 1873 and 1895 was quickly outlined and nationally delivered as an archetypical negative for reproduction across the country. Richard Ohmann makes much the same point about the political unity of literature and composition in "Reading and Writing, Work and Leisure," where he creates a significant list of educational and economic events in 1893, "plus or minus one" (11). In these years, *The Dial*, a widely popular national journal, published a series of articles about English curricula at eighteen colleges and universities. The Harvard Committee on Composition and Rhetoric published its report damning the writing of its entering students, which "gave the English reform movement 'its strongest impulse' " (11). NEA appointed a Committee of Ten, which established reading and literature as the primary goals of school curricula. The 1893 depression bankrupted 150 railroads by 1894. Wage cuts and strikes involving three-quarters of a million people followed. Sears Roebuck, General Electric, and US Rubber were founded (11–13). We can add to Ohmann's list of facts some equally important indications of their social background. For example, in Milwaukee as in other industrial trade centers, nineteenth-century immigration had resulted in a severe threat to the Anglo-Saxon upper class. A Polish militia unit was formed in the city; its dominant newspaper was written in German. The potential for social unrest gave the "new university" good reasons, by the lights of the state and its traditional Anglo-Saxon puritanical origins, for focusing on vernacular literary ideals supported by the "test" of English composition. Echoing Eagleton's analysis of English agendas for literature, Ohmann infers that the new university began in these social conditions "as if it had been planned by a national authority" (16). "English took its modern shape, in the 1890s, by privileging two of its possible contents—composition and literature." Composition, he says, "spread like kudzu, mainly because its utility was incontestable—in principle, that is" (17).

But the principle at issue here was not composition's industrial utility, which a traditional Marxist would naturally highlight, so much as it was the contribution of composition to establishing English as a whole symbolic system. Together, literature and composition were the united duo of literary ideals and initiation, or indoctrination, that Eliot had automatically joined in his plan for a New Harvard. Were economic utility the issue in composition's spread, its tight connection to English literary study would eventually have been powerfully questioned, with results other than those we now address. But the two pursuits of literature and composition were joined immediately as "high" and "low," advanced and elementary. Equally to the point, they were one bourgeois effort at delight and instruction, leisure and work—a necessary but nonetheless unified "division of labor" in Eliot's desires to satisfy within a designated "new elite."

It is crucial to notice that the "composition" of this two-sided unity is elementary, insofar as it is always thought of as *freshman* "work," not as the study of writing throughout college. Unlike earlier rhetoric, taught at upper levels throughout a continuing university curriculum, composition has logically always been placed in a very different "larger" context, the curriculum of English that it completes as Eliot intended. This particular placement of writing instruction clarifies both its earliest practices and its status as against the rest of institutionalized English studies.

Composition is clearly a site for the "low," in all its senses. As an intrinsic portion of the new American educational system, composition shared in the same tendencies to institutionalize functionally "pure" systems that characterized the entire nineteenth century. Its organized inclusion in the new curriculum was an example of enclosing formerly "undiscoursed" or domestic societal functions in new, rigid definitions of them as established practices, a movement that has been described in many studies by Michel Foucault. Asylums, hospitals, schools, barracks, prisons, insurance and finance houses— and among these, the quickly prominent new discipline of

English—arose in the late nineteenth century to assure the maintenance of bourgeois reason. Obviously, the new logic of stratification and licensing that Eliot was trying to form for Harvard was not singular in his time. It appears again and again in many settings where unorganized and strictly functional activities take on systematically regulated identities as elements in an objectified culture (Stallybrass and White 22).

This is to say that a new institution of writing, in the form of "composition," lifted out of their indigenous contexts a variety of disparate parts: grammar based on lessons in classical languages, graphic conventions largely standardized by printers, pedagogical practices first designed to teach translation, "model" texts, the aura of gentility around privileged ("standard") oral usage, and practice in "composing" that had once been a small part of a larger, continuing oral rhetorical curriculum. These excavations and their collective relocation in one curricular entity formed a distinct institutional appropriation of written language. Composition and "literature" (which was made up from a similar list of practices from classical language study and from applications of rhetorical terms) were joined to provide a necessary distinguishing boundary, a way to stratify diverse participants in one of America's dominant functional interests, writing.

As Foucault often pointed out, this kind of enclosed unity requires "outsiders who make the insiders insiders." Like the carnival, composition's moment of origination involved allowing it to act as a relay, a metaphoric switch that diffuses the "center" throughout lower, metaphorically *and* actually rural orders (Stallybrass and White 38). Composition curricula contained (and still contain) Platonic shadows of the higher Reality of national, race, and universal ideals that, as we have seen, those who began literary studies consciously planned to promote. As the symbolic national domain of "literature" was suddenly produced over and against the actual public realm, a newly identifiable, low, and now alien "writing" took on the status of the "Imaginary" that Freud described. Nonliterary writing by the unentitled acquired, that is, implications and connotations of murkiness and mythic danger. In composition, literary authorship could be openly compared to the inadequacies of popular writing and especially to inadequate student authorship. Like early American popular writ-ing, institutionalized writing-as-composition could be implic-itly demeaned as unequal to writing from the advanced elect.

As in many instances in cultural history when ordinary language has been taken into an organized vision that defines it as the language of "outsiders," composition offered a way to suppress, while noticing, "the body." The grotesqueries of handwriting and of paragraphing described in the Harvard Board of Overseers' report (one boy indented regularly, every five lines) were gleefully found and reported with the sympa-thy and understanding we might expect of young boys looking at a circus fat lady. These faults and others like them were snickered over, as they still are, so that they came to represent an "Other." And by virtue of their place in a new system that would now define "pure" vernacular language, they were newly repressible. They took on "dirty" associations that the nonelect, nonpredestined student could embody. The earliest composition student, after all, was not Shakespeare: he could not be excused for spelling his own name six different ways, even though Shakespeare may have done just that.

Composition, I am suggesting, focused on (while its new handbooks simultaneously formed) correct written vernacular language, as a matter of politeness and good breeding. It followed what Pierre Bourdieu called "the whole trick of peda-gogic reason" (quoted in Stallybrass and White 95). That is, it appeared to require only insignificant personal concessions, in the form of a "polished" surface of language, while it actually stripped from new students and a nation of unschooled poten-tial writers their needs and desires to create significant pieces of writing. No consequential criticism of the new university, of its implicit discriminations among students—or by exten-sion of new processes for organizing and stratifying many functions in society—would be written from this repressive new institution of the mother tongue. The surface of writing, what the institution wanted to see, would constantly say "aah." The purposes and practices for the composition course, which are amply documented, indicate that it was set up to be a national course in silence.

If I am at all right about this, we might do well to rewrite our history in terms of the actual discontinuity represented by establishing composition courses and later research around them. Composition met new social needs, quite accurately. It embodied no theory and no precedents for later twentieth-century versions of it that neoclassical rhetoricians have retheorized. Neither was it consciously set up to practice nineteenth-century faculty psychology, at least not in the institution of the course devoted to freshmen.

The Logic of Early Practices in Composition Teaching

This theory of an originating function for composition and its discontinuity with the intentions of precedent pedagogies offers a political perspective that allows us to reread some of the earliest practices in composition courses. From this perspective, we can infer that early teaching habits were not "errors" in regard to their fairly explicit intended outcomes. They served obvious purposes that are hidden by mourning the decline of unified rhetorics of one and another sort.

For instance, the early and continuing obsession in composition with mechanical correctness, which Robert Connors and others have painstakingly described (see Connors, "Mechanical Correctness as a Focus in Composition Instruction" and "The Rhetoric of Mechanical Correctness"), can be understood as one aspect of the kind of fussiness that will always color proper opinions of a carnival, in this case the new sideshow near literature, student writing. But scrupulous early attention to mechanics was also a sign of the more general novelty of *written* rather than oral presentations of significant language (see Kitzhaber, "Rhetoric in American Colleges" 330). After centuries of examination by oral recitations, subjecting students to close scrutiny of their written language implied that a new "objectivity," an element of nineteenth-century corporate reformations of the ties among people, was displaced into the schools. There writing could serve as a formal means of relative evaluation. Its distance from a human source might permit "nonstandard" speakers, like Abraham Lincoln, to enter into discourse communities they might not otherwise find open. In writing, there is hope that one may "speak" in some sense anonymously, without stimulating prior prejudices about regional or class differences that color a reader's responses.

But yet another distancing aspect of written texts is that they appear to prevent personal appeals from their writer. Writing makes an object of a student's language, and usually without at all objectifying a composition teacher's judgment of its writer. Consequently, the practice of attending to mechanical errors allowed written texts to become instruments for examining the "body" of *a* student, not just *the* student body. This attention allows a teacher (an "auditor" in both aural and accounting senses) to examine the student's language with the same attitude that controls a clinical medical examination.

Consequently, whatever clinical distance a written text might place between a teacher and the student's person was compressed by transferring images of recitation onto the situation of written examinations. In the continuing view that a student's written language reveals personal flaws as readily as his speech, the quality of the student can be identified with the correct or incorrect quality of that student's texts. The embarrassments that students were meant to feel after corrections of their (appropriately) "mechanical work" placed them well within the range of shame that idiosyncratic speech, or the body, can evoke. Writing, in fact, exposes errors and infelicities that speech might elide.

Thus a pedagogic obsession with mechanical correctness also participated in a broadly conceived nineteenth-century project of cleanliness. As Stallybrass and White explain this project, it was undertaken in all good as well as bad faith to convince the masses of their dirtiness while saving them from it. It used the figure of separation between human and animal in an impulse to promote scrubbed surfaces. This distinction between human and "animal" also, by persistently observing and surveying an "Other," made the body of the other permanently visible. It raised the issue of contamination from the pointedly unwashed masses, while also, of course, placing them in the dangerous site of the physically messy carnival, a place desired but officially shunned (Stallybrass and White 25–35).

Once again, this perspective on practices in composition

may appear forced. But it takes no creativity to recall the language of judgments from the Harvard Board of Examiners or continuing uses of such language in describing flaws in student writing. The designations that Mina Shaughnessy pointed out (*Errors and Expectations*) of "remedies," "clinics," "diagnosis," and "treatments" to "clean up" the errors of students have complex connotations that can be historically placed in an entire social agenda designed to convince an institution of its control over the language of citizens while persuading those individuals of their flaws. As in traditional Christianity, the metaphoric precedent for established literary study, a conviction of sin is necessary for sanctifying redemption to have force.

The actual new writing assignments that enacted this focus on mechanics were also subtly related to graphic details. Actual pedagogies for composing, in the sense of turning out whole pieces of discourse, have at least distant origins in ancient rhetorical exercises, which were used as transitions from grammar instruction in the schools to university-level preparation in oral discourse. In classical curricula (at a transitional site always argued over by the *grammaticus* and the *rhetor*), these assignments had two purposes. As D'Angelo and others have made clear, the earliest "composition" exercises gave students practice in the topics of rhetorical invention, the probes of comparison, contrast, classification, and the like. These common topics were supposed to provoke the student's memory of commonplaces—what others had already said effectively in similar public situations. Curricularly transitional compositions were assigned as warm-ups for composing public speeches. Their actual written status was not an issue, although the occasions for which they might be delivered orally were explicit in their presentation. However, the grammatical correctness of their sentences *was* an issue, because students in higher education before and throughout the nineteenth century had been prepared to speak in Latin, to read Latin and Greek, and to translate proficiently among classical and vernacular languages—all processes that require syntactic and grammatical expertise.

To achieve both of these purposes, what we might call "precomposition" practices in composing often treated moralistic and global subjects. They included topics like "Disease," "Comets," "Evanescence of Pleasure," "The Domestic Life of the Ancient Egyptians," "Curiosity," and "The Dice of the Gods Are Loaded" (Kitzhaber, "Rhetoric" 174). In instruction designed to test students' ability to call up common wisdom and to demonstrate grammatical and syntactic fluency in more than one language, such topics made sense.

But the assignments in our concern, newly established composition courses, changed. Reasoning about these changes usually attributes them to positive educational "reforms" without questioning their equal participation in the institutional constitution of a new course for a different sort of student. In what appears to have been a progressive attempt to allow the romantically conceived active learner to write "better," new criteria for making assignments took over. These criteria said that topics for writing should be of "interest" to students and should be about subjects that the students "knew something" about. These criteria were strenuously promoted in the later nineteenth century, when courses in "daily themes" began and invention was no longer included in textbooks, which instead began to supply lists of theme topics. Albert Kitzhaber's history of composition claims that "the reaction away from the old types of composition subjects became almost complete" ("Rhetoric" 173). In a move that could with fairness be characterized as from the sublime to the ridiculous, students wrote about "Our Newsboy," "How I Learned to Like Good Music," "The First Snowstorm This Year," "A Twenty-mile Ride for the Doctor," and "Condition of the Roads in This Neighborhood." Observations from personal experience and narratives about them replaced any purchase on participating in public discourse that the student might once have had.

Consequently, both the written status of mechanically marked compositions and the content of those compositions were now reduced to objects of inconsequentiality. The vernacular writing that had been taught in the earlier nineteenth century had had something to do with the kind of writing that those in high schools—and for some time that those at upper levels in college—might do as active participants in American communities. But the new freshman assignments both infantilized the entering student and exposed him to invidious, no matter how inaccurate, comparisons with the elite group who had formerly made up the student body—and who had not had to take freshman composition. This elite group had not known much more about composing in their native language without benefit of commonplaces than the new pool of students did. Their classical education had required some Latin composition, but not much English writing. Harvard's Boylston professors had lectured on composing, at least at first, to seniors, not to freshmen.

It is common to attribute both the intense focus on mechanical correctness and the new assignments that took little preparation for teaching to the kind of work that is demanded when a teacher must read the writing of two or three hundred students at once, in the well-documented conditions Harvard and other universities set up for teaching composition. The "work" of composition identified by Ohmann was no Marxist emblem, but a staggering number of essays whose correction was all anyone had time for and which invited irritation with any errors that impeded reading. But it is also important to notice the kind of subject that the content of this work load made of composition, not just of compositions.

Even a scholar like Frank D'Angelo appears to miss the character of this content in his "Nineteenth-Century Forms/ Modes of Discourse: A Critical Inquiry." Here D'Angelo shows that textbooks used before those written for these new students and courses listed genres of discourse that an actual writer might want advice about—letters, fiction, essays, theses, and orations. These functional categories were divided further into more specific purposes like news letters, business letters, ceremonial letters, friendly letters, histories of law, popular scientific prose, and criticism, which often included publishable reviews (32). But D'Angelo infers from his evidence only that "description, narration, exposition, and argumentation . . . existed alongside the more numerous categories in the nineteenth century, and were later separated out" (33). He says that since these four modes are so problematic, they should be abandoned. It goes without saying here, and unfortunately everywhere, that a new purpose for beginning courses must have had something to do with the disappearance of practice in writing generic documents that a student might have to produce outside a classroom, the site where the theme and the modes have their only life.

The disappearance of "generic categories" or varieties of writing assignments that D'Angelo has traced exemplifies the abandonment of a genuinely rhetorical (in the sense of public) impulse in writing instruction in both high schools and colleges. This leveling into modes rather than actual purposes for writing results in convincing both students and teachers that their already demeaned "practical" instruction further has no actual practical purpose, except by rather oblique metaphoric extensions that suggest (as rhetorical education never had) that writing can be undertaken and executed well without a specific goal in mind. The modes therefore assimilate composing into spiritual rather than functional aims, "ideals" like those that were established for literary study. They further mystify "English." They divorce writing from the mundane— or active—reasons that students will write, just as increasingly aesthetic views of literature have substituted formalist for rhetorical categories of analysis. We consequently mistake a cause for a result if we attribute new composition assignments and textbook treatments of them to numbers of students. Instead, those numbers and textbooks precisely fit the purposes for establishing such a course at all. Both the earliest "theory" behind composition and its practical implementations divided written texts from actual writing situations.

From this perspective, early composition practices harmoniously supported their culture's vision of public writing. Students were writing only for a surface gentility, only about "personal" experiences that immediately exposed their genteel or more humble origins to their teachers, and only in the form of the modal "theme," which has its only life in English courses themselves. These political—not "rhetorical" or "philosophic"—ways of appropriating language into the hegemonic common sense of the new university, with its program for naming two kinds of recipients of new education, comprised a whole system. Its diversion from the actual task of learning to write consequential discourse is clear.

These claims about the logic of mechanical obsessions, personal topics, and the ways that "modes" level and trivialize purposes for writing have support from the ideas and practices of two successive holders of the Boylston Chair at Harvard, Ellery T. Channing and A. S. Hill. These faculty members were enormously influential spokesmen for two distinct ages of discourse instruction. Channing, in his lectures to *seniors* at Harvard between 1819 and 1851, promulgated a view of writing that is startling for its insistence on democratic education in discourse production:

> When we read the history of the most democratical states of antiquity, we are constantly struck with the controlling influence of a few leading men. . . . The orator, the commander, his elevation and fall, these are the important incidents and personages that are constantly thrust upon our notice. . . . But when you look at society now, you see everywhere a disposition to place the security of nations and of every individual on the broad foundation of laws and institutions. (14–15)

For Channing, modern rhetoric had to do with *writing*, the more egalitarian discourse that at least moves rhetoric's fatherly oral tropes into brotherly printed relationships. He lectured on "A Writer's Preparation" and "A Writer's Habits," making the assumption that significant discourse would be written, if largely on the basis of *reading* "good books." It is enormously significant in light of the incipient entrenchment of a literary "center" that Channing, taking criticism to be an evaluative activity, went into some detail about the problem of allowing reading to stifle "originality," as he did about allowing "good" reading to unify the curriculum and character of education. "That a student is exposed to perils from his constant association with great writers is not disputed. . . . A man may be discouraged by contemplating excellence" (198–99).

Channing clearly thought that reading should serve, not stifle, what students would themselves think and say. Its purpose was not to promulgate "race ideals" and stop at that. He made a distinction between students, for whom studying "is to be the . . . *business* . . . and not the ornament" (205), and the adult, who "has a prominent object, of a very grave character and quite unconnected with literary delights, to occupy, excite and govern his mind" (205).

But Channing's balanced attitude toward literature in the life of the whole adult was formed at a time when social change had not required both principles and a test. Adams Sherman Hill, who had been in Eliot's class, was appointed by him to replace Francis James Child in the Boylston Chair in 1876 and remained in it until 1904. Hill had been a journalist and shared President Eliot's concern for English studies, especially composition. He revealed much of his attitude toward composition and a "real" (classical) education in his statement that until a boy "knows how to write a simple English sentence, he should not be allowed to open a Latin grammar" (quoted in Kitzhaber, "Rhetoric" 99). Hill is known for having a sharp tongue and dulled empathy, for expanding Harvard's English staff, and for recommending that sophomore rhetoric, which had been the only course required of postfreshmen, be put in the freshman year. He was finally successful in this latter goal. In 1885 the prototypical freshman English course (English A) began. With Eliot's encouragement to privilege as "the first subject . . . the English language and literature" (quoted in Kitzhaber, "Rhetoric" 54), Hill and his course pointedly forced the academic discontinuity from which current composition takes its context and character. In the move to the freshman year, writing was firmly placed in the site for winnowing and indoctrination that has located it for the century since. This move shows how the link between Harvard's earlier entrance exam and a freshman course was forged, locking the status of composition tightly in place across the country.

The examination had, of course, been important on its own. It was a way for the student to demonstrate that he came from a school where the teachers had prepared him with the literature on Harvard's canonical lists and with "correct spelling, punctuation, and expression, as well as legible handwriting; . . . failure in any of these particulars will be taken into account at the examination" (quoted in Kitzhaber, "Rhetoric" 57). As the catalogues of many institutions reveal, forms of this examination became the most powerful instrument for discriminating among students in higher education. But the exam also was placed to insure that Hill's new *freshman* course, which defined most of the issues now comprising composition studies, was on basically corrective, remedial ground. In this freshman course, Hill's infamous *Principles of Rhetoric*, which begins with a section on "grammatical purity," replaced Campbell's quite different *Philosophy of Rhetoric*.

For our purpose, it is important to notice how linking "the" exam to "the" course was closely tied to newly central vernacular literary study. Hill believed that literature taught composition, that "unconscious absorption" teaches how to write, significantly "as one acquires good manners by associating with gentlemen and ladies" (quoted in Reid 255). It is no accident that the still dominant modes—description, narration, exposition, and argument—include two clear translations of literary strategies, one of science-oriented explanation, and one of a classical rhetorical aim. This proportion of emphases among the modes has everything to do with the proportion of courses in each mansion of English, although many course syllabi since show that exposition and argument can also be exemplified, and one supposes can be taught, through only belletristic examples.

But to highlight this common perception, we need to look more closely at the problematic relation between an act that is thought of as "merely writing" and engaging in "authorship," the privileged creation that everything about composition appears to oppose or negate. Toward the beginning of English as both literature and composition, the new profession worried with this issue as it has not done since.

As Donald Stewart has shown, the early "pedagogical section" of the Modern Language Association produced papers, questionnaires, and reports that show how "composition" was thought of as opposed to, or at least quite distinct from, "authorship," the concept that might be taken to be closest to the ideals of current composition theorists. "Rhetoric" was in effect folded into composition, which was equated "with grammar, spelling, and punctuation and, not surprisingly . . . an elementary subject, not worthy of scholarly study" (Stewart, "Status" 735). It was the "art of writing clearly and correctly about ordinary matters and with such limitations as you expect in a good business letter. . . . Mr. Cornford [author of *English Composition*] sets out to teach schoolboys literary thoughts and write them down with literary force and grace; is it well to teach the literary art to English schoolboys? We do not think it is well; . . . *it is alien to the genius of the nation"* (*Proceedings*, 1902, viii, quoted in Stewart 742; my emphasis).

Others in this exchange, notably John Gerung, wrote textbooks that contained a great deal of instruction in invention (Crowley, "Evolution"). Despite the blame he has taken for some of the faults of "current-traditional" teaching, Gerung told his MLA audience that composition "however humble its tasks, is veritable authorship. . . . To put the student frankly on the basis of authorship . . . is to impart immensely greater reality to his study of rhetoric" (*Proceedings*, 1902, viii, quoted in Stewart 742). But it is also clear from this exchange that Gerung and others, as Hudson would later, distinguished rhetoric as an analytical art.

It is not very relevant to equate the "literary thoughts" or "literary art" mentioned in these records with nonfunctional belletristic writing. Although these arguments about the purpose of teaching composition had much to do with entrenching literature and establishing national ideals about its perfection, they were not based on a disagreement about whether composition students should actually aspire to literary greatness. As curricula in universities across the country in the earlier twentieth century show (see below), courses in "description" and "narration" included both writing short stories and using expository techniques. But the students' propriety in or ability to create influential but only belletristic writing was not the point about "authorship" that was argued.

Those who opposed Gerung about the students' potential for authorship thought of writing as "practical," or applied, and established *reading* as the goal their departments should pursue, although some in the middle significantly noted that Gerung might be right about fostering authorship in the exceptional student, but was wrong about the majority (Stewart, "Status" 742–43). The important revelation in these MLA *Proceedings* is that a plan was explicitly mapped out for denying, not for promoting, both old and new systems that might lead the majority of students into producing significant discourse of any kind. This plan had to do with the so-called capacities of, and equally with the desire to control, the majority of unevenly prepared students who were newly continuing in high schools and being admitted to colleges. "Writing," in the sense that composition's naturalistic historians have supported it, was not being taught to entering students, and few objected because its ancillary relation to studying literature was taken to be obvious.

All of these ways that vernacular literature became privileged in "English" recall lessons from the *New England Primer*, with its overt moralism and puritanical devotion to discipline and rigid standards for their own sake. It takes no extensive documentation to distinguish this strain in literary ideals derived from the New England bias and their projections onto distinctly new composition teaching in universities. This influence, more than Hill's reputed model of ill humor, gave composition an especially unpleasant flavor—decisively bourgeois but always aspiring to social elevation as a sign of salvation. A puritanical, unrelievedly serious tone infused the new devotion to literature and its imagined ability to make students "absorb" felicitous expression, so that Hawthorne's dark forests and Melville's chorus of whale-devouring sharks were ready to haunt, not delight, the writer of a misspelled theme.

The Rise of Composition: History as Catalogue

I have been arguing that composition was not established as a failed set of practices or a diminution and debasement of classical rhetoric, but as a consciously selected menu to test students' knowledge of graphic conventions, to certify their propriety, and to socialize them into good academic manners. It accomplished this by making both teachers and students vividly aware of the enormous difference between student writing and that of the (doubly meant) "masters." But the composition I mean in this argument, the now "classic" freshman course, was not the only sort of writing that English departments took on to guarantee a place for their politically practical mission, to apply Arnold's, and later Leavis's, religious associations with literature to the nation's war wounds and industrial sordidness.

University catalogue descriptions of English show the extent to which public forms of writing were institutionalized by new departments of English in their early decades, as they do the developing image of one universal freshman-level composition course. Over the period from 1920 to 1960, we see both an enormous variety of writing courses and their leveling into the generic forms that replaced them as New Critical literary principles became entrenched after World War II. In the documents selected for examination (from fifteen geographically separate research universities that now offer significant coursework in composition or creative writing[1]), we find the self-images of rapidly entitled curricular structures, which may admittedly have differed from actual departmental practices. But these seventy-five documents, which were selected to emphasize the programs of research universities where graduate students provide teaching, may be taken as speech acts that create institutional definitions of composition and other kinds of writing instructions, make departmental structures official, and enact requirements. They provide writing instruction with its own "language"—patterns of content, entitlement, "delivery," and pedagogy that have increasingly enclosed composition in its now normally ancillary status. These are not records of the philosophical bases of instruction like those examined by James Berlin in his *Rhetoric and Reality*, but a print ethnography of institutionalizations of written language.

The universities whose catalogues I examined were Arizona, Berkeley, Colorado, Cornell, Georgia, Harvard, Iowa, Kansas, Michigan, Nebraska, North Carolina, Oregon, Stanford, Washington, and Wisconsin-Madison. Most of these seventy-five archived documents name the teaching faculty (professors, associate professors, and assistant professors) and the lower or unranked staff. Over the period from 1920 to 1960, these departments went from an average size of 15 to 31 faculty members, and from 29 to 51 in ranks below them. The departmental sizes relative to each other obviously varied quite a bit, but in general the pattern of doubling in size is constant.

1. The primary source for interpreting the relation of creative writing courses to programs in English departments is Debra Monroe's 1985 M.A. thesis, "Fact and Fiction: Distinctions between Composition and Creative Writing," directed by Donald Stewart, University of Kansas. I am indebted to her for allowing me access to her primary sources, the seventy-five catalogue excerpts analyzed here.

The catalogue descriptions of English, which evolved into an increasingly literary curriculum, show the centralized composition that histories have addressed to be *one*, but not necessarily the overriding, kind of writing that English first included in its curricula. Especially in the earlier decades, a surprising variety of writing courses was taught. In 1920 Berkeley taught both "oral and written discussion of selected authors" in its 1A/B course and "Business Practice" for "precision and directness" in 1C/D. In the upper division, it also taught Advanced Business Practice, Critical Writing (primarily reviews of contemporary authors), Frequent Writing, Essay Writing, a course in "Essays in Literary Backgrounds" to be written on a different historical "period" each year, and verse composition, a course common at many of these schools. In 1960 Berkeley was teaching the 1A/B sequence of "training in writing" and introduction to literature, and 41A/B, "Writing in connection with reading important books." It had instituted a new rubric of "Advanced Composition" that included short story, verse, critical, and narrative and descriptive writing; an "advanced" writing category primarily for teachers; expository and critical writing courses; a new advanced composition; and a section of "advanced prose" for teaching assistants, readers, and honors students in other departments. But all of these classes were subheadings of the same course, which had begun in 1940–41. At the 300 level, "Problems in Teaching English Literature and Composition in Secondary Schools" was also taught.

The change that occurred at Berkeley, as it did at many other schools, was not so much to reduce the appearance of numbers of writing courses as to increasingly identify introductory writing courses with the result of reading "important" literature, leaving individual purposes for composing to more advanced courses. In 1940–41, Berkeley taught 74 sections of its 1A/B course, 4 of Masterpieces of Literature, and 17 sections of literary sophomore survey. In 1930–31, Michigan (with a limit of 20 students per class) taught 54 sections of English 1, 39 of English 2, and 6 of its sophomore composition for those who got a B or better in 1 and 2. Few of the other schools, in only a few of the years examined, documented how many sections were taught in catalogues that also served as their class schedules. But their stated requirements and the large numbers of unranked teachers responsible for implementing them suggest that Berkeley and Michigan were not teaching proportionately more sections than most.

In any case, as the professoriat grew in these schools, the writing curriculum generally became less diverse and more focused on literary texts, while the literature curriculum, particularly at the graduate level, became larger and more indicative of individual faculty interests. At the University of Wisconsin-Madison, which in the early 1970s discontinued freshman composition and fired its graduate assistants to quell a strike, the change over this earlier period was from eleven distinct courses to six. The 1920–21 curriculum included English Composition, Freshman English (for agricultural students), Freshman Rhetoric (required of the rest), Sophomore Composition, Argumentation ("lecture, textbook, practice, exercise"), Argumentative Addresses, Commercial Correspondence, Advanced Commercial Correspondence, Junior Composition, Advanced Composition (narration and dramatic writing), Technical Composition, and an upper-level graduate rhetoric course. The 1960–61 catalogue lists only the Composition (a noncredit course in "fundamentals of writing"), the Freshman English, the Intermediate Composition in a couple of versions, and a Composition for Teachers.

Even at Michigan, often justifiably singled out for its model sensibilities about writing, changes tell the same story. In 1920–21, before Fred Newton Scott's distinct rhetoric department was integrated into English, the department had only three courses possibly related to writing—"1. Literature in historical outline"; "3. Old English" ("to provide . . . a solid basis for the study of English grammar," including *Beowulf*); and "9. Modern English Grammar." From 1930 the department's offerings were divided into four categories: English Composition, English Language, English Literature, and Rhetoric and Criticism (described as assisting "the discovery of how expression becomes most effective," which Hudson would have approved). The number and variety of courses related to writing in the earlier years is impressive. In 1930 Composition was offered to freshmen; to sophomores with good grades in the freshman course; to juniors as Writing of Verse, Report Writing, and Junior Composition ("careful revising of original work"); and to seniors as short narratives and as Critical Writing. The Rhetoric and Criticism division offered Rhetorical Analysis ("the study of literary methods by analysis; fundamental principles of criticism"), Techniques of Novel Writing, Diction and Usage, Ancient Rhetoric and Poetic, and Medieval and Renaissance Rhetoric and Poetic. But by 1950, in new course groupings by levels of students rather than by content, the department offered only Freshman and Sophomore composition, Creative Writing, Advanced Exposition, and Criticism.

It might be argued that the tendency I report was merely to "streamline" the curriculum, a political agenda in any setting but one that is usually interpreted only as "clarifying." But other indications show a politics afoot. For one thing, it is obvious that rhetorical criticism and analysis gave way, after about 1950, to "literary" criticism in a formalist mode. Rhetoric had been taught at upper levels, usually in the ways Hudson suggested, and had often named lower-level writing courses. But its offerings appear greatly diminished after World War II.

In addition, faculty members in specific courses would retire or die and not be replaced with others in their field. No one with the precise interests of either Lane Cooper or William Strunk (of Strunk and White) replaced either of them at Cornell. Strunk's 1930 course, "English Usage and Style . . . the study of the theory of good English, the study of words, idioms, and pronunciation, and related topics," does not look much like Assistant Professor Jones's 1940 version, "English Style and Usage . . . history and theory of English syntax" and "analysis of English prose forms, with practice in writing." Also, as graduate students did more teaching, their work was to be controlled and simplified. At the University of Washington, the Freshman Composition faculty members were snappily separated from the others: "Associate Professor Lawson in charge." (At Georgia the only 1950–51 course in writing, "2xy. Composition," was listed as under the supervision of "Miss Dumas and the Staff.")

It would be an error to dismiss this pattern as merely a totalizing growth of literary dominance, although that is easy enough to see. Patterns *within* broadly conceived composition studies also changed. "Speech" having left English in the 1920s, courses in "oral and written" discourse or in oral interpretation ("Public Discussion and Debate" at North Carolina in 1920) were dropped or separated into a new division in a department, as at Stanford, where a "Division of Public Speaking" appeared in 1930–31. But in addition, discrete descriptions of motives for writing in the 1920 and 1930 catalogues were folded together later on. From 1940 to 1960, catalogues provided generalized definitions of writing by its own faculties, who were now distinguishable from creative writing and literature faculty.

Notably, these sources do not persuasively indicate that the "four modes" were treated in the earlier twentieth century as four parts of one rather misguided definition of mastery in writing. Instead, the four elements of description, narration, exposition, and argument appear to have been used at first to represent discrete interests and intentions.

At Colorado in 1920, when there were eighteen different courses listed under "English Language," "Oral Interpretation" was listed under Literature. Again in 1930 Freshman English was described respectively as "textbook, themes, oral expression" and "textbook, exercises, themes, conferences." (It is notable that throughout these catalogues course descriptions very frequently refer to "conferences" and to individualized attention to students as the guiding pedagogy.) In 1941 the Colorado course became "Composition: Exposition, Description, Narration" and "Composition: Exposition and Argument," the latter taught for pre-medical and pre-business students. At Iowa in 1920 "Constructive Rhetoric," "Description and Narration," "Exposition," "Rhetoric," "Composition," and "Essay" were separate courses. In 1930 the freshman courses were "1. Art of Writing" (practice in writing and the study of literature, required for all freshmen) and "109–110. Advanced Rhetoric" (writing and analysis of English, to learn "the inner technique of prose composition," including euphony, rhythm, and sentence patterns). In 1950–51 the freshman students had the option of taking only essay writing *or* demonstrating satisfactory work in fiction writing. Not until 1960 were the courses in composition listed under a separate heading, where they became Exposition 1 and 2 (writing "expository and informal" essays) and Technical, Business, Advanced Exposition, and Advanced Technical Writing.

At Kansas in 1920 the freshmen studied Rhetoric 1 and 2 ("written exercises with study of rhetorical theory"). The sophomores, juniors, and seniors were offered separate courses that included Principles of Argumentation, Narration and Description (preparation for criticism and versification), Exposition, Advanced Argument, Literary Criticism, Essay Writing, Prose Invention ("Theories of literary art, with practice in original writing"), and Advanced Composition. By 1950–51 Exposition, Technical Writing, and Essay Writing were the only separate offerings. By 1960 Kansas was still offering "Advanced Composition. Practice in writing essays with emphasis on problems in exposition: analysis, classification, comparison and contrast, and definition," along with "Narration and Description. Practice in writing descriptive and narrative sketches and the personal essay. Reading of short stories, essays, and other types of literature." "Writing the Research Paper" and "Technical Writing" were the other courses, offered to advanced students.

Often a university composition requirement covers a year, or two quarters, and its faculty must conceive separate courses to fill the time allotted. Often, unfortunately, this is done without much reference to a content that represents mastery of writing abilities in a reasoned developmental sequence. Nonetheless, these examples of changes that leveled the non-belletristic writing curriculum were not extraordinary. They represent fairly clear distinctions among the lowest level courses in "elements," "fundamentals," "basics," "principles," "preliminaries," and other early ideas of writing that appear to have coherent but separate motives and histories. At the University of Colorado, groupings of "English Language" and "English Literature" were listed sequentially in 1920 and 1930, without much duplication in faculty or any sign that the separately listed courses were interrelated. By 1940 Colorado had a department of "English Language and Literature (including Speech)." At the land grant universities, including Berkeley and Stanford, "scientific" and "commercial" courses had been diversely included from the outset.

This evidence clearly shows bases for some new interpretations of the history of composition. Composition has not been a poor or a preservative version of classical rhetoric, or a unified application of the modes and of mechanical correctness, or an indoctrination to monolithic literary values that appear designed to counter other professional interests—*except* in its introductory form. Undulating and distinct curricular purposes comprise "English" and the writing taught in it. In other words, we must focus on *freshman* composition as the center of academic interest in writing to see it as the "test" before the "principles" in Eliot's stratification of students. Without this focus, we would be forced to revise common assessments of English departments, which appear at these institutions to have accepted many sorts of writing instruction as a loose coalition of curricula at least until the 1950s. These catalogues do, however, reinforce the view that freshman composition was instituted for, and has continued to be provided for, "failures."

At almost all of the schools represented in this sample, and at many others, students are "excused" from composition on the basis of "success" in passing an examination. Catalogue after catalogue shows that the old Harvard exam has become the freshman course's "equivalent," a test that can be substituted for college-level writing instruction. The catalogues also show that the course will be imposed discriminatingly on certain categories of students. At Georgia, for instance, "The Elements of English" (including, magnificently, "business correspondence, a review of grammar, composition writing, and the reading of selected classics") was required "of one-year students in Agriculture who are not eligible to enter English 1." Elaborate (not to say rococo) systems have been established so that such students in agriculture, business, education, pharmacy, engineering, and other less gentlemanly professions take separately described versions (at Nebraska with different numbers of hours) than those who major in English or who can be excused from this instruction altogether.

It cannot be stressed enough that these systems around freshman composition were not devised to tell precisely where a student should *begin* to write in college, but to send the message that Eliot, the Harvard Board of Overseers, and A. S. Hill had in mind. The language of failure, deficiency, and excuses is universal. At Washington in 1920, for instance, "1–2–3 Freshman Composition" says "the word [sic] done in this course is regarded as belonging rather to the high school than to the University. Those whose preliminary training has been superior are excused from the course on examination. A grade of 'A' in course 1 excuses a student from course 2." In this fortunate fall, easily imagined as a classic Freudian slip, composition's mission is again made clear—to teach a different "word." This word is not the privileged and accepting interchange within literary ideology, but the one that tells deficient nonmajors how incompetent they are to participate in literary/literate elitism. The others will never have to hear this word, on Eliot's assumption that they already know it, like Boston aristocrats who *have* their hats.

It makes little difference what the avowed content of such a course is, given its presentation. It should be emphasized that these systems do not characterize a remedial course whose supposedly miscreant students Mina Shaughnessy so acutely portrayed in *Errors and Expectations*. This institutional apparatus applies to the credited introduction to postsecondary discourse that could, conceived differently, introduce students from various social and economic backgrounds to the linguistic diversity, and to the distinct privileging practices within this diversity, that are ahead of them.

Nonetheless, students whom the institution expects to, and who themselves expect to, succeed in college have rarely come near the freshman course, except in very recent global requirements that offer no exemptions (see chapter 3). Generally, the ideology that has been institutionalized as the setting for composition reenacts earlier discriminatory practices that kept all but upper-class boys out of Harvard and Yale in the early nineteenth century, when Channing lectured. At the "new" Harvard and at its public imitations across the country, ostensibly founded to educate contemporary students differently, composition has provided a continuing way to separate the unpredestined from those who belong. It now does this either definitively, by encouraging them to leave school, or more vaguely, by convincing large numbers of native speakers and otherwise accomplished citizens that they are "not good at English."

By helping to make this inadequacy the tenor of academic textual production and by providing a way to distinguish insiders from outsiders, institutions of writing instruction have willingly marginalized the majority of students. Composition is thus easy to explain as an obvious place for safely containing negative attitudes toward or internal anxieties about the perfections of literature, its immediate surround. And this theoretical hypothesis can be verified by actual, "catalogued," clues. The pictures they paint of great changes being made in quite brief intervals indicate a subtext of anxieties about retaining new professional gains, about clarifying (indeed, finding) a theoretical basis for research, about demonstrating a faculty's importance, and particularly about contrasting the immorality of error-ridden writing to the perfection of literature. Michigan, for instance, consistently published a long credo stating that "literature, *broadly defined*, presents the best that has been thought and said in the world" (my emphasis). This statement may have caught the attention of Nobel hopefuls in other departments, but it certainly was read by entering students.

Similarly, it is no wonder that the argument that reading literature could teach writing would be taken up at early MLA meetings, not to demean publicly approved good writing but to elevate literature to the public status writing had held in an earlier American culture. Michigan's claim for literary study does, after all, sound much like the arguments that Isocrates, Cicero, and Quintilian made about training the orator who would be able to use literature to deliberate the state's interests, although practice belies this reason for making it. But whatever motives have formed positive or negative language about composition, it is clear that these motives should include the actual results of the course in its English department contexts. It is a place where failure is named, where it is "disciplined and punished," and from which the elect are excused.

But if we consider that it was not entirely necessary for the field of composition itself to take up *freshman* English as its center, we must again look at a choice *as* a choice. We need, that is, to be alert to ways that composition as a field cooperates with the purposes that established the first freshman courses despite the field's frequently stated objections to the results these purposes have entailed. For instance, if the freshman course is allowed to characterize the entire historical conduct of writing instruction in higher education, we inadvertently comply with poor treatments of faculties who provide this instruction. Additionally, if we look for a history of "composition" as a history of its freshman conduct—the mechanical, modal repressions that naturalistic historians of composition focus on—we cannot find a legitimizing past to support either neoclassical or anticlassical theorizations of current teaching.

Even more important, we cage ourselves by identifying with the freshman enterprise. Doing so accepts that composition is an ancilla to literary study, an acceptance that leads us to ignore the legitimacy that disruptions in nineteenth-century educational history temporarily gave to many kinds of writing, including the "creative" sorts that are rarely mentioned in composition history or research. By making this choice, the field of composition inadvertently cooperates with a bad story. It becomes an introductory dunking game placed before the serious drama of later study. In this guise, composition is not the supposed irrelevant opposite, but a necessary photographic negative, the "Other," in the recently developed literary contexts where it has been taught. As both of these historical chapters suggest, composition's own version of its historical legitimacy in rhetoric and its limited self-definition as a freshman course allow new departments devoted to the "best" written language to perpetuate the claim that they can judge, and dismiss, the majority's perpetually worst.

Part II

The Carnival in the Great American Theme Park: Established Composition

Introduction

The historical part of this study suggested that composition, defined as the field around a freshman course, began in a political moment that was embedded in ambivalence about how to assimilate unentitled, newly admitted students in the late nineteenth-century "new university," which was in turn formed to address its era's social, economic, and political changes. When composition as we know it best was established, a certain kind of good sense shaped early practices that now appear to be insupportable ways to teach and to learn to write. Punitive diagnostic exams, an obsession with mechanics, and personal theme topics that revealed the student's origins and linguistic propriety while exposing his writing's "body" were all excellent mechanisms for establishing a necessary circus of writing. Freshman composition was, in these senses, a ferociously practical but theoretically inarticulate, component of new American literary studies.

Composition students, composition teaching, and ways of organizing both have since then defined the space of a seemingly inconsequential sideshow. This space, as the next part of this study explains, contains a dualistic institutionalized entertainment where covert, risky/risqué impulses toward and from the language of the majority may be acted out. In its atmosphere, many anxieties about the privileges of certain spoken dialects and written artifacts can be displaced, or translated, to control descendants of Eliot's imagined potential recipients of education in the now traditional "new" university. This control complements apparently different intellectual "principles" that are assigned to the study of literature, an equally new enterprise. Early composition practices and their established progeny play against a "serious" (unified, purposeful, idealistic, and ideological) literary study of vernacular texts.

It is also reasonable to argue, extending Shirley Brice Heath's reasoning (chapter 1), that composition was established in its carnivalesque aspect to regulate writing that accomplished domestic exchanges among American citizens by placing it under the bourgeois gaze of an institution. Most of what students of composition have been instructed to write since the late nineteenth century cannot be found "in nature." It stays on the margins of textual worlds in which knowledge and politics interact, where actions take place with increasing fequency without regard to the "essay."

These origins also divorced writing instruction in universities from the history of rhetorical education for participation in public forums. Composition practice has not emphasized education in conceiving whole pieces of discourse, the instruction that Channing at least partially offered to Harvard's graduating seniors when it was still assumed that only an elite would be admitted, and would receive certification, by exclusive postsecondary institutions. Seeking legitimization, historical accounts of composition often suppress this separation. Many in the field of composition emphatically claim that they extend supposedly "natural" ways to continue exercises between secondary and advanced levels in ancient rhetorical education. Stephen North's *The Making of Knowledge in Composition* and James Berlin's *Rhetoric and Reality: Writing Instruction in American Colleges, 1900–1985* are but two examples of how historians and theorists emphasize continuity from rhetorical education at and after the beginning of composition. But we find this continuity primarily in the claim for it, not in the actual spirit and requirements of composition courses, which were not intended to, and did not, replace earlier rhetorical education.

Although Berlin, North, and many others who accept their premises offer ways to comprehend composition as a whole system, a historically validated and still "developing" field, I will continue to view it primarily as a unique entity, not only insofar as it has characterized the new university's historical discontinuity with earlier educational practices, but as it has formed a continuing special circumstance that is not completely or very pointedly explained by analogies with rhetorical education. This emphasis on the uniqueness of composition, particularly in its ties to agendas in literary studies, reveals political situations around four of its fundamental components: composition students, the field's formative research emphases, its common images of its teachers, and its relation to institutional administrative structures. Looking at composition as an instructional and professional discontinuity from earlier practices also provides a way into defining the results of its practices for students and faculty. This perspective will, I hope, make the field available for more than merely cosmetic re-formations of its situation and results.

As an institutionalized academic site, "the great American theme park" has become a permanently established but marginalized scene. It is now in many ways *actually* removed from its earliest embedments in literary studies by virtue of having its own consequential identity and professional discourse, but it is nonetheless *symbolically* no less implicated in literature as the "Other" that the social goals of textual canonization imply. Numerous theoretical perspectives address this dualistic process of apparent separation that joins one entity to another even more closely in new forms of hegemonic common sense. Descriptions of the historical workings of patriarchy, of the sociology of stigmatized groups, and leftist political critiques offer useful analogues for comprehending the simultaneous separation and regulation that situate the theme park that composition now occupies.

But composition is, because of its universality and identity with written language, the most inclusive political drama. It mediates between textual and social concerns that are divorced, as if by decree, in current theoretical approaches. Consequently, its carnivalesque status remains most historically and theoretically revealing. As Stallybrass and White explain the late nineteenth-century regulation and curtailment of carnivals and fairs in England, which produced new laws and customs but did not eradicate the feared impropriety of the festive, the carnival became simultaneously regulated and disowned. This tension between possessiveness and rejection, a cultural norm in treatments of any group outside privileged status, characterizes each of the four topics taken up here—students, research, faculty, and institutional structures.

But this process is only sketched in descriptions of emergent composition theories, classroom techniques, and movements in composition in the twentieth century (e.g., Berlin, *Rhetoric and Reality*). Such treatments do not consider the "migrations, concealment, metamorphoses, fragmentations, internalization and neurotic sublimations" (Stallybrass and White 180) that now contribute to the established status of composition. These terms show how the events chronicled in the catalogues that were considered earlier—changes in English faculty interests, in curricular offerings in writing, and in a distinct curriculum for "rhetoric and criticism"—have submerged loose coalitions in English departments into more pointedly "unified" groups. These new groups, those in "literature," in "language," and in "rhetoric/composition," represent earlier and less organized traditions that in many settings have been transcoded into mutual competitiveness and criticism.

We can, of course, only partially explore the results of these transformations. They are apparent in images associated with literary study and with composition, like the adoption by literary criticism of rhetorical terminology (e.g., figures, tropes, even "unity," "coherence," "narration," "style") and the concurrent use in composition studies of remedial medical terminology (e.g., "clinic," "diagnosis," "lab"). They are evident in stronger borders between composition and literature students, lines drawn as canonical texts in literature have begun to use transgressive language in their new surreal and "experimental" forms. Freshman reading assignments now rarely expose students of writing to texts that are not clearly distinguished from literature, from which the low-status course in composition more frequently avows its difference even while it remains a jealously guarded staple of literary departments. The student of composition is by these means protected from, and excluded from, contemporary literature's critical, often angry, perspectives on established systems. In the process of practical "liberation" from literary readings, composition focuses on models and traditions that do not radically critique their own self-preserving structures.

These and other examples of apparent changes in composition practice suggest that as the textual carnival, composition allows its surroundings to place it in the situation of a periodic ritual (Stallybrass and White 189). That is, the place of composition as an established, and now often physically distant, locale for the low implies that literature now occupies a symbolically safer site for engaging anxieties about the perfections of literary texts, and for addressing its current uncertainties about the status of the scholarship devoted to them. Maintaining composition as a field, and course, divorced from the language and intellectual politics of contemporary literary study supports the governing category of literature, affirming that there is a language (and a purity of initiation into it) "other than" literary activity. The few autonomous composition programs across the country, by virtue of their separate faculties and students, equally suppress similarities between writing any consequential discourse and authoring literature. At a distance, these programs rarely escape the images and agendas for "good writing" in the earliest networked contexts of social and economic politics that defined unentitled writing.

These images are, however, now significantly blurred, as are the images of students, faculty, and institutional structures that typically provide both with leadership and rewards. These topics, and the comments on them of participants in the survey, remain in oscillation between enclosed and open views of what it means to teach and to learn to write.

3 The Subject of Composition

The subject of composition is at least a twofold prospect. Traditionally, we have thought of an academic subject as a body of knowledge, like mathematics, that stands by and for itself, and we have assumed that its students "take" it. This sense of a subject as content will be considered here as a recent theoretical movement within composition studies, the "paradigm" of process theory and practice. This paradigm has moved composition from a purely applied, practical set of ways to inculcate propriety to a field claiming equality with other academic fields. But to understand the political implications of this theorizing, we first need to attend to another subject of composition.

Content, the body of knowledge within a field, also implies a human subjectivity of a particular sort, a characterization of those who learn and profess its methods, solve its problems, and take seriously its most prominent issues. And this subjectivity works to create a field's content, often in covert ways. A "subject" is thus not a static body of knowledge, but an affective space. It includes students in a particular mode of relations to each other and to their world. The "content" of any field is realized only in relation to those who participate in it.

The Student's Subjection

Examining the earliest place of composition in the curriculum of English studies gives us a fairly clear idea of the original student who was thought to be the object of composition instruction. In the last quarter of the nineteenth century, "the" course in composition was designed to test the suitability of a newly admitted group for an education that was still explicitly a privilege. As Eliot described him at Harvard, this student would demonstrate his suitability for this privilege. But this was not to be done (at least not in A. S. Hill's early implementations of the freshman course) either by reassuring the institution about prior experiences in vernacular composing or by demonstrating a capacity to produce discourse that might compete with already powerful positions. The test of composition showed propriety and good manners in regard to the student "body," the surface of his writing.

As we have seen, the original student of composition was thereby defined by Harvard's entrance exam as the lower and in some ways the "animal" order, in need of scrubbing. A decidedly nonspeculative testing instrument, whose forms quickly multiplied, became entrenched as both national "standardized" examinations and as local instruments for "placing" students in a hierarchy. The entrance exam set up national and local systems that for the first time excluded the most fit students from requirements that they systematically extend their knowledge of how to compose, thereby more clearly assuring that the student who took composition was to be corrected and remedied before admission to "regular" courses of study. He—and later she—was either to be made fit for the entitlements within these regular curricula or finally to be excluded when he or she revealed the absence of an essential but limited quality—suitability for privilege.

This early student of composition, as catalogue descriptions of writing courses and programs across the country from 1920 to 1960 show (see chapter 2), might additionally either be, or not be, an English major. This discrimination, understandable enough from the perspective of a department's need to describe a specialized course of study, nonetheless served to separate students further into two coded groups: those who would eventually receive and assimilate the gentlemanly "principles" that literature provides to unify the elitist university's subjectivity, and those who would not. These two groups have often been characterized by the differing kinds of writing instruction they will receive. "Professional" majors at some land grant institutions (e.g., Georgia), those who are implicitly designated as unable fully to assimilate cultural ideals, take courses especially for them, even at the winnowing freshman level. These courses teach specifically expository writing to "communicate information," not to explore or analyze aesthetic experiences. English majors, on the other hand, may have to take a general freshman English, but may not be required to take later courses in any but critical writing, if at all. Thus institutional boundaries between human and not quite human, which composition first drew, have been rebuilt between two kinds of composition students, the not quite and the even less suitable, with the latter group in some measure imagined to be hopelessly "low."

These administrative practices, like the persistent habit of exempting some but not other students from requirements in composition, define composition as a particular kind of universal test, a task to be got out of the way. This work, at least as these processes of testing and placement define it, does not clearly build the ideological "center" that English departments were constituted to maintain, nor does it precisely meet the needs of its "insider" students. Insiders are excluded from composition in curious ways that can be justified only, if at all, by a belief in "vocational" tracking. It is, for instance, only administratively practical to separate students of English from students of diverse sorts of writing. And it is also only the logic of this particular practicality that excludes well-qualified freshmen from writing requirements, and from writing opportunities, throughout undergraduate education.

But in addition to expressing administrative practicality, these classifications of students and exemptions for some confirm that the student of composition has a distinct and overtly constructed identity. Testing instruments and further classifications have identified the person whom Eliot, Hill, and later avatars have required to take the course. But they have also characterized certain people who are required to approximate a distinct persona at least temporarily, when they become visiting citizens of these carnivalesque structures. Elitist institutions that do not offer composition in the traditional freshman form imply that no student with such an identity, or with the need for it, attends the institution, despite the inevitable range of actual preparation for writing that the students admitted to these institutions present. This particular identity of the composition student, in its political, not educated, aspects, may in fact have been absent from (or unnecessary in) these institutions, at least before their admissions policies were broadened in the later years of this century and composition courses were instituted to "serve" a distinct group.

The powerful desire to define a specific character for composition students is also evident in common practices that take its students to be beginners in a continuous four-year progress of instruction. This imagined continuous and sequenced collegiate curriculum ideally includes mastery of literary principles that were equated with the national, race, and universal ideals in early descriptions of English. It has been almost impossible for practices in composition to shake early assumptions about this privileged situation for its ideal student, even now. But today, in addition to the possibility that some other "race" will constitute the student ideal, the typical college student is an adult, is at least as likely to be female as male, is unlikely to complete a degree in fewer than five or six years, and is most likely to be part of the approximately 60 percent of entering freshmen who do not graduate at all from the institutions in which they begin.[1]

Nonetheless, a perduring sentimentality still characterizes the typical student of composition as a young beginner. No widespread reform of required courses has focused on imagining the recipient of their instruction as subject to the contemporary facts of educational life, except obliquely in new practices for the Basic Writer whom Mina Shaughnessy constructed in *Errors and Expectations*. The student is imagined to be (and in participating in the course is generally *required* to be) a presexual, preeconomic, prepolitical person.

In concert with such shaky demographic assumptions, typical representations of the material content of composition

1. To cite but one example, the office of the Dean of Liberal Arts and Sciences at Arizona State University, Tempe, which is one of the fastest-growing universities in the country, reports that of any entering freshman class, 21 percent graduate in four years, 37 percent take five years to graduate, and the rest do not graduate. Of any ten students in any group encountered on this campus, only two would be enrolled the following year. Generally, in statistics reported by directors of admissions across the country, 60 percent of entering students do not graduate from the institution they enter as a freshman (Green).

courses contain another important, if subtle, implication about the student's needs. In retaining the image of "literary ideals" as the best result of a complete education, composition curricula reveal an appropriating assumption that versatile participation in academic and other discourse can be reduced to model processes resulting from a baptism by textual immersion. Modern goals for composition instruction apart from literary teaching only partially modify this early core premise. They emphasize that composition courses teach "critical thinking," "critical reading," and "good style." All three suggest the priority of canonical textual education that English was established to provide along openly stated Arnoldian principles. English, that is, is concerned with "the best" that has been "thought and said," two terms whose precision in composition theory as well as in its practices will become clear.

"Thinking," "reading," and "saying" are imposed on the student of composition to place fundamentally textual values in the center of extraordinarily diverse kinds of education. By presenting what is conceived to be a total but specific form of analysis based on examining texts, and further claiming that textual analysis is the best way to acquire an analytic disposition, composition courses assimilate and subordinate preferences among their students for other kinds of study that do not privilege authorized textual conversations. Especially in mathematics, scientific theory, and the visual and aural arts, verbal texts supplement but do not necessarily contain or generate results that count as "content." But the student of composition is positioned to learn that the need to communicate *about* learning takes precedence over many sorts of learning processes. The student must thus assume that nontextual forms of knowledge are supplemental to, or at least are contained by, textual precedents.

It appears, then, that something remains at stake in the premises that guided those who formed the identity of the earliest students in freshman English, despite its beginnings in entirely different curricular circumstances. Something depends on this student being conceived of as relatively young, relatively certain to take a freshman writing course as a freshman and before other studies, relatively sure of the financial stability and cultural norms that result in finishing undergraduate work in a regularly sequenced four-year period, and certainly needing to revere the values that nineteenth-century English programs were established to entrench. Obviously, one assumption behind this conception is that the composition student is beginning an adult course of indoctrination into social and linguistic propriety. But more than a pedagogue's direct personal friendliness explains the modern "you" who is now addressed in textbooks.

This "you" is a particular form of subjectivity. As Terry Eagleton says in "The Subject of Literature," a particular identity has been produced for the student of composition. This student has never been predetermined to "fit" but one monolithic community's requirements. In any particular characterization, a subject is called into being; it does not exist before that call as the "personality" of a person. Specific people respond to many requirements in various settings, taking on identities that promote their economic and social cooperativeness with the structures that sustain their culture. Thus "character" is never entirely unified, except in our textual, or discoursed, representations of it—for example, in an "authorial stance" or a "villainous character"—in particular discursive practices. A form of public subjectivity is never self-created. It does not exist entirely as a "personal" choice.

Eagleton argues, however, that one of the specific requirements for the literary subject is that its human instances appear to create themselves independently, freely choosing this suitable mode of subjectivity. "The mode of subjectivity appropriate to our particular kind of society [will] deceive them [the subjects of this society] into believing that they do" choose it individually and personally (96). This is to say that literary subjectivity, and its transcoding as a lower form of composition student who must pass a test before higher principles are engaged, will take it as an article of faith that he or she is "independent" and "free" to choose within the controls the society establishes. In a composition course, for instance, this subjectivity may involve the student in freely choosing among topics for writing so that questions about the universal requirement "to write" at all, or about the purposes for writing essays, will be begged. A required subjectivity that automatically includes students in an imaginary world of texts will dominate other possibly nontextual realities.

Because this form of production reveals a great deal about the student, the teacher, and theories of composition, it is worthwhile to note that societies produce fairly well-constrained subjectivities to regulate and map individuals. Regulation includes ways to instill values and responses that best serve the society's maintenance of its particular form of order. In any culture, specific (if generalizable) objects of respect ("religion," "the flag," "mother"), specific motivations ("salvation," "property," "money"), and so on are used to provide this regulation. An individual female, for example, may be constituted as "a mother" and therefore as a person who will sacrifice her personal boundaries to attend to the frequent and private bodily needs of young children—elimination, cleanliness, nurturance. But the culture will also produce "motherhood," a symbolic domain that covers over these functions of a person in an image of *the* mother and places her in an idealized space of veneration.

Methods to instill such constraints in individuals also *themselves* produce knowledge of a society's human subjects. Credentials, certifications, licenses, degrees, even prizes ("Mother of the Year") all give the culture a way to "name" its individuals. In the case of the student, grades and a record of them will be kept to identify and describe that student as an object of the "grading system." Like medical examinations, these instruments make a person an object of scrutiny who may be more or less "normal." They were used in the eighteenth and nineteenth centuries, and have endured, to relocate formerly individual and interactive events in formal public structures, with the result that a person is particularized in relation to a standard or "norm" of health or achievement (see Foucault, "The Examination," *Discipline and Punish*).

Literature is specifically, Eagleton says, a "moral technology," equipped with both values and processes that create a subjectivity that is difficult to define. But this elusiveness also helps constitute its cultural function, to preserve "individuality" within fairly predictable, tight boundaries. Particularly, literature is a Kantian, "contentless" moral philosophy. It requires, Eagleton says, that its students neither embrace any particular set of values nor accomplish any but "universalized" actions. "It teaches us rather to be—let me rehearse some of the cherished terms—sensitive, imaginative, responsive, sympathetic, creative, perceptive, reflective. . . . The task of the moral technology of Literature is to produce an historically peculiar form of human subject who is sensitive, receptive, imaginative and so on . . . *about nothing in particular*" ("Subject" 98). In other words, the subject of literature (at least of literature taught in British schools) is endowed with "radically depoliticized" formalism. "Thus we just have subjectivity all by itself, as a value in itself, with no rigorously definable goals or functions" (99). And this subjectivity for its own sake, Eagleton asserts, offers a purposeless "freedom" and "creativity" that bind its students to the capitalist social order. "We are bound as firmly as we are precisely because we do not seem to be bound at all" (99).

In this view, both the characteristic "creative inwardness" (101) of literature students, or of English majors, as well as their persistent quality of thinking themselves "above" or "beyond" technology, industrialism, the proletariat, political activism, and a host of mundane concerns like the "test" of composition, are all precisely functional in maintaining and reproducing the culture. The value of creative inwardness, prominent in the literary texts about personal isolation that Leavis and the New Critics canonized, guarantees that the literary "center" of the curriculum will thoroughly depoliticize its most ardent students. Personal isolation from activism is also, I would argue, prominent in the displaced and transcoded version of this subjection that is imposed on those who take a literary freshman English, a course now universalized as a new form of postorthodox beliefs.

I might have said a "by definition" literary freshman English, for this entity need not be a course in reading or writing about "great" texts to initiate its students in this cultural subjectivity, although that content might be especially appropriate. The traditional freshman composition course, the textual carnival of correctness, propriety, and "good breeding," has served just as well to further the end of neutralizing the public participation of its students. It has supplied an ultimately repressive ideal, in the form of perfectly written texts, without exposing the precise ways these texts have become publicly successful, so that its students may measure their own inadequacies for full participation in the textual world. But even if we claim that this version of the writing class or of its practices does not even by extension represent the guiding theory of composition teaching now considered to create its best practices, we must acknowledge that almost any form of composition teaching fosters this subjectivity in its students.

Setting aside fairly solid evidence that "best practices" do not guide most teaching of writing in American higher education (Larson), we would have to qualify any claim that the subject/subjectivity called for by favored composition practices differs in any remarkable way from the one constituted by more traditional forms. The universality of the course, its continuations of early administrative structures, persistent silence about its results as apart from its stated goals, and its hidden unities all extend the subjectivity of literature in the current practices of composition.

It is now at least equally common for colleges and universities to require all students to complete some kind of writing course as it is for them to require any form of literary study. Many universities have given up a standard requirement for literary surveys in the process of diminishing "general education" requirements that once unified the first years of the curriculum (although, as Harvard is a witness, such requirements have recently been reinstated in many places). But in almost every setting (notably excepting some elitist institutions), some form of freshman composition is treated as a "god subject," necessary instruction for entering students and at times an equally important one in later requirements. (Again using Harvard as an example, its policy is without exception that "if God comes to Harvard, She takes writing" [Marius].)

Considering this almost universally conceived importance for an academic site that at its establishment was demonstrably carnivalesque, it is likely that in addition to providing the means to support graduate students and being the winnowing device that Kitzhaber said it was in *Themes, Theories, and Therapy*, some result for/in students in contemporary composition courses is imagined. One result might be, again considering this universality, that the student will learn to write well enough to fulfill assignments in college or, to use the language of theories often stated by composition professionals, to assume the identity of an active learner and later professional. But this result, in whatever language we choose, is at least disguised in descriptions of contemporary programs in writing, which seem no more direct about their students' active participation in discourse than they might have been in Hill's time.

In contemporary writing programs, at least those selected as exemplary models by the Modern Language Association and in Carol Hartzog's *Composition and the Academy*, a project partially supported by the national Writing Program Administrators' group, very little is said about purposes for writing courses that relates to the writing that students do. The supposed god subject seems to have little to do with preparing students to do the writing they may have to do, or may want to do, in the "social communities" they are now prominently imagined to occupy. One reason for this may be, as John and Tilly Warnock discovered in 1977 at the University of Wyoming, that students do not very often receive writing assignments in their first two years of college. The greater portion of college writing is assigned to seniors and juniors. And faculty, at least in the study the Warnocks reported, think of writing as important in a "career," but not so important in an academic setting, which is only natural if they do not assign it there (4).

What is more salient, however, is that only John and Tilly Warnock, of all the respondents represented in Jasper Neel's 1978 *Options for the Teaching of English: Freshman Composition* (18 articles), in Paul Connolly and Teresa Vilardi's 1986 *New Methods in College Writing Programs* (28 articles), or in Carol Hartzog's 1986 *Composition and the Academy* (44 programs in the Association of American Universities), appear to have asked how much writing or at what time actual pieces of writing are expected from students or graduates. That is, administrators in these ninety-two prominent programs appear to have needed no evidence to support the universal "need" for writing instruction. That need appears to be "felt," not an urgent reality that has to do with actual writing situations, except in imagined but largely undocumented postgraduate settings. Even if we were to argue that recent emphases on cross-curricular writing have increased the frequency of writing assignments across many campuses, a fair inference is that it is not the habit of those who guide writing programs to discover how much writing, what kind of writing, or what locales for writing create expectations of their students.

This kind of discovery was attempted in the now defunct writing program of the University of Michigan's College of Engineering Humanities, where faculty members inferred that senior rhetoric, not freshman composition, would best serve students. These students were characterized, notably, as "quite literate by the usual standards of measure" even after a freshman composition course that was perceived as having "failed to improve the writing skills of freshman students" (Neel 118). This evidence quite vividly recalls Eagleton's description of the objectless subject of literature, for even in contemporary composition teaching that appears to have set aside literary agendas, expectations within its courses or of its students are not clearly linked to writing the students do for themselves in other settings. We can discern references to actual writing only in extensions of pedagogies that promote process for its own sake, which we might justly compare to "subjectivity for its own sake" in the literary form of subjectivity.

Issues raised by this "process for its own sake" will become clearer as we look at process as a new theory of composition. For now, it is important to notice how the dominant ideology of composition continues to relocate, translate, and displace the "subject of literature" in its orientation toward a sensibility rather than toward the full, highly political experience of an external world. The universality of freshman composition, its continuing practice of exempting students who are in current sources still referred to as "strong" (as opposed to "weak" or "poor"), and its administrative divorce from evidence of students' actual needs to write—all these suggest that composition has become a cultural *site* like original literary English, an at least potential locale for the "center" of education. In this new center, agendas for teaching writing do not address "literacy" in the senses it has most often been measured, as an indication of capacities to transmit property, create it, or take political action. The *academic* subject of writing instead addresses the modern "individual" who has little at stake in the culture's organization, commerce, or politics. We can see the perduring implication that composition, like literature, is a site for values, attitudes, and "qualities," not in fact for anything like the determinate list of "practical skills" that it purports to instill.

This additional similarity between traditional literature and composition deserves attention, for it comments on motives for the supposed incoherence of the composition curriculum that Kitzhaber described. In the terms Eagleton and others use, it would be questionable even to look for a "content" for a course apart from a kind of subjectivity, supposing that a value-free body of ideas or neutral processes might exist apart from an academic institution's desires for a particular *kind* of thinking resulting from study in any discipline. But if we do look for this value-free corpus, we will find evidence to support Kitzhaber's findings of supposed incoherence in Richard Larson's recent reinforcement of this judgment and in the variety of courses in writing traditionally offered at upper levels. Everything denies that there is a compact range of material, or even of processes, to which college students of writing will be automatically exposed.

This diversity, which can be strongly supported on the basis of "the nature of writing," appears natural. Various emphases on universal themes, on history and theory of "language," on "argument," or on preparation to read complex works and respond to them fit the complexity of writing. Just as we could not expect a literature major from one school to have read precisely the same works as one from another, so too we could not reasonably seek unity among academic programs designed to allow students to write and to subject that writing to correction. Even an idealistic desire for "coverage" includes, in literature or in composition assignments, a diverse range within historical, generic, and critical categories.

But this comparison highlights an additional congruence between the subject of composition and the structure of literary subjectivity. It reveals an assumed and standard, if sub-

merged, "content" in composition, an essential core of principles that is only shallowly hidden by diversity in promoting
them. We find the carnivalesque variety that Kitzhaber made
a point of criticism if we ask teachers which textbooks and
what writing assignments or readings they require. But if we
ask what the purpose of writing courses is, we now get one
unified answer, the same "resounding intransitivity" that
Eagleton found in the subject of literary studies. A sensibility,
now promoted by teaching writing processes for their own
sake, remains the unified and recognizable form of subjectivity
that composition universally claims to instill. As the NCTE
Commission on Composition described it in 1974, composition
will "help students to expand and enlarge their worlds, to live
more fully" (219).

Those programs whose publicity suggests their idealized
status reveal this unifying ideal quite clearly, verifying that
composition has displaced literary values to reproduce the
subject of literature in the composition student who has few
publicly involved reasons to write. In their generalizations
about programs in the introduction to *New Methods in College
Writing Programs,* Paul Connolly and Teresa Vilardi infer that
"Freshman English is becoming a writing course, in which the
students' writing is the principal text. It is also, with increasing
frequency, a reading course in which construing and constructing texts are taught, as Ann Berthoff urged in *The Making
of Meaning,* as complementary instances of the imagination
'making meaning.' Where handbooks are used, they are
treated as reference tools, not course syllabi" (3).

The elaborated truth of this summary and its connection to
a unifying literary subjectivity is clear in the twenty-eight
descriptions that followed this introduction. Repeatedly, the
freshman writing course is described as a course that connects
generalized "reading, writing, and thinking." It is a place
where "writing and reading [are] the two converse processes
of constructing meaning" (17), where "good writing and close
reading go hand in hand" (30), where "personal knowledge,
experience, and curiosity motivate writing growth" (40),
where "the human person" unifies processes and products
(90) and students "explain their insights" (91). At one school,
rhetorical situations for writing were (in light of current the-

ory, it is said) "demoted . . . from ends in themselves to means to an end" (108), an end that appears to include workshops, peer reviews, research, shorter assignments, and modeled processes of writing. At another, writing courses "help students understand their own writing processes" and "use writing as a tool of liberal learning, particularly as a means of understanding what they read, of thinking critically, of clarifying values" (124).

Although these descriptions of pedagogies that focus on methods of writing clearly improve on earlier emphases on correctness and grammar, their most prominent quality is an emphasis on intransitive *processes* that appear to have no particular products as results. Nor does this emphasis on processes include measures of their mastery. It is not clear how changes in the performance of these activities are perceived to be changes, except as a product might measure them, or how much change in the now valued activities at the center of the course is counted as a success. Even if measurements are implemented in these programs, results are not prominent goals in the courses described.

More important, however, these descriptions reveal the completely self-referential quality of a displaced literary subjectivity. In imitation of Eagleton, it is fair to infer that the composition course values the student for activity, reflection, and "meanings" that are entirely contained in the community constituted by the classroom. These are not activities that *do* anything in particular, that reflect *on* anything in particular, or that have "meaning" *about* anything in particular. While students now engage in reading each others' writing, these descriptions almost scrupulously avoid mentioning how they come to assess it in any systematic way or how they locate their own writing and their "assigned" readings in any structure of beliefs about writing.

It is tempting to infer that contemporary composition has gone literature one better in creating the sensitivity for its own sake that literary studies has required of students. It has, that is, removed a canon of ideologically joined works that instill ethnocentric, logocentric, or any other congruent set of values and has substituted for them an almost entirely formalistic and intransitive vision of writing. The subject of composition, in both senses of "subject" that I am using, divorces writing from any claim on a value *system* and instead contains it in "valuing" or "processing" of language that is even purer than the literary subject's perspective on specific literary objects. In its emphasis, for instance, on "meaning" without reference to meaning *to*, the course extends what Jane Tompkins called in "The Reader in History" the New Critical desire to give priority to meanings that are entirely within written language.

Applying Tompkins's chronological view, we can see ways that composition now extends the almost failed project of literature, which she says managed in the nineteenth century to overcome obvious needs for a historical contextualization of its "facts" by creating "authors" who were, in the critical view at the time, "transcendent." Literary studies, cooperating with its own quasi-religious social purposes, overcame claims that literature might change the consciousness of humankind by defining the poet as an isolated nightingale, "lonely and ineffectual." It greeted the placement of literature in the center of nationalism, where it was claimed to be its "most important resource," by speaking of it as (and by permitting it to be) "one of the worst possible ways to make a living" (217). In each of these seeming contradictions, the theme of "literary" alienation from the action, movement, power over environment, or intellect was repeated. Literary subjectivity, and now the subjectivity inevitably created by allowing composing processes to become purposes for writing, focus on the author/writer, not on the results of authorship or of writing.

As Tompkins notes, the literary project almost failed. From her point of view and from Eagleton's, it was intended to reproduce Kantian philosophy, a relocation of the universality and regulations of human "spirit" once accomplished by organized religion. But these desires were revitalized in later New Critical formalism, which defined the text rather than its author as an object of knowledge, "as meaning not doing," and made describing this object "the supreme critical act" (Tompkins 222). In this move to purified interpretation, literature "denies the existence of any reality prior to language and claims for poetic and scientific discourse exactly the same relation to the real— namely, that of socially constructed versions of it. All language, in this view, is constitutive of the reality it purports to describe, whether it be the language of mathematical equations or that of a Petrarchan sonneteer" (224).

By focusing on texts and on textual processes, composition appears to have without reservation taken up the formalist, or structuralist, project that preserved and continued nine-teenth-century literary estrangements from active cultural participation. It has gradually renewed these practices and formed theories that imitate the spirit of New Critical detachments from rhetorical engagement, if not the overt New Critical denouncement of it. At least as composition programs are represented in prominent models, they have divorced the student from any reality but the now objectless activities of responding to and generating written language. In *English in America*, Richard Ohmann praised this tendency to place writing processes in the center of the composition course and to help students "generate ideas," hinting obliquely at how freshman composition serves the self-contained sensibility of literature: "Perhaps I was asking students to be free, critical, and creative in a situation where society was asking them to be of service, docile, and limited" (142). But no contradiction inheres in these two sets of expectations, in "freedom" and "creativity" as against expectations from "society." Both fit objectless mental states to the society's expected docility, passivity, and containment of its students' writing.

Tompkins suggests for literature an obvious (a "rhetorical") alternative, "a shift away from the analysis of individual texts and toward an investigation of what it is that makes texts visible in the first place" (225–26). Her proposal recalls the language of Robert Scholes in *Textual Power* where he points out the deficiencies of Stanley Fish's failure to say exactly how certain texts become prominent, as well as Michael Apple's complaints in "On Analyzing Hegemony" about the depoliti-cizing effects of process-oriented pedagogies (see Introduction). Tompkins proposes that an alternative to formalistic analyses of texts in literary studies would be to look for a more radical theory of language as constitutive of a greater reality. This theory, like Greek rhetoric, would acknowledge that "mastery of language [is] mastery of the state" (226). Language, she says, is a form of power, and understanding discourse means understanding its relation to power. But composition teaching as it is described by its most current practices stays with the earlier, conventional literary project, defining written language as a self-contained site for "meaning" that is only within it and its students' processes. This emphasis, as Scholes, Tompkins, and Apple discretely point out, covers up everything that empowers the student or, more pointedly, disempowers the student writer.

When we compare this historical movement in literature to available narratives about practices now promoted in contemporary composition, it becomes easy to see the kind of subjectivity that composition now implies. The composition student is expected to experience processes, activities, strategies, multiple perspectives, peer groups, and evaluations that have no articulated relation to actual results from a piece of writing. These expectations may give us pause, even when we discount Richard Ohmann's complaints in *English in America* (e.g., 183–90) that the student of composition is constructed to be a "problem solver" and thus a tool of military-industrial sensibility. One program in *New Methods* (Connolly and Vilardi 26–28) does explicitly require this "problem solving." But even if we reject Ohmann's traditional Marxist complaint about such a requirement, we nonetheless may become uneasy about the fit between a self-referential subjectivity and purposes for writing that teaching processes for their own sake cannot address.

The subjectivity of composition now created by its model programs appears to result for its students in an infantile and solipsistic relation to the results of writing. Denied the imagined social privileges once associated with mastering the ideology of a literary canon, the student is nonetheless constructed by extensions of modern literary theories. The student is taught to contain all reality in writing and in unarticulated interpretive theory, without reference to analysis of the changing reasons others have written, to the results of writing beyond the classroom, or even to a unity in the teacher's authority. A discordant position in regard to this orientation in *New Methods* demonstrates how vividly this identity for the student guides others:

1. Exposure to a variety of ideas presented from a variety of viewpoints seems more likely to encourage divergent thinking than does total immersion in the kinds of egocentric, almost therapeutic reminiscences and reflections advocated by those who naively equate creativity with spontaneity. . . .

2. Exposure to a variety of thematically organized media seems more likely to promote genuine involvement, and thus effective communication, than does total dependence on the printed page. . . .

3. Writing assignments that are argumentative or persuasive and that contain a research component seem more likely to develop critical abilities than do assignments that elicit unexamined, unqualified, and unsupported descriptive, narrative, and expository writing. (Connolly and Vilardi 66–67)

Clearly, this contentiously phrased position does not overturn the values of traditional composition, but it does explicitly reveal a difference between the character expected in "process" settings and the one that might be called forth in alternative contemporary settings. It shows, for instance, how self-involved the student is in a matrix defined as his or her own "thinking," not defined as testing ideas against customary, authorized views. As Althusser would argue, a difference between "thinking" and struggling among ideas implies that "ideas" exist abstractly, and are shaped by consciousness, not in a struggle among positions in specific discourses (136). This divergent program description also opposes abstractness, in its reminder of how often the student of composition is placed in a textual, monomedia world of information unlike his and her ordinary and academic experience of multiple visual and other nonverbal languages for learning. Finally, this description shows how divorced students' writing may be from a desire to make cases, convince authorities, or change anything outside the self or the interpretations of peers.

As Ohmann described the student revealed in composition textbooks in a criticism that nonetheless gave priority to the "theme" and to its statements in a classroom, "the student is almost invariably conceived of as an individual. He [sic] acts not only outside of time and history, but alone—framing ideas, discovering and expressing himself, trying to persuade others, but never working *with* others to . . . advance a common purpose" (*English in America* 149). More recently, Kathleen Welch has pointed out the continuation of this spirit in text-books: "The textbook-bound classroom as it now often exists—in spite of Ohmann, Rose and other critics—promotes passivity. An alarming number of texts focus on the wrong issues of technical rhetoric and ultimately encourage a belief that written language is valueless" (279).

I have said that the required subjectivity of the composition student is infantilized, which I take to be obvious not only from characterizations of the composition course as a transition to college life and its reliance on pedagogies often used at much earlier levels, but also from the persistent objectification/subjection of the student that follows from requirements, from placement and "diagnostic" exams, and from the absence of choice among the emphases or conduct of sections of one course taught by those described in class schedules as anonymous "staff." At one university where no one is exempt from the freshman sequence, the goals of this sequence might have been taken from the statements of early American college presidents at Yale and Princeton, who would have applied similar desires to their seniors. They are "to provide freshmen with a common educational experience, to assist them in making the transition from high school to college, and to introduce them to [the university's] curricular goals" (Connolly and Vilardi 90). Nothing is said in this description of a course in humanities about teaching the student to write (either transitively or intransitively), but the goal of unifying students within the institution's ideology is explicit, as is the fact that the student has no choice about this indoctrination.

But when a significant percentage of students are exempt from writing (a trend that is declining, according to Connolly and Vilardi [3]), those who take it are also reinforced in child-like passivity by becoming part of an undistinguished mass who may not choose their own exposures to writing except, often, on the ground of what hour they will experience it. In Carol Hartzog's survey of 44 writing programs, she found that 37 had statements of principles and goals and that 34 provided a common syllabus, although only a relative few required its use (35–36). For all the supposed diversity of the course, then, it does not appear that a student is permitted to experience it as a divergent or idiosyncratic or unconventional instrument in his or her community, but as a site for unifying and leveling differences.

This is not to reject emphases like those in the NCTE position statement on developing the individual by developing individual uses for and fluency with the written word. But it is to be extremely cautious about these emphases, because their most vocal representatives claim that writing will develop a "personal voice" that speaks to no one in particular, in no particular settings, and to no particular purposes. If one's "voice" is developed to be "heard" only among a peer group, its range and volume are more modulated than unexpected situations and their power relations will tolerate, as feminist theorists and the experiences of women verify.

Without sentimentality, we can also see that current practices in composition create a problematic personal situation, not just a logical problem, for students. Emphases on the self-contained act of writing may add to, not substitute for, earlier discriminatory practices in composition. The student is still subjected to the demeaned status accorded those who first took composition at Harvard and sat for its Board of Overseers' exam, as shown by frequent references in current descriptions to the "strong" and the "weak" and their separate treatment. But now the student is placed on trial by a required composition course that not only exposes and corrects the body of his or her writing, but also implicates that body in narcissistic, self-directed manipulations. Although many contemporary practices foster "communication" in addition to personal experience writing, the community in which messages are sent and received is imagined as isolated, homogenized to the members of one class (those who are all in the same "course"), and exempt from the responses of traditional conventions about who will be "heard" within textuality. Almost every attempt to make student writing more "relevant" to experience outside the classroom undercuts itself by denying that the actual test of power (or "effectiveness") from a piece of writing is how visibly it accomplishes precisely stated purposes among those who do not know its writer/author from immediate interactions. Thus the student subject of composition now has no verdict, to extend the metaphor of the trial and test from Eliot, at least no verdict that appears to count beyond a now cooperative and isolated community where competitiveness is anathema.

This is not to argue for more stringent requirements or for reinstating the acceptance of publicly humiliating practices, but to recognize that the almost universal subjectivity required by current composition practices differs from that expected in the introductory and later courses of other disciplines. In those settings, the student is expected to compete, to master material, and even to solve problems whose answers may be either correct or incorrect. A universally "important" writing course (if one course were to serve at all) to prepare students generically to "be" writers in these other settings and afterward could acknowledge and analyze these demands and their implications for the writing student. It need not isolate the student's writing in a world constituted by "processes" and content that are consequential only within it. The creation of the student might, again, have more to do with writing as a transitive, not intransitive, verb. This point at least distantly raises the question of how teaching practices are related to "science," the "hard" or testable alternative to humanistic/ humane self-definitions of composition, but composition has in no way rejected science for its own self-definitions.

The Subject as a Paradigm

The student subjectivity I have described is now taken to be validated by a model in which established composition finds itself constituted as a discipline: process teaching and its program descriptions reflect what is commonly described as the "process theory" from which they follow. But process teaching among students and process theory among professional groups cooperate in a complex way that requires careful examination. The subjectivity required by process teaching is only partially a result of process theory, which has been aimed more at the *profession* it has formed. But this profession, largely because of the model used to describe its theory, is now in an ambivalent, blurred relationship to its most immediate surroundings.

Like histories of writing instruction that equate composition and a unified classical rhetoric, models and "paradigms" that legitimate composition theory and practice have had many well-motivated sources. They improve teaching by placing it on intellectual ground. According to Maxine Hairston's seminal article "The Winds of Change: Thomas Kuhn and the Revolution in the Teaching of Writing," the primary value of establishing a paradigm of "process" in composition was to provide a space for systematically discovering and describing how writers actually write (85). This model, she argues, has led teachers away from analyses of the product of composition (although only these products often remain measures of processes) and has encouraged them to intervene during the process of writing, when actual benefits can result.

Certainly the descriptions of model programs cited earlier appear to verify this particular shift. Workshops, drafting and revision, peer review and evaluation, and emphases on "critical" reading and "thinking" all portray classrooms where writing is treated as an ongoing act, not as a product to be corrected or even analyzed after its completion. Most of these descriptions openly claim their association with the process paradigm, and now we even have "Competing Theories of Process," the further extension described by Lester Faigley's title for his investigation of three categories of "expressive," "cognitive," and "social" emphases in the performance of writing (528).

There are, of course, many slips between the cup of program descriptions and the lips of the majority of teachers and students. But even this slippage emphasizes how important it has been for the field of composition to create for itself a symbol system, by claiming its possession of a "paradigm" like those that centralize the activities of other professional groups and well-established disciplines. As Gerda Lerner points out in *The Creation of Patriarchy*, all marginalized groups suffer substantially, not only socially, from being excluded from "history." Those on the periphery of dominant social orders and outside their cohesive "stories" need their own alternative symbol systems if they are to prevent their absorption into anonymity (222–23). Hairston's lengthy review of Kuhn's argument and Robert Connors's perceptive analysis of it in "Composition Studies and Science" both highlight how important it has been for composition to take this way toward legitimating itself, not in this case by extending the ancient discipline of rhetoric as a credential, but by creating a new area of inquiry that can share the substantive and social status of contemporary "science." As Connors says, "*the tacit message of all of this borrowing* [from Kuhn] *is that composition studies should be a scientific or prescientific discipline*" (5; Connors's emphasis).

This legitimacy, if not a scientific identity, appears to be the most clearly achieved result from paradigm theory in composition. As an insider, Faigley unself-consciously claims that we may assume "the recognition of the study of writing as an important area of research within English" (527). He, like Stephen North in *The Making of Knowledge in Composition*, uses the kind of classifications that are necessary to define "schools" and professional groups on which a discipline's status depends. Composition is, at last, a "subject" in at least one sense its professionals desire.

It is worthwhile, therefore, to clarify the sort of subject composition has become by virtue of choosing this model. The questions that I take to be most relevant are whether a paradigm shift has actually occurred, what its quality is, and how it has, or has not, created an intellectual subjectivity/ subject of composition that has specific consequences for the field's intellectual politics. Granting that this new model has modified the earliest subjectivity of the composition student in limited ways, and that it has modified many composition courses, there are still open questions about the quality of differences resulting from process theory. One of these questions was best raised by Donald Gray, who in a review of the articles he published as editor of *College English* said, "When I was told that I was living in a paradigm shift, I didn't feel the earth move" (150).

We might use Gray's allusion to explore the first and second questions, the issues of magnitude and quality in the shift that process theory has achieved. It is not only true that a perceived shift from a "current-traditional product analysis" to process research must be qualified by findings in comprehensive surveys of teaching practices like Richard Larson's Ford-sponsored research, which does not make the extensiveness of this shift apparent. In addition, even research that is clearly based on process theory suggests that there are ways that the earth has not moved so much or in precisely the ways that many avow that it has. Research in composition is not generally undertaken, as Kuhn's model of a paradigm shift would say it would now be, to verify a new, normalizing theory based on a revolutionary idea that sets a new set of problems for the field. Dissatisfactions with old ways of solving problems in composition teaching have joined with new material and social circumstances for this teaching, but results from these interactions are of a particular and limited kind.

In a political analysis of the subject of composition, it is clear that process theory, by focusing on "what actual writers do," celebrates new tools used in classroom and other situations for writing, tools that were not available when composition courses began. The situation of the teacher in contemporary classrooms involves much smaller classes than those that were originally formed for correcting students' written exercises. But activities in these classrooms—multiple revisions, group work, and personal interactions—are possible only because actual technologies of writing have changed enormously since the late nineteenth century. Just as the telescope and the microscope have been credited with paradigm shifts in science, so too have cheap paper, ballpoint pens, word processors, and disposable textbooks created a new situation in which writing can be reconceived. Nonetheless, they did not necessarily form new theory. While new possibilities for sustaining the actual processes of writing over a lengthy time do change teaching, the attempt to describe these actual processes as a comprehensive theory of textual production raises some additional intellectual problems.

Ideally, these tools and the teaching situations they encourage would direct attention away from the problems of those who write to make a correct record of individually conceived if conventionally executed speech, or thought, and toward the problematics of "writing" in the sense that modern technologies, contemporary philosophy, and literary theory have diversely redefined the word. But this result, a move from one theoretical image of writing to others, is not at all clear. To the question of whether a paradigm shift has actually occurred, we must answer "not quite." A realistic history of writing suggests that "process" is serviceable mainly as an affective improvement in the classroom and as a way of granting composition a qualified academic legitimacy. Viewed from both historical and theoretical contexts, however, process theory has not yet provided an accurate or even a very historically different theory of contemporary writing, even if we grant it partial paradigmatic status.

It is first at least arguable that research into "the composing process" is not turning up data that is generally "true," or at least not data about actual writers that has been explained in a broadly historical interpretive context. (Detailed summaries of this research, and its conclusions about the recursive strategies of writers, have been thoroughly stated and explained elsewhere.) The historical context of vernacular language education indicates that written products have only in the last century become the goal of what we have called, in panhistorical flattening, "writing instruction." Oratorical training, from Aristotle through most of the eighteenth century, was for the purpose of teaching citizens to speak in public. Writing, the act of making marks on a slate or page, was taught and later used for two purposes, to aid reading and to practice for oratory.

For the first of these purposes, especially in the grammatical and spelling exercises that were taken from their origins in rhetorical education and moved into the earliest composition courses, "writing" was a way to visualize spoken language. For the ancients, fragmented remnants of texts were to be memorized, recited, and later incorporated in students' speeches. Later, in examples from the sixteenth century that have often been repeated as the inherited unconscious of vernacular language teaching, schoolmasters might interchange the word "spell" with the word "write." They meant when they mentioned "writing" that the student should know what a word he might hear or say would look like, not be able to actually produce the word for original compositions. *After* the traditional elementary rhetorical curriculum (where early composition at Harvard and elsewhere did not go), students practiced composing and delivering speeches, but they were not "writing" to produce actual documents, except as records of what they would say or had already recited. Thus the earliest social uses of writing as an aid to reading, and instruction in writing for this purpose, were very different from those we might describe now.

The second purpose for writing in educational settings, practice for using the rhetorical common topics like comparison and classification to organize and invent the matter in speeches, gave "writing" another place in traditional education, between discrete grammatical and rhetorical instructional programs. From the eighteenth century to the twentieth, as the locus for public influence from elite groups of graduates moved into print and written manuscripts, many rhetoricians claimed that their work applied to writing as well as to speech. We have evidence for these claims in the changing emphases of Hugh Blair, Richard Whately, I. A. Richards, Chaim Perelman, and Edward P. J. Corbett. Each of these theorists and others, in specific historical circumstances, further moved oratorical rhetoric from its actual speech situations to descriptions of language events that take place in visible words, not in speech or personal interactions (Miller, *Rescuing*). Later rhetorical education, as Channing's *Lectures* at Harvard exemplified, took actual writing more seriously than its classical pedagogy had, analogizing writing with speech and thereby establishing the metaphor of spoken discourse that still controls images of composition "activities" even now.

But in view of even this brief summary of changing social purposes for writing, we have to infer that in any version of applied rhetorical theory it made a great deal of practical as well as hegemonic common sense to promote the now excoriated "vitalistic" practices in current-traditional composition classrooms. Even the emphasis on correctness in the first college composition courses was an appropriate way to deal with an actual piece of writing. Until recently, writers with good training in memory and outlining could first compose what they wanted to say and then linearly record it, despite interference from their quill pens, difficult parchment paper, and complicated tools for erasure. We would overlook history entirely if we imagined that process-oriented teaching is a sign of a "humanity" toward the student that could always reasonably have been applied, or if we inferred that process-oriented research turns up "actual" (cognitive or expressive or social) processes that are not bound in time to specific material and social circumstances.[2]

Consequently, recent claims in process theory and in program descriptions that interaction with written language is a way to generate even objectless "meanings" is only possible now, in a precise historical moment. For earlier "writers," the generation of language was usually experienced as remembering words or as performative improvising that took in oral practices like the gestures and facial expressions taught in elocution, the popular eighteenth- and nineteenth-century version of rhetorical instruction. Historically, the visual and physical stimuli that accompany actual writing were not absolutely necessary for voiced language to produce more language.

Even if we grant "process" de facto status as a paradigm, we might exercise caution about how much and in what ways this recognition of technological changes has actually changed the subjectivity of composition. Novel process theories achieve what Marshal McLuhan described as the tendency of any new technology to relocate, but not fundamentally change, an old practice. But the new description in composition of "what writers do" must also be seen as only a partial theoretical move toward defining a model of composition that actually shifts the field toward coherent views of its designated object of study. This partiality is not completely explained by calling the field "preparadigmatic." That designation suggests that an old and a new theory (for instance, Newtonian and quantum physics) compete in a lively exchange, as process *theories*, not classroom practices, have not competed with other, well-described alternatives. "Current-traditional" or "product" theory appears to have been created at the same time that process theory was, to help explain process as a theory pitted against old *practices*. On investigation, "product" and "process" share underlying assumptions about the "prob-

2. Alvin Kernan, in *Printing Technology, Letters & Samuel Johnson*, offers an excellent description of the conditions that promoted modern written authorship. See also my *Rescuing the Subject*.

lem" that each approach to teaching has addressed: student (and other) writers.

To summarize their commonality, both product and process participate in one theoretical paradigm for discourse generation, the traditional Western paradigm of "presence" that gives priority to speech over writing. Both preserve one underlying model of what happens when writing is accomplished, by reiterating the situation of the ancient "orator," a now displaced speaker who theoretically can control the meaning of the written language he or she produces. Both approaches, that is, privilege speech situations, as classical rhetoric did, in ways that distort how contemporary acts of writing are distinctly contextualized in everything that impinges on what actual writers "do." Both participate in some measure in the perduring belief that writing is a container for speech and for thought, a medium rather than its own specific, and often precedent, "message."

It is possible, of course, to object that the open, collaborative atmosphere in process-oriented teaching does define a text as an overdetermined result from various interventions, multiple processes, and the responses of others. But process-oriented research, at least in its cognitive and expressive versions, persistently investigates the processes of individuals whose thought and reactions to responses are the object of study. Even in the work of those who investigate writing as a *social* process—scholars like Patricia Bizzell and David Bartholomae, who appear to embrace deconstructive theories—the instrumentality of the writing course is tied to results in its classroom situation, which is imagined to imitate a broader, but nonetheless depoliticized, social and material context where analyses of power are disconnected from writing. This theoretical program openly supports institutions of academic discourse production without appearing to recognize desires to subvert or destabilize them.

These theorists and others whom Faigley associates with them (Bazerman, Myers) have ignored the political implications of writing as the site of power that Tompkins, Apple, and Scholes describe. They see discourse communities as sites of articulation for community discourse practices, as choirs singing many parts in harmony. Social process theory defines the "community," which as Raymond Williams has pointed out has no "opposing" term (Faigley 538), as a group whose separate and unconscious class, economic, gender, and social desires will not oppose the negotiated settlements that constitute the order of things for these scholars. Social process theory does not work to "unmask [the] claim to speak on behalf of everyone, saying in effect: 'we are all the same; we all speak [or can, and with proper training *will* speak] the same language' " (Macdonel 7).

The social process theorists have, that is, accepted poststructuralist views that written words are socially construed, not fixed in their meanings, and that texts negotiate within specific textual communities. But this acceptance does not give significance either to student writing or to community processes as sites for struggle against these textual worlds that actually produce ideas. This further political contextualization of student writing as a way of connecting "ordinary" to "discoursed" spheres that inevitably oppose each other has not been accomplished fully in any view of process. Even theoretically advanced textbooks (e.g., Bartholomae and Petrosky, *Facts, Artifacts, and Counterfacts*) aim finally to bring the student and the student's desires within academic conventions. Robert Brooke's "Underlife and Writing Instruction" is a first effort at revealing struggles of students against these conventions, but no source I am aware of analyzes the resistances either of students or teachers to reveal the sources of larger community authority or its appropriating results, except to show students' exclusion from full citizenship if they do not learn conventions.

I am not suggesting that the proper application of social process theories would end in talking students out of the desires that first bring them to college, to learn institutional conventions that appear to be keys to "success." The issue is what they will learn *about* such conventions. If students are not asked to analyze "the conventional" and are not required to perceive both conventional and unconventional language as relatively successful strategies in varying situations, they will develop no self-consciousness about the language games they properly wish to master.

As Dianne Macdonel points out in *Theories of Discourse,*

this oversight is similar to the practice of teaching students vernacular "grammar" without reference to the larger Latin grammar system that makes it meaningful. Soon after the French Revolution, the "ruling middle class chose the French half of a dual French-Latin grammar as a State grammar for the instruction of all. . . . This led to a system in which the primary-school pupil learnt—and still learns—the national language under the form of a grammar [system] largely meaningless in the absence of instruction in Latin" (30–31). Macdonel goes on to draw the relevant lesson from this example, that those who receive a "complete" education study "comparative grammar—and thus [gain] a full understanding of the generative schema of the national language" (31). Social process theory, at least in many versions, similarly would teach students only the "basic" process of society itself without a necessary contrastive analysis of varieties of social process or of struggles among these processes from which ideas and actions occur.

Both product and process views of writing also implicitly or explicitly continue to describe a "student-centered" but independent individual, whether as isolated or as part of a community. This writer still "originates," "generates," and "conceives" discourse, in metaphors that remind us of active male sexual reproduction. Within the fairly inconsequential, intransitive world of process that creates the students' subjectivity, each student is still an agent of writing that, like speech, can be taken to be a self-determined "responsibility." Similarly, the collaborative peer group shares responsibility for self-contained "meanings" whose limited "meaningful" results they are imagined to be able to control for the "audience" they have become and analyzed.

In both models, sources of power and privilege in evaluative judgments, canonizations, or actual results from writing go by the board, although in the process approach the student is left even without deference to a single authority whose arbitrariness might be instructive. Both views assume in related ways that there is a *goal* text, a final version that could accurately re-present intentions, and that this version can result from, and cause, linguistic clarity. Both product models and expressive and cognitive process theories assume that words refer to settled (even if negotiated) meanings, intentions fixed in language and correctly or incorrectly interpreted by a writer or an audience. These meanings could, that is, be identified definitively and be clearly communicated.

In each of these models, then, with some qualifications for social process theories, a basic intellectual assumption is that meanings reside "behind" a text in essentialized "minds" and that there are secrets to "grasping" them. Both models agree in theory that meaning could, if Edenic (or contrived technological) innocence were possible, be spoken better than they are written. As Plato insisted in the *Phaedrus*, readers could learn more if they questioned the text's originator, which Robert Zoellner later suggested they do in his extended "talk-write" pedagogy. In the process view, these questions are the very fabric of instruction taking place through conferences, workshops, peer groups, and revisions that place writing processes firmly in a realm that gives priority to speech and to speech situations that students of composition will rarely encounter. In the product view, these questions were answered by the "secret" of authorship, in which student subjectivity would not share. But reform from one to another view does not change the assumption that meanings, not actual consequences from silently disseminated writing, are the interesting focus of composition research. This is the assumption of literary New Criticism and other formalist theories, which focus on "the text itself" rather than on its relations to power.

As Faigley inferred, this critique involves accusing process theory of "failing to deal with key concepts" (537), which I would define with him not only as "class, power, and ideology," but additionally as the actual difference between learning to write in specific and complexly loaded situations and basing this learning on theories that provide a generic and partial model of what actual writers do. The process model excludes writing that may still be quickly conceived and executed—that is, written under enormously important time constraints—or that will expose an individual writer to judgments that no one else will suffer or benefit from and that he or she may never know about. These situations are the full content of what I would take to be "processes" of the subject of writing, if not of its academic tradition in composition.

As both a course's content and the subjectivity of the student, "writing" might provide a genuinely different focus for the field of composition. It would encompass the historical sensitivity that Faigley links to understanding the politics of writing. It would require research like that of Bazerman and Myers into the situations of historically located composers and writers. But it would additionally see the interest of these discursive practices in the struggles that form them and in their broadly conceived consequences, not in the "meaning" of their words or their place in supposedly coherent mental or disciplinary biographies. This subject is neither the student subjectivity nor the object of expressive, cognitive, or even the social versions of process research.

Although a genuinely new paradigm for composition could deal openly with the complex and *specifically written* textual privileges that contemporary writing actually entails, none of this is to say that process research has made no difference in the intellectual politics of the profession of composition. It is first of all clear from this critique as well as from countless other sources that the process model has, as New Criticism did for literature, stabilized a field that originally was a loosely connected set of untheorized practices claiming origins in rhetorical theory, religious reading instruction, and the study of classical languages. This analogy with New Criticism is important. Process theory might also be called a result of leaving biographical and moral criticism of ancient texts to analyze them in a way that could claim "scientific" status. For instance, if we agree with Maxine Hairston that Mina Shaughnessy's *Errors and Expectations* represents the field's "essential person . . . who asked [the essential] question" (82), we can see how process theory took its first methods from New Criticism. In Shaughnessy's work, student biography was taken to be the precedent for examining "the text itself" as a product of the student's mind that could be illuminated by linguistic, grammatical, and symbolic systems uncovered by "close reading." Composition research to examine "the writing (process) itself" followed this lead.

But in calling composition a discipline, its professionals also appropriated the same scientific spirit that led New Critics to claim that literary language is separate from ordinary language or from what Wellek and Warren designated as "rhetorical literature" (15). Given a literary "medium" for analysis, New Critics could claim that they had an object of investigation, the workings of literary language in literary texts, and that they could discover self-contained "meanings" in this language. Given the "purified" (ahistorical, intransitive, theorized) "processes" of writers, composition has become able to make the same claims—that it has an object of study and that it can discover self-contained "meanings" in the act of writing.

James Berlin's survey in *Rhetoric and Reality* of trends in the 1960s and 1970s also shows that after New Criticism had thoroughly defined the teaching of literature, process theory increasingly pushed toward similarly pure considerations of "authorship." By looking at texts to find the systems encoded by their errors, by privileging subjective rhetorics, and by turning to cognitive and other brands of psychology, composition has added to its focus on correctness a concern for the whole text as an independent structure formed by "forces." It has followed New Criticism in sustaining a vision of writing as an independent medium for thought, not as the play among texts that are more or less visible, for specific reasons, in a textual politics.

When we ask a final question about process—How has it created an intellectual subjectivity/subject of composition that has specific consequences for the field's intellectual politics?—we need to return to the political situation of composition among its closest neighbors. Like New Criticism and later literary theory, composition has claimed a broad interpretive privilege, but it cannot support its process model in post-Shaughnessy studies without causing conflicts in its own professional sphere. Shaughnessy's clearly literary approach to student texts did attract the support of the literary establishment as it had not been attracted since the earliest MLA meetings. But the definition of the field's research as "interdisciplinary" that followed her call for further investigations of students' processes (17) and the use of quantitative methods from fields outside the settings where composition was almost exclusively taught have associated composition with another sort of credibility altogether.

Extrapolating from Stallybrass and White, we can see that process research after Shaughnessy has turned up yet another ambivalently transgressive aspect of the carnivalesque. It has, that is, assured the intellectual placement of composition outside the recognized, incorporated "city" that it originally completed and has thereby assured that the field will be identified with foreign methodological languages whose origins are uncertain and whose purposes and desires are consequently suspect. Close reading, Shaughnessy's method, was given over for statistical and other empirical designs whose credibility within the academic homes supporting this research was nil.

We need not review the many philosophical objections to these methods or to their resulting particularized conclusions to see that their benefits to the field's entrenchment (and to its capacity to receive grants from agencies biased toward these methods) has blurred the politics of composition. This emphasis has given composition a professional subjectivity that paradoxically undercuts its strong desire for consequential status among those in its most immediate surroundings. The literary and other humanists whose form of subjectivity was in fact served by a composition conceived of as an intransitive process now find it more necessary to draw away from composition intellectually than they did earlier, when the field made no claims to require expertise in matters outside the model of their own *professional* subjectivity.[3]

To use Althusser's interpretation of ideologies, this move from composition necessarily reproduced "the conditions of production at the same time as it [was] produced" (Macdonel 28). That is, the field reestablished antagonism and estrangement in the very act of following literature's earlier way of overcoming them. In attempting to overcome the atheoretical, or covertly theoretical, early nature of composition, the field reinforced its separateness. Removals of its most prominent research from humanistic rules of evidence, replacements of

3. See the Appendix for verifications of the professional conflicts created by the professionalization of composition as a discipline with a "paradigm."

literary vocabularies, and substitutions of behavioristic for ineffable literary subjectivity have constructed a place where new composition research re-forms antagonisms even as it attempts to reform its field. This reiteration of the estrangement of composition from its parent discipline occurred as a result of its new professionals' attempts to demonstrate their equal claim on the structural characteristics of a "serious" study.

Claiming to have a new process paradigm for composition also appears to support Althusser's claim that ideologies, in this case the research ideology in current composition, do not emerge from inherent motives or attitudes within a particular class, but from inevitable class conflicts. Without its status in relation to literary ideals, composition would not have moved into an alien social scientific realm, or necessarily have "moved" at all. Ideologies emerge "from between the classes" (Macdonel 34), so that composition might both give credit for its partial theorization as process to its first relations with literature and look forward to fuller theorization as the result of inevitable new class struggles that will take place internally. Among what Stephen North has called "practitioners" and "experimentalists" in its own professional structure, a similar set of movements can be expected to occur.

But in literary studies, the hegemony of New Criticism and its intransitive scientific spirit has relaxed at just the time when composition has been entrenching its own versions of these intellectual and affective projects. Consequently, if process theory continues to ride this literary subjective coattail, especially while dragging one foot in the methods of unfamiliar scholarship, it has little choice of a destination even more distant from the city of literature. It may move, as Stallybrass and White have claimed the local carnival did, to "coastal" locales far distant from the urban centers that established carnivals began to threaten (179).

Currently at least, composition studies avoid political alternatives like those that Tompkins and others have suggested for literary studies in three specific ways. First, the new field of composition has not widely accepted responsibility for research into the actual consequences of various historically determined processes of writing. Second, it has not taken responsibility for showing students the variability of writing processes, nor has it shown how their variety connects to particular contingencies in larger cultural systems that privilege some writers over others. Finally, it has not claimed a part in teaching students to analyze these privileging mechanisms. In one of the most prominent offshoots of process theory, for instance, the National Writing Project that engages high-school teachers in every state, process has even further been made the only content that teachers, not students, must learn. Consequently, composition is subject to the critiques now applied to New Critical and structuralist literary studies. But even New Critics have difficulty seeing the fit between their formalism, which largely remained unarticulated, and the research results of those in composition who describe validity, duplicability, statistical significance, and other operations on empirical data.

It might also be argued that process research undercuts one of its symbolic purposes, legitimizing in its immediate surroundings a long tradition of composition practice. Insofar as they have attempted to embrace one dominant model for research, ambitious members of the field have attempted to privilege empirical studies of individual processes to define legitimate research methods. In discriminations that many of this same group have objected to in literary studies, many have proposed that these methods define *all* genuine research in composition. A locution that designates "research" as the "hard" branch of the field, separate from historic and interpretive studies, discounts humanistic interpretive approaches to student texts. For instance, in George Hillocks's recent *Research on Written Composition*, the only alternative to "positivistic and scientistic" research that is recommended is "experimental" research, curiously in a statement that "we cannot afford to reject one mode of research in favor of another" (246). Many other process researchers have assumed an off-putting macho privilege for abstract models over interpretation and contextualization, both of which they criticize for their totalizing intellectual hold on literary theory.

Neither the various process theories nor historical studies that tie writing to historical rhetorical theory have left much room for interpretive theory in composition, an approach that might permit the field to answer some important political questions and to gain support from the peers it wishes to persuade of its value. It is obviously the bias of this study to give priority to interpretation and, therefore, to suggest research methods that use data from analyses of actual social situations, privileging mechanisms, discursive practices, and verifiable outcomes from writing. But even disallowing my bias, it is clear that the subject/subjectivity of composition as an intellectual pursuit is still largely maintained in its closest context, English studies, as a subsidiary carnival of the text. It remains one step behind newly emerging intellectual legislation from those who license and regulate it.

4 The Sad Women in the Basement

Images of Composition Teaching

One of the chief characteristics of composition, at least of composition perceived as teaching, has been that it fills the time that others take to build theories. Creating a process paradigm, despite its incompleteness, has been a monumental achievement because its existence *as* theory historically marks a new era in which composition professionals have room of their own, space to write their own story and become included in "history," not just to pore over student writing to find its faults.

But it remains to speculate about why a space for research and theory building has been filled with assertions that professional teachers of composition, taken and taking themselves seriously, work in a symbol system described as a "paradigm." That specific form takes them even further from the immediate and powerful community around them, their colleagues in literary study. It might be argued that this choice was made because such a model for observing writing lay ready for application and that composition professionals took it up because they agreed that writing is a "behavior" of autonomous individuals. But other models for studying other conceptions of writing were equally available. The choice to describe the past and present in composition as "current-traditional" and "process" paradigms, explanations of writing as a set of observable actions, is very much like the choice of "rhetoric" to explain composition history (see chapter 1). Its particular sort of authority also invites interpretation.

We cannot refuse this invitation, for as Gerda Lerner stressed in *The Creation of Patriarchy*, already established symbol systems are provisions that even enslaved and socially powerless males commonly adopt to identify with other males who have power and wealth. She comments that historically, "what was decisive for the individual was the ability to identify him/herself with a state different from that of enslavement or subordination" (222). But as they established their research, composition professionals did not choose to identify their work with the traditions of those who held power in their immediate surroundings. Their choice to risk a move even further from literary studies is, in English studies, both "different" and suspiciously, because overtly, "scientific." Its alienation from root metaphors in literary study can help us further understand the subordinated identity that it was meant to remedy, the established identity of those who teach composition.

At least one contrast between theories presented as a "paradigm" and promoted or objected to as they relate to "science" and early identities of composition teaching is their difference in regard to traditional images of masculinity. Words like "hard" (data, science), "tough-minded," and "rigorous," like the word "test," fall on the right side of our most common images of power. Not "everyone" in composition consciously chose these distinctive metaphors over another symbolic code they might have applied from a broad "English" or from specifically literary study. Many have taken exception to it; many are appalled by its "difference," if not entirely by its symbolic forcefulness. But everyone in composition has in some measure benefited from this symbolic choice, just as all women have (again, in some measure) benefited from feminist theories that decisively separate them from earlier, traditional representations.

This choice attaches composition to a form of power that clarifies the more traditional and accepted identity of the composition teacher, an identity deeply embedded in traditional views of women's roles. Apart from self-evident statistics about the "feminization" of composition (Holbrook), many theoretical positions and the self-perceptions of individual composition teachers confirm that composition teaching has been taken to be "worthy" but not "theoretically" based, culturally privileged, work (Appendix: Survey). To overcome this ancillary status, composition professionals have found it entirely reasonable, if not entirely successful, to redefine their hitherto blurred identity in more crisply masculine, scientific, terms.

As the last chapter suggested with the example of "motherhood," individuals are "placed," or given the status of subjects, by ideological constructions that tie them to fantasized functions and activities, not to their actual situations. These ideological constructions mask very real needs to organize societies in particular ways. For example (here, *the* example), the identity of the female person was created as "woman," the opposite, complement, extension, and especially the supplement to male identity. This traducement was first necessary to organize cultures for their survival. A female's particularity or her ignorance of such category formation could not at first, and has not later, excused her from a cultural identity devised to ensure group survival. She responds by virtue of the call for womanhood, not consciously *to* it. This particular "hood" cloaks, suppresses, and finally organizes individual female particularity.

Similarly, when we look at the particularity of people (of both sexes) who teach composition, we may find enormous variations in their interests, education, experience, and self-images as teachers. But when we examine the ideological "call" to create these individuals as a special form of subjectivity for composition teaching, we see them in a definitive set of imaginary relationships to their students and colleagues. Particularities are masked by an ideologically constructed identity for the teacher of composition.

The female coding of this identity is, in fact, the most accurate choice if a choice between sexes is made at all, although the large proportion of women hired to teach composition does not simply cause—or simply result from—cultural associations that link nurturance to teaching "skills" of writing. But we cannot overlook the facts. As Sue Ellen Holbrook infers from her statistical analysis of this "Women's Work," it is likely that about two-thirds of those who teach writing are women (9). In 1980, 65 percent of the participants in the NCTE College Section were women, in comparison to 45 percent women participants in MLA (10). Drops in doctoral enrollments in the 1970s and 1980s have been decreases in *male numbers,* not in numbers of females, so concurrent drops in full-time tenurable appointments have affected women most directly. Women, by and large, fill the temporary jobs teaching composition that are the residue from declines in "regular" appointments (see chapter 5).

In composition research, the hierarchy that places women in a subordinate status is maintained: men appear to publish a greater percentage of articles submitted to *College English* (65 percent); books by men dominate in selective bibliographies (approximately 70 percent); male authors overwhelmingly dominate in "theoretical" (as against nurturant, pedagogical) publication categories (Holbrook 12–13). Holbrook's analysis of these demonstrable proportions and of the historical position of women as faculty members in universities gives her good ground for inferring that "men develop knowledge and have higher status; women teach, applying knowledge and serving the needs of others, and have lower status" (7–8).

Economic determiners obviously have had a great deal to do with these dispositions among the actual genders of composition teachers (see chapter 5). But imaginary relationships of all teachers of composition to their students and colleagues are complex, not simple results of a one-to-one correspondence between kinds of "work" and patriarchal images of men and women. For instance, no one can take issue with evidence that the origins of English studies required that those who taught composition would contribute to the survival of a whole group. Just as "it was absolutely necessary for group survival that most nubile women devote most of their adulthood to pregnancy" (Lerner 41), it was absolutely necessary that the earliest English departments devote a significant portion of their energy to fulfilling the vision of them Eliot imagined at Harvard and that others took up: offering quasi-religious literary principles *and* a test of composition.

As I have said, we cannot be reductive here: composition teaching is not precisely, at least not only, "imaginary" womanhood, as I will explain. But the inference suggested by evidence of early huge composition classes, of the few people appointed to conduct their teaching, and of "leadership" in composition programs from one person over multitudes of students (like A. S. Hill's at Harvard or of "Miss Dumas and

Relation of Promotion to Field of Specialization

When asked if promotion is related to field of specialization in their departments, 62 (71 percent of the 87 who
answered this question) replied no. One qualified by stating that "it is, I believe, related to sex." (Four did not
answer; 7 were unsure.) The 14 respondents who replied
yes (22 percent) included 2 who stated that composition
appears to create a privilege for promotion. Three described their departments as accustomed to differentially
evaluating work in "the many mansions" of scholarship;
1 said that "the department must promote to full professor
in five years, no matter what"; and 1 echoed responses to
questions about tenure difficulties with "no, not yet."
Four others, however, spoke of various kinds of normal
and extraordinary field-related prejudices:

> 1. Yes, partially due to relative new entry of composi-
> tion; we have no full professor in composition.
> 2. Some departments will never change their negative
> attitude toward composition as a specialty. . . . They [peo-
> ple in composition] have grudgingly been afforded a cer-
> tain status. The central administration is very aware of our
> strength in the composition/rhetoric area and is extremely
> supportive.
> 3. The Chair debated the authenticity of a national
> award that a . . . book . . . had won (but not the award
> won by a poetry book of a colleague). Thus, he denied my
> promotion but supported that of my colleague.
> 4. While work in composition is worthwhile, literature
> is better. (Appendix, p. 229)

the staff" at Georgia [see chapter 2]) is that a great deal of
delivery from a very small (conceptual) input was required of
English departments from the outset.

It is interesting in this regard that we also have heard so
much and so often about the "victory" of Francis Child at
Harvard in giving over rhetoric for literature when he threatened to leave for Johns Hopkins in 1875 (e.g., Corbett, *Classical
Rhetoric* 625–26; Kitzhaber, "Rhetoric in American Colleges"

55; G. Graff 40–41). A. S. Hill was brought in from his newspaper career to manage composition in 1876 so that others' literary study would not symbolically sink under its weight. His task was to manage the actual "work" that Richard Ohmann has described ("Reading"), in a position that became a symbol of the management of "work" itself. In this regard, it is unlikely that presidents in new, vocationally justified land grant institutions, or anyone else, would have permitted English departments to thrive without well-managed labor from composition teaching. Along with evidence in discussions like William Riley Parker's, Wallace Douglas's, or James Berlin's of "where English departments come from," the small sizes of early departments in comparison to the numbers of students to whom they were required to teach composition point out that this teaching, if only at first, helped justify new English departments. It was loud in their ideological "call."

All of this evidence points toward how a cooperative brotherhood within English studies first *necessarily* separated and subordinated the teacher of composition in those departments that were well enough supported to establish a division of necessary labor. This division would by definition be inequitable, considering the ideological motivations for including composition in literary English that explain its rise. And in smaller settings, where work could not be divided among different people, the work of composition could be compartmentalized from the leisure or "play" of literature. Single individuals, those who have taught both subjects in largely undergraduate institutions, have identified themselves as members of "literature."

Francis Child's rearrangement of his teaching duties to include research and to focus exclusively on literature thus also became part of an emerging symbol system in English. Escaping rhetoric and composition teaching was an early sign of an institution's ardent regard for individuals. Using Lerner's terms, we can describe this privilege as a symbol in the "American Academic Dream," an internalized goal for those who felt themselves enslaved and poor or who accepted the association of composition with all of the "low" qualities that had been meant to apply to its students. But the important point is that, like women in early communities that depended on their production of live births, composition teachers were at first necessarily placed where they would accrue subordinate associations that were no less binding than those still imposed on women.

Obviously, this historically created role for composition teaching also loads the identity of its teachers with larger biases that were first associated with the whole of English literary study. The cultural identity of anyone in English shared the upstart, nonserious, vulgar (as in vernacular), dilettantish, and certainly nonscientific qualities ascribed to their new pursuits. But as performers in a site for illegitimate and transgressive textual activities that are inextricably linked to, but only placed beside, a newly established and unsophisticated community, composition teachers would not have been separately recognized at all in the larger academic world. The students in the course that I have called a course in silence were taught by those for whom a separate and recognized "profession" of composition was "unspeakable." Outsiders to English did not recognize composition as separate, as they still do not. Among insiders, it was a deniable subtext in a new discipline that was inevitably competing for publicity among established fields and hoping to be regarded as the guardian of national "ideals" with a worthy claim on time for academic research.

Consequently, the work of correcting spelling was at least partially uncompetitive with other symbolically constructed functions for English. Its mundane nature overcame any of its potentially positive associations with morality or serious intelligence in the "new" secular university. And this work was actually threatening to the time necessary to compete for symbolic academic rewards. Like any group or individual widely thought to be *nouveau,* literary studies needed to ignore an embarrassing root under a new family tree if that tree was to grow. The Teaching of Writing Division of the inclusive MLA was established only in 1973, well after a distinct insider group of self-identified composition teachers had formed the Conference on College Composition and Communication in 1949.

We have, therefore, at least two historicized identities from which associations with composition teaching would stem.

In actuality, composition teaching was work, and work of a particularly subordinate kind that *by definition within English studies* preceded the students' later exposure to cultural ideals in literature. It was literally "ground work." Ideologically, composition teaching had no claim on professional legitimacy, for it was not grammatical instruction in classical languages to transmit the Hegelian "spirit" of the past. The supposed low quality of its students and their writing, and its own mechanistic practices, had been constituted by the ideology of English to be illegitimate counterparts to ideals of content and perfections of execution that increasingly defined literary textuality. Over time, catalogues that describe developing English curricula in this century (see chapter 2) show that as even faint associations with classical grammatical instruction grew dimmer, composition was increasingly diminished and simplified. Concurrently, literary studies grew and became more complex.

These actual and imagined historical identities for composition teaching and its teachers have entrenched the imaginary identity around composition teachers. Their power over actual activities, like the power of womanhood over females, is not lessened by new facts. Although composition teachers now teach small classes relative to the majority of classes in other college-level subjects, their new ability to compete for research time, their publications, or the comparatively high salaries that some receive among their colleagues in literature do not automatically improve images held over from entirely different historical conditions.

The teacher of composition thus inevitably has at least some attributes of the stigmatized individual whom Erving Goffman describes in *Stigma: Notes on the Management of Spoiled Identity*. Goffman is a sociologist whose analysis focuses on interactions among stigmatized and normal individuals and groups within the same social situations, an arrangement that occurs in one department where ego identities from both literature and composition complexly conflict as privileged and subordinate, or healthy and "spoiled," identities. He is also a structuralist whose system of analysis identifies the stigmatized by their *relationships* with "normals," not by their intrinsic qualities.

Research Awards

Respondents overwhelmingly reported that their institutions and/or departments regularly provide one or another sort of support for research. Of 106 responding to the first questions, 85 (80 percent) answered yes or "occasionally"; 2 responded that support comes only from outside the institution. Thirteen respondents (12 percent) were in institutions where research support is unavailable.

The frequency of applications and success of the 89 who answered the three parts of the question about their own applications for research support show that 93 applications for research (not all to investigate problems defined as composition topics) had been made by this group in the previous ten years. One additional person indicated that she had "outside funding." Some respondents had applied and been turned down before later success; some had received more than one award. Although no control group from English or another humanistic department was used to measure this level of activity and 4 of these respondents defined themselves as "in" literature or as receiving grants toward research in it, a two-thirds (66 percent) rate of awards among this group defines them as aware of funding opportunities, active in pursuing them, and capable of competing successfully when they do.

In addition, those responding to these questions appear to believe that research awards in composition are made as often as in other fields. (See Appendix, pp. 230–31)

The "central feature" of these relationships is, Goffman says, "acceptance," which in fact appears to be the primary issue that current composition professionals identify when they discuss accomplished and hoped-for changes in their status. The stigmatized individual is treated so that "those who have dealings with him [sic] fail to accord him the respect and regard which the uncontaminated aspects of his social identity have led them to anticipate extending, and have led him to anticipate receiving" (8–9). The otherwise physical nor-

malcy of the deaf, the apparent masculinity of a male homo-
sexual, and by extension the Ph.D. in literature of a part-time
composition teacher will lead their associates and each of them
to expect acceptance in the group who share their larger "ego"
identity, a "felt" identity (105). But contamination from deafness, sexual practices, or trivialized teaching responsibilities
also means that they will receive treatment from others that
powerfully contradicts these expectations.

Goffman lists a number of typical responses to such treatment from stigmatized persons: they attempt to correct the
flaw; they use the stigma for "secondary gains," such as an
excuse for failures in other areas; they see the stigma as a
disguised blessing; they reassess the value of being "normal";
they avoid "normals"; and they develop anxieties, hostilities,
suspicions, and depression. We can find obvious instances of
some of these responses from composition teachers who apply
for full-time positions in literature, who imitate the elevation
of Francis Child by defining themselves as primarily graduate
faculty and researchers, or who avoid the Modern Language
Association because it remains "irrelevant" to their interests.
Naturally, each of these possible and actual strategies for coping colors encounters with normals and their groups.

Applying this analysis, we must emphasize that no feature
intrinsic to composition teaching urges stigma on its participants. The *discrepancy* between a felt identity and social treatments of those who allow themselves to be perceived as "in"
composition causes stigmatized relations. Thus when it is
"normal" to teach both composition and literature, as it is
for faculty in undergraduate four-year or junior colleges, or
normal to teach composition while engaging in graduate studies in literature or in creative writing, the stigmatic discrepancy
need not develop. Even when all graduate students must
teach composition and some faculty occasionally take it on,
the larger cultural or academic attitude toward composition
does not prevent it from being considered a perverse or abnor-
mal endeavor, one marginal to the "true" identity of members
of these groups. In these settings, however, some can treat it
as a joke, a source of shared good humor and complaints, or
as a temporary initiation ritual that "everyone" must endure,
a mark of maturation in trial by fire.

Perceptions of the Relative Status of Fields in English

The survey asked respondents to rank, on a scale of one to nine, eight fields (literature, literary theory, composition, rhetoric, linguistics, feminist studies, film, and folklore) and an open category ("other") according to their perceptions of these fields' relative status in their departments. . . .

The respondents clearly perceived literature to have the highest status in their departments. They most often placed literary theory in second place, and they placed composition or rhetoric (or the two combined) in third place, where it (or they) received 31 mentions (34 percent of 90 ranking these fields). . . .

Composition and rhetoric also held sixth place in these rankings. The seventh rank went to film studies, which was placed at that level 12 times. Folklore held eighth place, receiving 13 mentions (23 percent), and ninth place was held by "other."

Evaluated this way, data from these respondents suggest the following levels of status among fields:

1. Literature
2. Literary theory
3. Composition/rhetoric
4. Literary theory and composition/rhetoric
5. Linguistics
6. Composition/rhetoric
7. Film
8. Folklore
9. Other

That is, below the clear leader (literature), literary theory and composition/rhetoric appear to be vying for position in many settings, but composition/rhetoric has relatively low status (in sixth place) in many others. . . .

We can infer that these respondents recognized composition/rhetoric as a field as often as they did literature and that they appeared to be aware of recent elevations in its status. Rankings from 3 respondents were excluded from these data because they provided dualistic, past and future, rankings; these rankings commented directly on the changes perceived by the respondents. One only noted, "*I* perceive rhetoric and composition highly. The literature people don't." (See Appendix, pp. 233–36)

It is easy to see, therefore, that only individual composition teachers in a certain relationship to "normalcy" would be seriously stigmatized by this identity. While the entire activity of composition teaching is stigmatized in its historicized relation to literary centralism, many who engage in it can contain it, neutralize it, ignore it, and otherwise make it "all right." Temporary deafness, cross-dressing on Halloween, being assigned one composition course a year, or holding a graduate assistantship while completing a degree in Shakespeare do not permanently disable relations with the normal.

But it is one thing to go to the circus each year for entertainment, or even as part of one's family duty, and another thing entirely to run off to *join* the circus that composition was constituted to be. Openly displaying the signs that associate an individual with stigmatized groups, like openly engaging in any interaction taken to be peripheral to institutional purposes, inevitably disrupts normal social interactions.

We might infer from this distinction between the results of partial and full participation in a stigmatized, transgressive activity that one of the clearest operations of composition teaching is the cultural regulation and repression through stigma of particular kinds of otherwise normal activities— teaching and learning. Composition courses, from all of the evidence we have of their history, of the identity of their students, and of their choice of a research paradigm, *automatically* raise the issue of legitimacy. By this I mean that these courses and their teaching raise the issue of how an *actual* identity can take on imaginary associations that serve either privileged *or* marginalized cultural roles. The actual activities of someone who is learning to write, or of someone who is teaching composition, inevitably become implicated in a relationship to the imaginary perfection of literary texts. Both literary production and literary products are composition's "Other," the second terms in discrepancies between "the raw and the cooked" or "savage and domesticated" texts.

Given this foundational structure, we can extend Lerner's analysis of the operations of patriarchy to agree that a surplus of women or of live births, and perhaps a surplus of English Ph.D.s in literature, can make available human resources that have traditionally been closely regulated to guarantee that their scarcity will dispose them only in competitive and "proper" social circumstances. A surplus of females as slaves may in fact instigate prostitution, wherein commercialized sexual activity can fulfill symbolic (unlicensed, subnormal) cultural needs (see Lerner 133). But such a surplus can instead become the basis for newly normalized relationships, which a culture can afford to leave "unnamed" or even to elevate to the special status of "independence," "freedom," and "self-determination." In either case, permitting actions by this sort of surplus to remain outside established designations for proper and improper activities—that is, not calling its sexual activity prostitution—will mask the *actual* extracultural or extrafamilial situations of this surplus. Excess women, and perhaps excess Ph.D.s, may take on new roles that cloak their real status as surplus.

Consequently, it is even further possible that a surplus Ph.D. or a Ph.D. candidate in literature will take one of two paths: openly to choose the unlicensed, subnormal identity associated with composition, as many recently have, or more covertly to provide this teaching on a part-time, ad hoc basis while implicitly retaining a "normal" ego identity in a claim that "self-determination" or "independence" are his or her motives. This analysis from Goffman is in no way meant to belie the sincerity of such identity claims. But his structuralist model does explain one way that a group of individuals might *actually* derive their identities from composition teaching but also avoid its stigma through new and *imaginary* legitimizations for it.

Additionally, as Goffman points out, an imagined exemption from a stigma like this one can even further affect the actual conditions around stigmatized status. The surplus of Ph.D.s who have taken up composition teaching as one way to engage in transgressive behavior without actually joining the circus now have special professional grants, organizational fee structures, organizations, and support from professional position papers like the Wyoming Conference Resolution on the status of part-time composition teachers (Slevin 50). All show that normal people may respond to a new imaginary identity for the deviant. Dominant, already accepted groups may, that is, provide new *actual* relations that are within a "normal" range. These dispensations and expressions of concern have resulted from imagining normalcy for marginalized groups of part-time, traveling "gypsy" scholars. New institutional structures incorporate purveyors of the carnival into larger cultural systems, so that it always remains outside and suburban to an established city, not an independent force that might become parallel to it or competitive with it (see chapter 5).

Such responses do change actual conditions for one kind of composition teacher, just as feminist theories have contributed to actual benefits for women by urging social services and legislation to benefit those who are marginalized by virtue of being single, divorced, or lesbian. As earlier references to Althusser indicate, ideologies emerge from a struggle *between* classes; they are not positions that a class will inevitably take from within itself.

But no new actuality can entirely revise the identity state of those who choose the first path, openly devoting themselves to a deviant identity as composition teachers or further becoming researchers in composition. Again, Goffman helpfully points toward the condition of this person:

> Even while the stigmatized individual is told that he [sic] is a human being like everyone else, he is being told that it would be unwise to pass or to let down "his" group. In brief, he is told he is like anyone else and that he isn't—although there is little agreement among spokesmen as to how much of each he should claim to be. This contradiction and joke is his fate and his destiny. . . . The stigmatized individual thus finds himself in an arena of detailed argument and discussion concerning what he ought to think of himself, that is, his ego identity. To his other troubles he must add that of being simultaneously pushed in several directions by professionals who tell him what he should do and feel about what he is and isn't, and all this purportedly in his best interests. (124–25)

Goffman hereby suggests that we look even more closely at the situation of these individuals who overtly claim to be *in* composition as its teachers and who are academically placed where they could not be imagined before model building, and finally paradigm construction, were undertaken (see Berlin, *Rhetoric and Reality*, chapter 7). The professionals surrounding these teachers—their colleagues, their (usually male) privileged theorists, and administrators who form and enact insti-

---

Difficulties with Tenure in Composition

Among the 34 who answered that they had perceived problems with tenure related to composition as a field, only 1 attributed the difficulty to problems with the quality of a particular person's work. . . .

Among responses classified in table A–8, 12 respondents explained specific instances of difficulties that they perceive as related to having composition as a field. Very difficult personal situations were revealed: 2 were promoted before tenure, then suffered from second thoughts of colleagues about actually tenuring people in composition; 2 people reported results from an institution that, they say, "routinely passes over people who spend too much time on composition"; 1 reported that she "made changes in the program," then left her position after warnings about receiving tenure; 3 reported similar difficulties when appointments to administer composition were later not "counted" for tenure; 1 said that she had, in an unprecedented departmental action, been put up for review two years after the beginning of her appointment; 2 other less specific cases involved releasing all of the people in composition, or some of them, while retaining others in literature. One person was told at hiring that he would never be promoted or allowed to serve on committees because he had been hired to teach writing courses. But he witnessed changes from this situation in his department to active hiring in composition. Nonetheless, he reported that a more junior colleague in composition had been reviewed first by the usual three outside reviewers, then by three more because the first group was perceived as "too complimentary." (See Appendix, pp. 220–21)

---

tutional structures—all contribute to a particular kind of blurring in their experienced identity, the conflict that Goffman quite accurately describes as both a contradiction and a joke. As Stallybrass and White say of the "Maid and the Family Romance," both "service" and "motherhood" converge in the call to this group from traditional ideology.

But composition teaching is not simple "motherhood," in service to father texts. The social identity of the composition teacher is intricately blurred in a matrix of functions that we can understand through the instructive example of Freud's description of the "feminine," which was formed at about the same time that composition courses and their teaching first achieved presence in the new university. Despite the problematics feminists point out in his work, Freud's description of associations that contain ambivalently situated women can be seen as a reliable account of nineteenth-century sexual mythologies, offering us historical access to early and continuing images of the gender-coding of composition teaching.

Freud dreamed of his family nurse, whom he later transformed into "mother." The nurse in the dream "initiated the young Freud in sexual matters" (Stallybrass and White 157). But later, in Freud's writing about "femininity," "the nurse has been displaced by the mother" (157). In a series of statements, Freud by turns associated seduction and bodily hygiene with motherhood and the maid, at one time calling the maid the most intimate participant in his initiations and fantasies, and at another thinking of these matters in relation to perfect motherhood. Stallybrass and White infer that because the nineteenth-century bourgeois family relegated child care to nurses, the maid both performed intimate educational functions and had power over the child. "Because of his size, his dependency, his fumbling attempts at language, his inability to control his bodily functions" (158), the child could be shamed and humiliated by the maid. But paradoxically, it is more acceptable to desire the mother than the maid, who is "hired help," so that actual interactions with a nurse/maid might be fantasized as having occurred with the mother.

Without stressing prurient comparisons between the "low" work of composition and this representation of intimate bodily and other educational functions (although in nineteenth-century sociopathology they were certainly there to be drawn) it is fair to suggest that this symbolic blurring still encodes the role of teachers of composition. It explains some otherwise troubling contradictions in their habitually conceived identities. The bourgeois mother and maid, that is, both represent comfort and power. The mother was the source Freud turned to for explanatory information about the maid; the mother was also, with the father, an authority. The maid was an ambivalently perceived site for dealing with low, unruly, even anarchic desires and as yet uncontrolled personal development.

Even down to the reported problematic of leaving the "home" language in a requirement to "'forget' the baby-talk of the body" (Stallybrass and White 166), a developmental stage associated with the maid, we can see an oscillation between images of mother and maid. Leaving the maid represents foregoing infantile freedoms for the embarrassments that the mother/power figure is likely to represent, as she did when the child moved on to formal Latin lessons in the process of leaving the governess for the schoolmaster (a process that Freud's Wolf Man found crucial). By the obvious analogy with learning vernacular language again, as a formalized system, the composition student's teacher combines the two images of mother and maid. This powerful but displaced person blurs anxieties over maturation that must inevitably accompany a move toward public language.

Consequently, one figure of a composition teacher is overloaded with symbolic as well as actual functions. These functions include the dual (or even triple) roles that are washed together in these teachers: the nurse who cares for and tempts her young charge toward "adult" uses of language that will not "count" because they are, for now, engaged in only with hired help; the "mother" (tongue) that is an ideal/idol and can humiliate, regulate, and suppress the child's desires; and finally the disciplinarian, now not a father figure but a sadomasochistic Barbarella version of either maid or mother.

By virtue of all the institutional placements of composition teaching that were described earlier, it is clear that the individual composition teacher is a culturally designated "initiator," much like a temple priest/ess who functions to pass along secret knowledge but not to participate freely in a culture that depends on that knowledge. Strict regulations, analogous to those devised to keep "hired help" in its place, prevent those who introduce the young to the culture's religious values and rites from leaving their particular and special status. These mediators between natural and regulated impulses are tied to vows, enclosed living spaces, and/or certain kinds of dress. (See Lerner, "Veiling the Woman" 123–41.)

But this initiating role, whether it is described in terms of religious/sexual initiations or as the groundwork under discursive practices, is unstable in any context. It was never worked out in regard to codified culture even in ancient times, when the socially separated *grammaticus* and *rhetor* argued over who should initiate students into rhetorical composition. Thus the teacher of composition is not assigned only the role of initiator, which might involve the care, pedagogic seduction, and practice for adult roles provided by nurses in bourgeois homes. In addition, this teacher must withhold unquestioned acceptance, represent established means of discriminating and evaluating students, and embody primary ideals/idols of language. This initiator, who traditionally has a great deal at stake in the model-correctness of his or her own language, must also *be* the culture to which the student is introduced.

This embodiment in rules and practice exercises, the rituals of language, displaces actual discourse. It requires the student to keep a distance. If there is an Oedipal situation in regard to working out an imagined young student's entitlements to full participation in cultural "principles," the composition teacher is the Jocasta figure, the desired and desiring but always displaced representation of maturity. In the terminology of psychopathology, this teacher is called into an inverted neurotic situation, one that displays the *social* irruption of *psychic* processes, not the more usual "*psychic* irruption of *social* processes" (Stallybrass and White 176).

Some might counter that this structure contains the imaginary identity called for from any teacher of any introductory course claiming to initiate students into "essential" cultural knowledge. But the composition teacher consciously and unconsciously initiates students into the culture's discourse on *language,* which is always at one with action, emotion, and regulatory establishments. This teacher is always engaged in initiations to the textual fabric of society and thus will always be in a particular and difficult relation to the powers that overtly regulate that society. Although the fairs that permeated social life in Europe were broken up and discontinued in the process of regulations like the Fairs Act of 1871 in England (Stallybrass and White 177), actual carnivals do not disappear. "Fragmentation, marginalization, sublimation, and repression" (178) keep them alive. Similarly, the identity first imposed on teachers of composition is held over, even after their mechanistic and very obviously regulatory earliest roles are revised and are in fact contradicted by many stated goals, practices, and actual situations.

Doubts about the plausibility of this explanation of the composition teacher's blurred identity may be lessened by common responses to these teachers, which should reveal its force. Like the carnival, composition teaching still is often acknowledged as "an underground self with the upper hand" (Stallybrass and White 4). It is an employment that in the majority of its individual cases is both demeaned by its continuing ad hoc relation to status, security, and financial rewards, yet given overwhelming authority by students, institutions, and the public, who expect even the most inexperienced composition teacher to criticize and "correct" them in settings entirely removed from the academy. The perduring image of the composition teacher is of a figure at once powerless and sharply authoritarian, occupying the transgressive, low-status site from which language may be arbitrated.

Continuing associations of composition teachers with "Miss Grundyism" also reinforce this claim that as an identity, composition teaching codes the individual of either sex as a woman, the inheritor of the "pink sunsets" image of literary initiation that has in the last quarter-century largely been removed from the self-perceptions of literary professionals by their own "theory." In this way also, the existence of composition within English permits literature to displace and translate an older social identity onto only one of its parts. Composition is a site for residues and traces from earlier literary identities that first coded English as "female" among "hard" disciplines.

If we return to the original question I posed in this chapter, the question of why composition professionals would have chosen a "process paradigm" that appears to estrange them from English studies, we may answer that this choice emerges from their blurred identity and from strategies for coping with its nonetheless clear stigma. The choice of a "process" "paradigm" for research appears to, but finally does not, represent a contradiction in terms. On the one hand, associations with "process" extend and in fact enlarge the subjectivity for its own sake that removes students and their teachers from the need to verify, validate, and find significance in "results." "Process" thereby reinforces the composition professional's claim on a "normal" identity among colleagues in literature, expressing a desire that is difficult to shake. But on the other hand, associations with a scientific "paradigm" give value only to verified, valid, significant "results" from research. This member of the pair of terms reveals yet another mechanism for coping with stigma, in the form of a desire to elevate stigmatized status to a place that is imagined to be above the identity of the "normal."

The juxtaposition of these terms does not, I would argue, unconsciously preserve androgyny and thereby give equal privileges to two terms of a pair that is symbolically female and male, yin and yang. Instead, the choice of this seemingly contradictory pair in a new description of composition teaching and theory contains two equal preservations of the historical (traditional, hegemonic) situation of composition. *Process* practices extend and preserve literary subjectivity, while their explanation in a *paradigm* theory extends and preserves the anxiety about status that has always been associated with English studies, both in regard to the perfection of elitist texts and as a professional concern about identity in relation to older, "harder" disciplines.

As in other examples, composition professionals inevitably re-create the conditions that first established their identities. Persistent attempts to change these conditions without changing the basic structure of high and low that sustain them leave composition in new versions of traditional values. Stallybrass and White summarize such moves in a judgment whose importance cannot be overstated: "The point is that the exclusion necessary to the formation of social identity is simultaneously a *production* at the level of the Imaginary, and a production, what is more, of a complex hybrid fantasy emerging out of the very attempt to demarcate boundaries, to unite and purify the social collectivity" (193). They claim, that is, that by separating itself from an objectionable entity—the stigma, for example, of "mere" teachers of composition engaged in "grotesque" untheorized work—a group necessarily produces a "new grotesque."

We see this process in action in regard to composition teaching and theorizing, both of which have appeared to exclude formerly acceptable literary agendas as well as "soft," unorganized theories of composition or interpretations based on work that is not really "in" the field. But the production that occurs simultaneously with this attempt to mark boundaries, unite, and purify a field of composition also is a process of exclusion, the very process that otherwise dedicated teachers of composition object to and take as their motive for change. Consequently, the theories I have applied to the identity of the composition teacher may appear to describe a condition that is past or clearly passing, not one that is held over in a complex set of continuing interactions that slowly move the teacher out of a sweat shop and into respectable professional modes. Nonetheless, the nature of this movement is too clearly implicated in reproducing the conditions it wishes to revise to be celebrated with unqualified assertions that "change" has occurred, as new institutional blurrings of the identity of composition also demonstrate.

5 The Institution and Composition

Bread and Circuits

Composition is now undeniably an academic entity. Its systematic management and competitiveness in established systems for recognition and reward imply hope that it has, or will soon, overcome the carnivalesque quality of the position it was designed to hold. Many still state unself-consciously (as Carol Hartzog does in *Composition and the Academy*) that "composition is not—at least not yet—viewed as a field of study equal to others" (141), that "the department confers a kind of academic legitimacy" (143), and that composition does not have "the standing of an established scholarly academic discipline" (144). But an active self-consciousness about the status of composition studies and its professionals controls many other conversations, which portray both composition research and those "in" composition as elements in a newly recognized and perhaps entirely "new" discipline that differs from its traditional forms and corrects their ancillary status. To understand fully how novelty and change may redefine the status of composition, we need to explore the extent of these differences and their corrective energy.

As is not true of women's or of ethnic studies, the novelty of composition has no obvious sources in larger political changes in the 1960s and 1970s that might have improved an earlier status. These new fields that are specifically "political," like imported European discourse theories that dig around the roots of formalist American literary studies, have had support that composition cannot claim. Rearrangements of privilege in the larger society, Gerald Graff proposes, may diminish the marginalization of more obviously political fields, "since they have outside political ties" (252; see Macdonel, "The End of the 1960s" 8–23). But the novelty of current composition has more to do with movements within its originating traditions—

142

objections by neoclassicists to New Critical displacements of rhetorical criticism in the 1940s and 1950s and precedents for "process" in the work of Rohman and Wlecke and Janet Emig. We might argue that theoretical "novelty" is in fact not at all an issue in composition because current turns toward process theories of writing signal a "return of the repressed," a reemergence within English studies of disguised rhetorical instruction that is now closely adapted to the alternative paradigm of "writing" described in chapter 3. But even if we take composition theories to be new, we cannot automatically link this field to others that have arisen from social changes that explained and supported them.

Obviously, a (new) "literacy crisis" occurred in the 1970s, along with certain institutional shifts that responded to the quantity of graduate students in English, the unlikely prospect that these graduate students would be absorbed into literary teaching, and the proliferation of postsecondary required composition courses in new colleges established after World War II. But quantitatively motivated expansions of composition instruction and the number of people involved in it do not mean that writing is a new academic concern or that it has theoretically interacted with political and social change as gender or ethnic studies have. Nor does the "growth" of composition mean that it is less marginalized in new institutional structures that now facilitate and constrain it. In fact, as we will see, at least one new institutional path for composition teaching included marginalization in its formation, reproducing the most traditional stigmas of its teachers in response to priorities in "new" budget planning.

Because composition was established long ago *to be* a low site where certain students, corrective teaching, and inevitable anxieties from nineteenth-century claims for vernacular textual research could be displaced, it has always been openly recognized in the "high" site it is placed beside. But it now has a professional nomenclature, visibility, and a complex new relation to the ecology of supply and demand in this academic setting. It is defined by "programs," not courses, and has "specialists" rather than only teachers. Departments offer graduate degrees in the field (Chapman and Tate); funding agencies award grants for its research and program development. These novelties in a fully franchised version of the carnival have brought many advantages. But new organizations of its people and its knowledge about writing also raise further questions about its politically lowered place. They most pointedly bring up open anxieties about difference as they arrive in the traditional (and changing) "English" where they have always found their home.

A new institutional identity for composition both uses and is used by a variety of actual and symbolic structures. These patterns constitute the "bread and circuits" that this chapter describes. Funding and its administrative "circuits," symbolic and actual pathways that move to and from composition through the typical director of composition in an English department, symbolize autonomous power and active participation in the exchange between language and politics. This autonomy and participation are not, however, entirely straightforward advantages that now place composition on a line parallel to its neighbors.

1. Bread

In the academy, the relation between status and money is not a particularly inviting topic. Academics are always aware of how little wealth their profession accounts for in relation to a larger corporate and private economy, even if they are unaware of their organized structural complicity in this disposition. A strong component of humanistic subjectivity (in line with its Kantian moral philosophy) is that individual humanists are among the "independently poor." These juxtaposed terms complement each other, suggesting that the traditional humanistic subject's "standard of living" results from ineffable traits and independent choices that reinforce a passive relation to broad political and financial interests. Similarly, in the larger arena it has contructed, academic humanism tends to displace financial competitiveness inside the academy, and possible social influence outside it, onto other measures of its status, like the American post-Depression "top-out-of-sight" class that hides signs of its wealth (Fussell 19–20). Institutional actions that connect actual resources to status usually "go without saying" in this sphere, as basic preservative structures usually do go.

But we need to explore the relation between financial actions and academic status if we are to understand the strength of claims that composition has become a "new" entity. Both symbols and cash provide ordinary (daily) and extraordinary nutrition to a profession that by its own traditional definitions must submerge its consciousness that money influences its members' independence or their subjection. Financial processes that interact with both old and new symbolic dispositions of writing instruction in the academy reveal a great deal about the criteria by which change must be measured.

Budgets

Although the carnivalesque, ad hoc status of composition is not completely explained by the notoriously low pay of composition teachers, this condition for teaching composition is one example of an actual constraint that has maintained its original status. Another example is the relation between budget planning and the symbolically lower, not just financially unrewarding, domain created by large numbers of nonfaculty composition teachers. In this instructive case, a complicated interaction between symbolic and actual domains entrenched the low set of administrative priorities applied to composition at about the time when the field began to claim academic parity as a research field.

This group of nonfaculty teachers, often called "the rotating bottom," has become a national problem that departments and institutions recognize, but its creation *as* a group and the ways that that creation reveals the politics of composition are not addressed in most suggested solutions to its problems. As we know, academic institutions base their budgets on the number of people to whom they have commitments to provide salaries. Recent budget crises in a number of states (e.g., Michigan, Idaho, and Texas) demonstrate that significant reductions in academic budgets necessitate reducing the number of people who can regularly be paid with budgeted, or "hard," funds. Consequently, when predictions in the early 1970s foretold that student enrollments would fall dramatically in the following decade, those who controlled academic budgets responded to advice to keep their budgets flexible and to avoid commitments in permanent appointments. This forecast now appears to have had the same credibility as the Club of Rome's prophecy of imminent worldwide famine, based on its infamous misplacement of a decimal point in its calculation of world population growth. But its persuasiveness at the time had important results.

It is difficult to imagine the status of composition and its professionals if this prediction and subsequent refusals to add or replace faculty positions had not occurred. At that time, complex new structures for evaluating faculty, in the form of new committees and statements about "due process," cooperated with administrative perceptions that faculty might be economically dispensable. But if this cooperation between re-active financial planning and stringent processes for faculty evaluation had not occurred, possible alternatives to it are nonetheless unclear. On the one hand, if the positions of relatively large numbers of new assistant professors hired in the late 1960s had not been significantly transferred to three-to-five year appointments of "lecturers," "associates," "ad-juncts," and other terminal positions, composition might have claimed new, equal entitlements with literature in an easy permanent expansion of departments. But if the prominent career pattern of combining a literary research specialty with (just) teaching composition in the late 1960s had held among retained and replaced faculty appointees, a mass of new "composition specialists" might not have emerged at all.

In any case, this academic planning for significant enrollment declines that never changed the overall size of higher education in America greatly influenced the social and symbolic situation of numerous ad hoc, mobile scholars who earn their living primarily by teaching composition in temporary and often concurrently held positions. This is not, of course, to claim that a new class of academics sprang forth without precedent, nor is it to ignore actual declines that rewarded this sort of planning in specific cases. But it is to point to a situation in certain large departments of English across the country, many of which are large because of the hiring and "release" of limited-term appointees. Attitudes toward teaching composition that resulted in such settings also redefined

Faculty Ranks and Power

A large group of responses (23) connected tensions around composition to discriminations among various ranks of personnel, ranks that take specific privileged or underprivileged relations to composition teaching. Fourteen people mentioned tensions resulting from the place of tenured faculty over either part-timers and nonfaculty or over untenured faculty. In one case, evaluations by those with tenure over unranked nonfaculty were mentioned; in another, resentment of a tenure-track specialist director from untenured M.A.-qualified faculty was the issue. Two mentioned the unhappiness of part-timers about job insecurity, and 3 mentioned "remarks" by full professors that denigrated part-timers or others who teach composition (as the full professors in these cases did not). One pointed to the "guilt and resulting resentment" that stimulate these remarks. (Appendix, pp. 245–46)

a new quantity of composition students as only tentatively "accepted," whatever their admission status.

The underclass that their teachers inevitably comprised has reinforced earlier images of composition's place. But it has had an additional result. Those with insecure positions impose an enormous burden of guilt on the secure who had already associated composition teaching with the work of hired help in the mode of the nineteenth-century maid. This guilt encourages avoidance. People use such groups as scapegoats, as we can verify easily from treatments of the stigmatized and of large groups of politically displaced refugees. But guilt can also be reversed. The budgets of composition programs formed at the same time this budget planning took effect, programs staffed by this underclass of nonfaculty, might be thought of as seductive prizes. They could, that is, represent booty that could be transferred to more legitimate departmental interests after an imagined defensible ruin of the scapegoats' obviously illegitimate domain.

Both of these responses, guilt and predatory fantasy, contribute to broader concerns on the part of the Modern Language Association and the Conference on College Composition and Communication. These organizations, expressing their interest jointly through the Association of Departments of English, have suggested remedies for insecure teachers that would improve their financial and career situations by providing ways to censure and correct egregious treatments of them (Slevin 50). The Modern Language Association has also called on chairs of English departments to agree on a minimum percentage of courses to be taught by nonfaculty (Franklin). But composition specialists, perhaps in ignorance of the institutional budget planning that created this class, initiated a resolution (quoted in Slevin 50) in which they at least implicitly accept low status as the inevitable condition of these teachers. Their plan to set up committees to state policies about the treatment of this group acknowledges its commonly overworked and underpaid situation, and then attempts to improve its maintenance.

This well-intentioned solution may inadvertently reinforce the existence of such a class, not address the error in its creation or suggest means of improving the symbolic status that made its work, composition teaching, a particularly available object of this error. But whatever their outcome, few solutions were proposed until better futuristic budget predictions were clear. Now, evidently without realizing that academic appointments will be held at a reasonably stable or increased level in the near future, organizational responses add "fairness" and "equity" to an unnecessary insecurity. The underclass that was a "solution" to a problem that never occurred now evokes further solutions that diffuse guilt and ward off appropriation, but not responses that demonstrate what it might mean to withdraw this human resource, or its status, from higher education.

Meanwhile, the money that pays this underclass is "soft" money, which is to say that it has not been assigned to "lines" in regular budgets but to variously named pools that an institution might, in a crisis, relinquish. Like a place in a departmental budget for unspecified "TA lines," such a pool may not usually be used for other purposes, and it is usually not sufficient to hire teachers for the numbers of students who will in fact appear to take writing courses. This last qualification is important, for it points to a larger problem of funding composition classes and their ad hoc teachers that existed well before faulty predictions about enrollment declines. Composition has a particularly shaky relation to the ongoing commerce in its institutional settings, but its weakness is often unrecognized. In the commonly described composition "program" in an English department that employs nonfaculty to teach composition, composition professionals often argue against all of the symbolic and actual snobbery they encounter on two grounds that are rarely persuasive in any context, but are additionally in their situations only provisionally true.

First, it is argued, composition teaching occupies the *largest* instructional space in an English department. It regularly enrolls, at least in many departments that were until recently losing numbers of English majors, a majority of a department's students. It thereby appears to give a department's weaknesses covering strength. Second, composition is thought to be "cheap" for such a department and therefore to support not only itself but the department's ability to offer graduate programs, their small classes, or research leave for its scholars. Each of these arguments is correct, but only in a limited way that distorts how large composition programs create a financial burden that can actually reinforce common social and symbolic prejudices against them and the activity they represent. My reasoning for this statement cannot be generalized to all departments or programs. But this logic shows how arguments from some composition professionals for equality on the basis of "contribution" can inflate the actually limited heft of the nurturing bread they make. As Hazard Adams pointed out ironically in "How Departments Commit Suicide," composition assures that departments do not become "overfunded and underworked" (31).

In typical departments that appoint graduate assistants and other nonfaculty to teach composition, yearly budgets barely support faculty, supplies, a limited number of graduate assistants, and various supports for faculty development. They are too small to pay for teaching all the sections of composition that student demand usually warrants. Consequently, the institution sometimes provides supplemental funds for these sections as a special category of "enrollment demand" funds. But these funds are as often taken from the "soft" money in departmental budgets that results when budgeted faculty take leaves, receive grants, or leave a department before they are replaced. Composition courses do not, therefore, regularly "pay for" anything in such a department. Deans and department chairs who control their budgets usually take composition sections to represent a normal continuing departmental deficit, which in a large state institution can be as high as $50,000 each year.

Consequently, while money to teach composition classes is often "there" in the form of unspent regular funds, it is not money budgeted for composition teaching, "there" before the fact. It must be earned, saved, and accounted for by a department chair or dean, who additionally does not know how much of it to count on, or what the demand on it will be, until regular budget processes for a particular year have ended. Financial gains from composition teaching are hand-to-mouth gains where enrollments are translated into funding; small sections even at the low rates normally paid to ad hoc teachers often generate only enough money to pay for a section, not significantly more. But an exchange between credit hours and funding is not automatic, or even particularly common. Often, sections of composition will be supported by a college or an institution on the basis of a department's average class enrollments. These averages will often be higher in undergraduate literature courses that thereby "pay" for composition or that could be averaged with lower graduate class sizes. Together, these three cohorts of courses might comprise equalized financial contributions to a whole unit.

In other departments where "everyone" teaches composition, a budget for it will not be discriminated so clearly from general concerns about a department's whole effort. But even as only a special case in departments where large and often newly distinct writing programs are involved in a complete set of undergraduate and graduate curricula, this special curricular circumstance contributes to a continuing general perception that inexpensive composition "supports" the curriculum above it. This perception is not usually accurate, except as composition accrues symbolic support from its social mis-

sion and justifies the support of graduate students, as Kitzhaber noted in *Themes, Theories, and Therapies*. But in more
recent circumstances in which enrollments in lower-division
literature courses have risen concurrently with numbers of
sections of composition, these graduate students might be
equally well supported by relieving the financial burden of
understaffed literature courses.

These realities, the subtext for the treatment of composition, are displaced, as I have suggested, by cooperative views
that composition is a department's socially "important" work
and that low pay automatically frees already available funds.
These blurred perspectives misguide the attitudes of those
without information about actual funding situations at any
level of curricula. But considering that composition is also
placed in and under literary humanism, these realities are
vivid signs of the "open capitulation at the universities by the
humanities as agents of the minimization of their own expense
of production" (Spivak 109). By this charge, Spivak gives us
another view of the nineteenth-century agenda for literature
that Jane Tompkins noted (see chapter 3). Both suggest that a
powerful, central ideological site, whose object of study is
charged with the "legislation of mankind," has constructed a
self-identity that permits it to be a terrible way, plus a more
terrible way in composition, to earn a living. The fact that
departments and institutions around them labor with "soft"
financing for composition teaching exemplifies the tradition
of accepting relatively minor funding as its due. A normal
inequity in the humanities has been transferred to the low-
status site of composition. Composition studies is again implicated in the position that has traditionally preserved literary
humanism from details in the "real" world it claims to know
best, but to be free from.

A typical department chair thus might not separate composition from the department on the grounds that it "belongs,"
in the carnivalesque symbolic ways we have seen. But asked
about his or her budget deficit, a department chair might
cheerfully acknowledge that composition is a yearly burden,
a balancing act, and a drain on the department, in other than
symbolic ways. This same person might also, as some have, be
motivated to remove this actual burden from the department's

fiscal responsibility. Providing funds for composition classes can limit the number of visiting speakers, the research time, and the predictability of resources that would benefit an entire department. And from whatever source, this funding additionally requires that the department employ people who must be observed, supervised, and assimilated into a unit in whose survival and prospering they can have no stake. Where this situation exists, it confirms the perception that composition is not really "part" of the department, a root metaphor in many prejudices against it in its recently institutionalized forms, as we will see. Actual composition classes are treated by the department and its institution as departmental donations to a "larger" effort of initiation, but they are perceived in the composition community as exploitation that supports more privileged work. These conflicting perceptions diminish the image of composition within and outside it. An actual financial burden, therefore, can become a subtext that reinforces symbolic workings of exclusivity and self-denigration.

Grants

These ambivalent daily workings of the nutrition that composition provides appear to contrast with more clearly positive examples of the new configuration that composition now represents. But at the risk of reading too deeply, we can also see how other actual funds may similarly blur otherwise "normal" circumstances in a whole when they are digested in the carnivalesque site created for and by composition. A primary example is a grant awarded to a faculty member who is a composition specialist. It will usually release its recipient from teaching. It may bring recognition and prestige to the institution, the department, and the individual(s) who receive it, and it may also provide funds for secretarial help and for replacing the faculty member in classes. This replacement can be done at a much reduced rate; one faculty member on a year-long grant might allow a department to staff two or three times as many sections of scheduled classes as the faculty member would normally teach.

So far, then, it appears that a grant for research in composition benefits everyone around its reception, as it actually does. But in the humanities, where grants do not ordinarily support

---

Research Awards

This group also included 9 who saw composition research as having a *greater* chance of funding in their institutions and 1 who saw the process of applying over five years
as finally educational for the committee making awards.

Finally, in 48 responses explaining causes for institutional changes toward recognizing composition research,
the respondents portrayed the same patterns they perceived in conditions around tenure, but did so with a more
positive cast of mind. The sources of change, for instance,
included many of the sources for hiring. New faculty, once
hired, generate support for research. Sixteen respondents
attributed positive change to new faculty. An additional
11 mentioned administrative encouragement from deans
or vice-presidents, sometimes as the result of a grant that
motivated this support. New undergraduate or graduate
programs were mentioned as a source of increased research support by 9. (Appendix, pp. 232–33)

---

faculty salaries, grants to individuals whose academic field is
traditionally thought of as a kind of teaching that anyone
easily handles are both visible and ambivalent symbols. The
relation of the grant to scholarly achievement can be blurred
by the culture in which it appears. A grant might remove
a faculty member from administering writing courses, from
teaching required seminars for teachers, and from teaching
classes to which this person is the only faculty member assigned. If these results follow, the institutional setting—the
department, the program, even a college—confronts a structural gap or hole in its symbolic maintenance of the carnivalesque teaching of composition by those who are not faculty.
Thus although everyone actually benefits from a grant, its
advantages can disrupt the normal process that maintains the
symbol system around the "low." This result is not necessary,
nor is it necessarily made plain when it happens, but it is
implied in many settings by the new institutionalization of
composition in the face of its originally low status.

In *Class*, Paul Fussell gives us a window onto this particular blurring. His most upper class, the "top-out-of-sight," is "out of sight" not only in the vernacular slang sense, but actually unavailable to the gaze of lower classes. But the unavailability of a lower-class person (unless by removal to prison or a mental institution with walls as high as those around an estate) produces a cultural anomaly. Removing an essentially "exposed" and available identity, in the person of the composition specialist, calls into question the isolation to which grant recipients are normally entitled. The privilege is not absolutely straightforward, for it reveals unspoken assumptions about the "work" of those who are now detached from the environment in ways usually associated with "leisure." Removal may subject its recipient to responses that differ from more usual, good-humored jealousies, as in cases where any research in composition has been treated dubiously by colleagues who do not see it as equal, legitimate, or established within the symbol system of their setting.

To point this out is not to claim that this response is inevitable, as we could verify from many cases. If a "rule" can be associated with this interpretation, it is the reminder that composition was established *to be* a low-status site. It enacted clear social agendas to keep the masses in new universities and their writing in a socially low place. Consequently, new elevations by special endowments of funds, or by notoriety that has traditionally been normal in other domains, inevitably need "work" of a special kind to make them acceptable. Isolated individuals in composition, and the many departments that are now reconceiving composition's lowered place, undertake this work in light of new funds made available to hire and reward specialists.

The Rewards of Textbook Authorship

Officially, the labor of writing a textbook has often gone unrecognized in systems that support and reward other scholarly and creative work. Many research institutions do not "count" textbooks in personnel decisions or offer support that is otherwise allocated to help complete a scholarly manuscript. Salary increases after a textbook's publication are often

---

Recognition of Publications and Research

Of the 105 respondents who answered "Have recognitions for research and/or publication in composition been equitably visible in your department?" 75 (71 percent) answered yes, 13 (12 percent) answered no, and 17 (16 percent) judged the question not applicable. The 13 who explained either yes or no answers might again be separated into "neutral" and "negative" groups. Those 9 who were neutral included 3 who said, "We are recognized without regard to field," 1 who mentioned two people who had written well-known textbooks, 3 who said that no one does research or publishes at their institutions, 1 who said there are few recognitions of any kind, and 1 who answered (predictably, by now) "not yet." Among those 5 who answered negatively, 1 said that while recognition comes, research is done "on our own time." The remaining 4 comments were "writing is not considered a discipline"; "publications in composition don't have the same status"; recognition "is based on traditional literature"; and a summarizing "research in composition still lags behind in significance and acceptance." (Appendix, p. 240)

---

thought to be unnecessary because their authors are imagined to have become wealthy overnight.

But such officially sanctioned prejudices have recently received official attention in proposals from the MLA Commission on Composition and Literature that define textbooks as theoretical contributions equal to other research (Moglen and Slevin). The commission's opposition to systematic diminutions of textbook authorship does not, however, automatically give credibility either to these classroom materials or to their authors. What requires further explanation is the actual function of the textbook and the ways this function constrains the nature of its authorship. Composition textbooks have purposes in ideology beyond their substance, which necessarily result in their, and their authors', unequal recognition. This ideology is not limited to a set of beliefs about how to write, as Kathleen Welch has said, for it also defines the status of student writing, or its lack of status, in a larger society.

Typical criticisms of textbooks and their authorship reveal this larger system of beliefs, for they give us clues about how apparently unreasonable but systematic prejudices do reasonably fit the operations of ideology. For instance, Kitzhaber's criticism in *Themes, Theories, and Therapy* of textbook authors who engage in "cut and paste" (see Introduction) and his claim that they write only to sell to their own students bespeak common if unofficial prejudices against these books, which are taken *by definition* to be intellectually redundant. In the early colleges, whose practices were opposed by the research thrust of new universities, textbooks had been defended because their lessons could easily be keyed to daily recitations and because they reduced the possibility that students would become confused by reading too much (G. Graff 27). But their continuing regular and extensive use even in the new university did not indicate that they were held over only to suit differences between publishers in the way Kitzhaber implied. Considering that they are aimed at a large freshman and advanced market that is many times the potential readership of scholarly monographs, and considering the financial constraints on publishers, it is in fact unlikely that a textbook will reach only students in its author's institution. But three other results are equally unlikely: that a textbook will contain any really idiosyncratic view of the students who use it, that it will singularly define purposes for writing in the course it serves, or that it will bring its author "authorial" acclaim. (See Miller, "Is There a Text in This Class?")

Richard Ohmann has explained the monolithic view of students and of their writing usually implicit in textbooks, elaborating on views of composition students and their subjectivity that were described earlier. He says that composition texts create a student who is "defined only by studenthood, not by any other attributes. He [*sic*] is classless, sexless though generically male, timeless. The authors assume that writing is a socially neutral skill, to be applied in and after college for the general welfare" (*English in America* 145). Writing is conceived in textbooks, he says, to be "a generalized competence"

(145). These books treat the student and student writing as abstractions that will eventually have a social place, but that do not have one now (149). In other words, textbooks, especially those designated "introductory," are foundations for the subjectivity that composition, literary studies, and a broader society expect. Even substantial variations among them hide this superstructural aspect, their fundamentally constraining way of centralizing "transcendent" public identities.

Consequently, in the academic settings where they are used, both official and informal prejudices against composition textbooks and their production point to their enormously powerful doctrines and the need to preserve them. But this preservation is accomplished largely by removing precepts from ongoing societal interchanges. We would not, for instance, commonly argue about whether one textbook's "genderless" treatment was more or less unsexed than another's. To do so would begin an inappropriate scholarly conversation about why textbooks now promote neutrality in relation to gender, or describe the nonspecificity of writing processes, at all. Instead, we distance textbooks from normal discussions of research activity and withhold our own official and tangible rewards for them.

It follows that "authorial" rewards do not come to textbook authors. These authors can be compared (if only in relation to their symbolic functions and rewards) to the temple harlot described in *The Epic of Gilgamesh*, who "possesses a kind of wisdom, which tames the wild man. He follows her lead into the city of civilization" (Lerner 132). The temple harlot lived better than a common city prostitute, Lerner shows, on rewards for a sacred service that was distinguished from respectable full participation in society. Women in this and similar sacred religious functions received donations but were not officially maintained by the city they rarely entered (Lerner 130).

We consequently have more than historical reactions to textbooks to explain why their authors might create a felt disease if they claim normal recognition for the effort or the theoretical contribution a textbook entails, as though this contribution were of the same order as scholarly research or creative work. Examples of this discomfort are clear in the experiences of many who write textbooks. The labor of this writing and its results function discretely in a whole symbolic structure, and they do so by virtue of removal from comparisons with research and from ordinary sources of support. The textbook author's simplified, patient explanations of clearly political principles of writing address the "wild man" whom the student of composition is constituted to be. Those who take on this initiative function are often rewarded *only* financially, outside the visible symbol system of the departments they serve. They have done a basic ideological labor, which might be argued to be a "higher" labor, of sustaining an infrastructure of beliefs.

The support that replaces usual academic rewards is cooperation among composition professionals, the publishing industry, and the students who pay for their own books. This support is quite similar to the sort of exchange of service for payment that has always been associated with tribal and religious indoctrinations. It serves the larger social maintenance in which it is embedded, but it does so from outside the officially stated subjectivity of English studies, which claims

---

Possibility of Promotion

Those who were unsure about the possibility of promotion gave reasons that elaborated on these weightings of teaching and service. They also open up a perspective on answers to the question about whether departments relate promotion decisions to a field of specialization.

Among the 7 who were unsure about their promotions, explanations included "not until I have time to write a book" (this person gives workshops and writes pedagogical and administrative documents that are used internally); "the University is debating because I have published a popular composition textbook"; and 3 respondents who indicated that they had been kept in their departments without Ph.D.s and would probably not be promoted unless they met "normal" expectations. (Appendix, pp. 228–29)

intransitivity and passivity in relation to financial rewards. As a displaced system of recognition, it actually highlights the importance both of common ideologies around students and of the books that transmit them. It also supports the ideology that reduces, as Spivak noted, the "expense of production" in literary subjectivity.

2.   Circuits: The Director of Composition

Established composition, the new configuration I have renamed a great American theme park, generally has a proprietor or a manager who is responsible to the city that his or her entertainment serves. In the actual world of carnivals, this person ensured circumspection within his or her community, order among those who visited, and the distance, in many senses, that permitted a city to ignore officially the displaced values completing its identity. In established composition, functions similar to these are continued, although in a modified form. "The Big Four" whom Kitzhaber describes—A. S. Hill, John Gerung, Barrett Wendell, and Fred Newton Scott— directed composition in early times at Harvard, Amherst, and Michigan, with the generalized regulating results across the country that were explored earlier ("Rhetoric in American Colleges" 98–121). But settings that have created composition "programs" since then primarily require of their newly prominent directors not only this regulation, but a more complex set of results.

This position now acts as a relay or a shuttle through which we switch all the inherited and new vectors that composition entails. Its human embodiment, a "director" or "coordinator" in common parlance, is an emblem for many of the issues raised throughout this study. I have highlighted earlier the bourgeois gaze to which composition students and their writing are exposed, the intransitive subjectivity formed by composition among its students, theories, and teachers, and some of the institutional privileging mechanisms that keep unentitled writing in the place to which it was at first imagined to belong—subordinated, displaced, and as ineffectual in comparison to the moral claims made for its importance as the carnival was tame in comparison to bourgeois claims about its immorality. Each of these perspectives is superimposed on the image of a composition director who both transmits and receives ambivalent messages from each of these configurations. The director is the strong voice of tradition, but also of hegemonic re-form, who acts and is acted on in ways that help us define what it now commonly means to learn to write.

In her *Composition and the Academy*, Carol Hartzog did the groundwork for this interpretation of the director's position. She calls directors agents of change, praising "their own leadership in determining what would work, in knowing when to take risks and when to show restraint" (68). Hartzog repeatedly comments on how directors of composition work within existing structures, succeed in this work through political acumen, and devote themselves to detailed supervisory tasks. In her description of the positions held by directors of composition in AAU schools, she also documents their actual demographic equality with almost any other academic administrative group. Her sample of respondents, who held titles including "chair," "director," and "coordinator," were usually male and usually full or associate professors with tenure. They had been in their positions from one to seven years, with some exceptions (21–24). Like other academic administrators, all were regularly reviewed and found it difficult to find time for research. They had administrative support, released time, and the ability to delegate responsibilities to others who assisted them, served on committees, or provided ad hoc help.

In actuality, directing a composition program may require no more than ordering large numbers of textbooks through a bookstore, facilitating the selection of these books and of course plans among colleagues, and evaluating nonfaculty teachers in a pro forma way. In large programs with significant numbers of nonfaculty writing teachers, the director usually also writes the policy statements that unify teaching to the degree that it is unified, "trains" the teachers by explaining how to accomplish weekly assignments and by making supplemental resources available, and observes and evaluates these teachers. The actuality of this position, at least in schools where it has been recognized as a position, may also involve representing the interests of composition to a larger campus community. The director may be a figurehead, an advocate for departmental interests, and a mediator between students and teachers who negotiates teaching schedules and helps select ad hoc staff. This description, verified and elaborated in Hartzog's study, does not appear on the face of it greatly to differ from one appropriate for a department chair. Someone must do administrative work, and where composition is a significant set of courses, personnel, and requirements of students, it is efficient to place this work "under" one person.

We begin to get a sense of a difference that creates meaning, however, when Hartzog reports "attitudes." She asked her sample of directors to respond to the following questions: "On a scale of 1 (very negative) to 5 (very positive), how would you characterize the overall attitudes these groups or units show toward your writing program?" She then listed the following groups and units as categories in which directors reported numerically weighted attitudes: undergraduates, graduate students, writing faculty, writing program administrators, English department, home department other than English, other departments, campus administrators, and members of local schools.

One meaningful difference inheres in the question itself, which places writing programs in a position to be acted on, or "thought of," as colleges and departments are not. Those other units rarely evoke absolute "attitudes" of this sort and are not perceived to be responsible for pleasing so many constituencies. Responses to the question varied: "Attitudes toward writing programs are reported to be quite positive among four groups: the writing faculty, campus administrators, writing program administrators, and graduate students" (54), with the exception of negative attitudes on three campuses from graduate students. "Attitudes are thought to be somewhat less positive among three other groups—undergraduate students, other departments and English departments. . . . The ratings for English departments, *perhaps not surprisingly*, vary more widely than those for any other group: 7 ratings of 5 and another 7 at the low end of the scale" (54–55; my emphasis). (English department attitudes were listed on the negative to positive, 1 to 5, rating as *1* = 1; *2* = 6; *3* =

12; $4 = 16$; $5 = 7$. In other words, 19 directors reported that their programs were *disliked* or almost so by the English department and 23 reported that they were *liked,* or almost so.)

The variance among all groups appears to depend on whether a group's members think of themselves as directly implicated in the image and success of a program or whether they stand outside as onlookers who do not find a program blending into their own agendas in an academic "home." Clearly, programs (and, we can infer, directors) seem to please those who are "in" them—those who teach writing and those in the institution who benefit from symbolic associations with preparing students for the larger academic community. The ambivalence of English departments, perceived by the directors as almost evenly split between "favorable" and "unfavorable" judgments of their own writing programs, is an extraordinarily clear indication that the self-identification of a department is separate from the identity of its composition program. This "home" of composition programs may encompass its own composition program in its self-identity, but it may not. In Hartzog's view, the department's judgment often depends on the personal success of a director. But this choice could also be described as a systemic relation, in which a director and department may or may not have cooperated to define a program that does not threaten the self-perception of the department in question.

The sensitivity of this self-image is clear in the ways Hartzog's group of directors reported (again on a scale of 1 to 5) their difficulties in making changes. While modifying existing courses in their programs is "easy," making other changes (creating new courses, modifying programs, creating programs, changing writing requirements, even modifying existing writing tests) is difficult (57). Hiring full-time tenure-track faculty was reported as *very* difficult (i.e., rated 1) by seventeen of twenty-five respondents. Among a miscellany of other program changes, most directors had a great deal of difficulty with the following: "Arrange released time for faculty," "Make administrative appointments," "Change your program's administrative structure," and, with a bit less trouble, "Introduce faculty development programs" (58; see Appendix for further instances of these perceptions). In other words, Hartzog's

Hiring and Tenuring Composition Specialists

The remaining 80 (77 percent) reported some sort of changes in relation to hiring and tenuring composition specialists, but these have by no means always been positive changes. Linking attitudes to actions, departments become interested in hiring composition specialists (12 responses in both yes and no categories) either when they perceive composition to be a field or when administrative "leadership" and "pressure" create this interest (13 additional responses). They may conduct searches (3 responses), they may waffle ("some are for, some are nervous about it"), they may make composition hiring "a negative priority." When they do search, departments are changed by the process of the search itself (5 responses). They may evolve a pattern of hiring composition specialists (23 additional responses), with as yet undetermined results for departmental attitudes. Or they may hire one person with tenure and rank (1 response) or hire a person who is tenured later only under duress. Alternatively, the process of the search may solidify, or even produce, negative attitudes toward hiring in composition, with the result that the department hires someone else who is in literature (1 response) or changes search priorities (3 responses). (Appendix, p. 225)

directors demonstrate that changing an institutional self-definition around composition, or modifying composition in relation to one, is the task most likely to be threatening to the director's home. The only other change it appeared "easy" to make was working with faculty in other departments, who obviously have a specific and different systemic relation to a director, a program, and an English department.

In her chapter "English and Composition," Hartzog also quotes directors as they elaborate on this data. "I have heard tales of anger, frustration, and distress," she says in quoting the following comments (63–65 passim):

1. "Composition's status is not an issue on our campus—because it has no status";

2. "Some would consider these [writing program activities] janitorial services, but they respect the director's work in literary criticism and linguistics and they admire his political sense."

3. "There's still an undercurrent of anger and nervousness because composition is where all the action is, and all the energy."

Hartzog interprets attitudes and comments like these with balanced and qualified points; she is looking to describe directors as active agents of change, always "within existing structures," and finds positive forces propelling change in many senses. But the directors who report these comments and others like them might additionally be viewed as acting on and through a broader matrix of ambivalent attitudes and positions in which they themselves embody composition "in the academy."

Hartzog does not report some other well-known but decidedly different problematic conditions around directors of composition, problems that she of course recognized during and after her study (Hartzog, interview). These conditions include legendary nontenuring of directors who appear to have made significant improvements in composition teaching in their programs, but who may have offended graduate students and academic mentors who protect them. They encompass regular exclusions of directors from the ongoing central life of their departments as well as overtly negative behavior toward them. They take in the persistent attitude, expressed in jokes, criticisms, and sometimes open humiliations, that the director is only in his or her job because nothing else would suit or is there temporarily, under an execrable burden that no one in his or her right mind would want. They include being told that the "department" would not hire faculty in composition without pressure from above or that the department *had* hired someone (them) in composition, but only because of such pressure.

It is not likely that otherwise rational and cooperative colleagues act against individuals who hold many variations of a director's position without a reason. Nor is it likely that this reason has much to do with intrinsic qualities of the colleagues or of the director. Given the diversity of "problems" with various released directors, it is a department's predetermined but unacknowledged expectations of any director that are probably at issue. The same reasoning of course applies to common difficulties directors have with tenure, with negative groups of graduate students, and with what one of Hartzog's respondents and another respondent to my own survey call "a small, vocal, powerful, and increasingly bitter minority" (64) of the faculty. These are not likely to be difficulties from personal traits of a director or from the personalities of their nemeses; rather, an affective domain around the position creates such troubles.

The first inference we might draw about this symbolic domain is that directors of composition suffer from the same stigma as do other teachers of composition, but that now they additionally must absorb and convey both historical *and* current patterns that keep writing in a lowered, but now less openly acknowledged, place. The "Big Four" of the nineteenth century are still imagined to be embodied by today's directors, but negative responses they may have encountered are now more complexly loaded with the ambivalence that the "new" composition—its programs, its research, and its specialists— forces on traditionally clear diminutions of composition instruction. Now that composition has its own doctrines opposing prescriptivism and overwork, its directors emphasize the regulatory functions of these early role models only reluctantly or against organized, vocal opposition.

Most difficulties beyond the actual job description outlined earlier have to do with conflicting symbolic codes associated with composition in both its immediate and wider surroundings. One person, that is, mediates between "high" and "low" but is not meant to be a diplomat who is loyal to only one state. The director, like a token of any sort, additionally must display simultaneous and strong loyalties to both levels. This simultaneity can be specified in many ways. The composition director is responsible for teaching those students who are, by definition, taken only tentatively to be worthy of the principles that will follow the test of the course. This person is therefore both the conduit for the institution's continuing ambivalent vision of these students and the agent who must implement actual conditions (courses, books, "trained" teachers) that impose the subjectivity expected of them. But this person is also strongly motivated by the organized theories and practices of a new field actually to empower these students, who have been historically defined as only questionably entitled to this empowerment.

The composition director is further responsible for relaying the subjectivity of the teacher of composition to those teachers. This person establishes that individuals must answer a call, at least temporarily, to be stigmatized conveyors of the institution's view of students' needs. Unlike other colleagues who have chosen their teaching by preference and training, these teachers may or may not particularly display talent for or interest in teaching composition. Some will welcome the director's guidance in this direction; some will resent and resist it. Young teachers who have taught nothing but composition may discover their unsuitability for all teaching while conducting this course. And whatever institutional position they hold—teaching assistant, adjunct, associate, or faculty rank— they usually conduct and grade courses independently. All must be equally supported, validated, and honored because they are signs of an institution's claim to provide access to the later cultural principles without which the student cannot succeed. This success, as we have seen, is not necessarily linked to writing well in later courses or to graduation itself. The student of this introductory course primarily will acquire a subjectivity wherein writing is divorced from participation in active cultural roles.

In addition, of course, the director is placed where the various subjectivities and framed activities of all the disciplines in a university actually converge, at conjunctions of the languages of their differing discourses. Without arguing for an open analysis of these subjectivities and discourses, which would betray historical literary purposes for composition that still at least implicitly separate "high" and "low" writing, the director must nonetheless be knowledgeable about and accepting of at least "business," "technical," and "cross-disciplinary" students and discourse. Directors ideally avoid commenting on the superiority of their home departments' literary texts relative to aesthetic values or on the limits of this relative superiority. Instead of addressing such relativity, they advocate the generic "process" of writing that includes correctness, mechanical competence, revision processes, collaboration, and many other old and new mechanisms for teaching composition. Even in selecting models for readings, the director often conveys the belief that "good writing" can be recognized for qualities apart from its actual outcomes, apart from its verifiable appeal to widely separate and specific readerships, and apart from its author's reputation and good fortune within publishing institutions.

The "social usefulness" of a composition program therefore depends in large measure on a director's ability to leave the uses of writing undefined or tied only to generic processes, forms, and formats that are not openly implicated in social or political conflicts. A composition program's effectiveness will be judged largely by the level of correctness and propriety its students achieve in relation to the body of their writing. Its success will depend heavily on the level of comfort its teachers achieve in relation to their stigmatized status. It will not be judged according to the later successes of its students in writing anything in particular or by criteria outside the institution's social goals of initiation and indoctrination.

The director must usually accomplish each of these necessarily subverted persuasive functions without the ability to "direct" by setting new directions or by selecting open advocates for them over others. Like all academic administrators, a composition director maintains a circumscribed stream of activity, without independently deciding how to spend money on behalf of—and, therefore, how to redefine—a department. But the director is additionally a conduit for the institution's or department's sustenance, its "bread," with the ability only to magnify or diminish its nourishment of certain people or projects (like computer purchases). This function does not allow or require the director actually to spend or to withhold funds from particular people and enterprises, as a department chair may do. As Hartzog documented, "Even within programs that are budgeted separately, directors have

varying degrees of discretion" (19). The director of composition is not solely responsible for securing and managing funds,
or for withholding them from specific recipients.

Inevitable institutional, departmental, or individual guilt
about composition and traditions that separate high from low
can be transferred onto the person of the director. In the office
historically placed to convey simultaneous loyalty to opposed
emphases on propriety and on "growth" in the uses and users
of written language, the director is a mirror who reflects the
actual interests of a department, but who also reveals by his
or her "political acumen" the lineaments of exclusion and
privilege that mutely gather around the course in silence.
Much like the hidden picture of Dorian Gray, the directorship
assumes the burden of both the cultural "morality" of correct
writing and what it is fair to call the amorality of the ways it
has usually been taught. Evidence for this function of the
position arises frequently, in difficult relationships with graduate students and other nonfaculty teachers who transfer their
unspoken doubts about the place of composition onto the
position itself. By relaying various "levels" of morality in an
accumulation of opposing value systems that now simultaneously nurture and demean students and teachers, the director
becomes a focus for issues in a more diffuse morality. He or
she is Caesar's wife, placed over sentimentalized "freshmen"
whose specific political identities must be suspended to serve
their imaginary subjectivity in the course in composition. This
position is a switching mechanism, under pressure to trans-
code low-status practices into the highest institutional ideologies.

Much research would support the inference that no organization would respond neutrally to a person in such a position.
While an authority figure will be endowed with quasi-mystical
qualities and imaginary powers in any setting, as department
chairs always are, an authority over the "janitorial" and inconsequential activities required of large numbers of people who
do not accept the status of their low-life services is in a particularly difficult situation. Students resent this imagined source
of their ill-treatment by composition in an institution, as faculty and peers resent a power that is blurred by conveying
"higher" principles in partial and displaced forms.

This analysis accounts for some of the contradictions turned up by descriptive statements about composition programs. As Hartzog shows, the director of composition often writes "official" policy statements and syllabi, but these are not necessarily imposed on or followed in a systematic way by program teachers. Textbooks may be selected by directors working with committees, but they are often selected by individuals in the well-defined programs that Hartzog describes (35–37). In programs ranging in size from 65 to 465 sections per year (31), the "directors" only partially or erratically direct large numbers of students in learning to write. They are exposed to the "attitudes" (the gaze) of many diverse units and constituencies on their campuses, but significantly they are not questioned about their own vision of how well these units support their own projects. They, like the carnival of composition and its students and teachers, hold an object position. In programs that can be described along the authoritarian lines that "program," "director," and "attitude" connote, the director sustains the cacophony of sideshows that imitate but never entirely accomplish "serious" business.

Erving Goffman, in *Frame Analysis*, explains this sort of position as a mechanism for keeping others "in a stream of framed activity" (378), the metaphor he uses to describe the boundaries of public interactions. "If someone has the job of making sure that most participants are intensely involved in what is occurring, he [sic] may become quite carried away. What is fully involving for some will be overinvolving for a few. Indeed, that a few cannot keep themselves in control can be a sign that the many are fully engrossed" (380). The composition director, given this job of "involving" students of writing, teachers with various levels of experience, knowledge, and interest, his or her peers, and approving faculty members in other institutional units, will be counted successful if some become entirely swept up to focus on writing and its instruction as a "field," but will be unsuccessful if too many follow this pattern or if only a few assent to the ideology this activity requires. "If a torture show in a circus is to carry away most of the audience into the horror of it all, a few members of the audience may have to be carried away far enough to throw up" (380).

Obviously, on the other hand, if this torture show becomes "real" and defines what is outside it as the "show," it will threaten the vision of reality, and of play, held by the community at large. A director who presents composition as intellectually distinct from literary studies calls into question colleagues' assumptions about language, about their own subjectivity, and about the status they have achieved by disassociating themselves, in imitation of Francis Child, from composition teaching. But a director who presents composition as substantially embedded in literary studies, and thus capable of being equally well taught by "anyone," may be unable to justify the regulatory as well as substantial work that the position now requires. Anxiety about the boundaries of "reality" and "play" are at issue, as Goffman suggests. The prominence of the directorship in new programs that organize new knowledge while regulating a new underclass of teachers manifests this issue. Defining composition as a new "field" and appointing someone who will inevitably relay the existence of this field to its formerly "pure" surroundings threatens deeply held assumptions about self-identity and the borders between the "serious" and "ancillary" purposes of that identity.

The common debate about the legitimacy of composition as a "discipline" that Hartzog documents might also be taken as a sign of this anxiety about the boundaries of "reality" and "play." As Samuel Weber points out about similar relations between "literature" and "theory" in *Institution and Interpretation*, "the operation of anxiety as a *signal* would thus converge with a process of identifying and retaining such perceptions and representations so as to maintain their self-identity against conflictual desires tending to disrupt such identity" (29). That is, a specialized composition and its directors disrupt other established self-identities both "above" and "below" them, creating the results Weber attaches to "literature" as opposed to "theory": "phobias . . . symptoms, as well as 'defensive' processes such as that designated by Freud as 'isolation' " (29).

Persistent questions (and persistent answers to them) about composition's status as a discipline suggest that claims for its absolute legitimacy, entitlements, and recognition coerce

> ### Perceptions of Composition as a Field
>
> Fewer responses than we might imagine on the basis of answers about difficulties with tenure, 20 (15 percent) specifically pointed to the identity of composition as a field as a major source of tensions in their departments. The largest group among these, 15 people, explained this tension as a question about the authority of the field as against their untenured status, as against resentments of their achievements in composition, and as against a perception that "anyone can teach composition." Four people in this group further specified that this tension is between their own belief that composition is an equal academic field and their colleagues' perception that composition is "worthwhile" teaching, but not a field. "They see us," one said, "as the rude proletariat." (Appendix, p. 247)

those around it to perceive themselves differently, in ways they often find insupportable. The common ideological work of "attention to borders" (Weber 30), like the work of those charged to maintain borders around a framed stream of activity, shows that a great deal is at stake in keeping composition in an enclosed, if now not an entirely lowered, position relative to its departments, but not separate from them. The vast number of European carnivals has diminished since the late nineteenth century in processes of fragmentation, marginalization, sublimation, and repression (Stallybrass and White 178). Similarly, these processes have acted on an original interdependence between composition and literary studies in the ways that Weber suggests, creating the mobile and blurred patterns in the role of the composition director.

A directorship, like new process theories, represents "a return of the repressed" mentioned earlier as a manifestation of new versions of rhetorical instruction in both literature and composition. Establishing the directorship as a significant role has created an increasingly large actual and symbolic domain for composition. In that domain, teaching composition, disposing of its students, and even conducting research under a theorized process model are reimposed on their surroundings through new organizations and a new office that a director may only erratically and partially fulfill.

Stallybrass and White note that the regulated carnival in England was transferred to the seaside resort settings of Brighton, Scarborough, and other towns on the border of the country. But physically moving the carnivalesque to geographic edges hardly diminished its power to comment on and raise anxieties within orderly bourgeois culture (179). Similarly, by creating "directorships" held by people appointed only to these positions, new marginalizing processes can be discerned in the "change" now commonly attributed to composition. A directorship is relegated to the borders of its empowering setting, where its interactions, initiatives, and perspectives evoke response from both the "high" and the "low" to whom it transmits composition. As composition is now established, its director no longer mediates between it and the city from the lower position, but has become a filter through whom all that is "low," ad hoc, and transient moves, even as this filter represents the city's regulating gaze. But the director also figuratively represents vivid possibilities that unregulated texts, unlicensed writers, and literary discourse will unaccountably merge.

The role of current directors must, therefore, be accounted for in terms of the transgressiveness designated to, and feared from, student writing. "Carnival was too disgusting for bourgeois life to endure except as sentimental spectacle. Even then, its secular identifications could only be momentary, fleeting and partial—voyeuristic glimpses of promiscuous loss of status and decorum which the bourgeoisie had had to deny as abhorrent in order to emerge as a distinct and 'proper' class" (Stallybrass and White 183). This assessment recalls the impact within the entirety of English studies made by Mina Shaughnessy's quotations from remedial students. Her work offered momentary glimpses of the sort of writing that threatens the values and privileges of those who uphold the subjectivity of literature. It often evoked only embarrassed and voyeuristic involvement in its world.

"Basic" writing by disempowered lower-class students who

were suddenly placed where they too might receive the test and principles of a privileged education has only briefly fallen under the gaze of the establishment that hysterically avoids it. Ultimately, as I have pointed out about the development of the process paradigm, glimpses of this writing from Shaughnessy's New Critical perspective drove a greater wedge between composition and literature. These brief encounters called for a new boundary, which appeared in the form of the paradigm that removed composition even further from its origins. But the field's organized manifestations also require a "director figure," a person whose imaginary identity is a lightning rod absorbing differences and anxieties like those evoked by lost linguistic decorum, even while it engages the complex work of restabilizing relations between high and low.

Part III

Alternative Entertainments

6 On Seeing Things for What They Are

As the feminist critic Patriocino Schweickart has pointed out, the basic tenet of New Criticism has been that "one must stay within the terms intrinsic to (i.e., authorized by) the text" (172). Her reason for mentioning this fundamental principle of current-traditional criticism is similar to mine. "Standard" interpretation of the sort she criticizes has been a game in which we call foul on moves that do not find internal unity, coherence, and consistency in data from any entity we take to be a text.

But rhetorical and political criticism, the different bases for this study, value an opposing view. Here, the history, populations, and theories that comprise composition studies have been treated as a "text," not as a conglomerate of ordinary, seemingly trivial details. But matters that would appear in traditional interpretation to be outside this text have endowed it with "meaning," and more. By highlighting some traditionally unmentionable, "external" social and economic particularities and their superstructural implications, I have tried to show that taking composition teaching, theory, and some of its histories only on their "own terms" actually explains very little about each of them, even and especially in interpretations meant to pit tradition against reform. Neither Kitzhaber's specific complaints about the misconduct of composition in *Themes, Theories, and Therapy* nor patterns in more recent comments tell very much about the cultural importance of traditional or new composition. We need to suspend searches for their "intrinsic" implications in the history of the field's imagined mental state and look additionally at symbolic and theoretical contexts to explain undeniable fissures in this "text itself."

When we see the politics of composition for what it is, its

intrinsic facts lead into contradictions. For example, perduring moralistic elevations of the "need" and "important service" of universalized composition teaching contradict equally verifiable systematic denigrations of its students and teachers. Nor has this "importance" been attached to specific results of composition instruction. Within composition, pedagogical theory and legislated course requirements assert that writing instruction bathes students in an essential instrumental medium to foster their personal linguistic and social growth, but these structures do so simultaneously with persistent trivialization of actual demands on students to write and with disorganized forecasts about results from this learning. The self-contained facts also reveal continuing pedagogic claims that mastering conventional language displays intelligent moral propriety, but they do so against very different cultural elevations of consequential literary and nonliterary writing, which is often called experimental, unconventional, and even "revolutionary" at its moment of recognition. The "field itself" reports, finally, new energy, achievement, and expansion—but with resignation about a continuing struggle against constraints and about negative attitudes toward its intellectual persuasiveness and its disciplinary identity.

I have been claiming that contexts that explain these and other contradictory but undeniably forceful oppositions share a subtext of hegemonic desires, largely as ambivalent attitudes toward expanding higher education in the late nineteenth century, at the inception of the "new university." Continuing superstructural agendas for composition teaching maintain earlier necessary boundaries: a division between proper and improper language, gate-keeping separations between its entitled and unentitled users and uses, and an original, still entrenched national ideological function for "literature" or "English" as a set of unrealized ideals—a content and linguistic execution that the majority of ordinary citizens aspire to but never attain.

Identifying this particular context for early and developing composition has placed this study in an uncomfortable relation to "common sense" and "best practice" about American writers and writing. But acknowledging this context also makes it clear that composition studies are *necessarily* embedded in contradictory conditions. From the perspective I have taken, all of these examples gather easily around the cultural site that houses "other" writing. This writing symbolically completes and highlights culturally designated perfections, inspirations, and achievements. It and its traditional corrective treatments are framed to create a dually defined corpus that does not, by definition, fulfill our best expectations.

This new story of composition explains systemic discrepancies that cooperate to accomplish purposes that the new universities took as their warrants when they attempted to relocate the spirit of the old colleges in a new demographic and curricular situation. Composition courses, for instance, must communicate to both their students and teachers the continuing and growing primacy of vernacular *written* language in American culture, as they do. But they must also communicate that only a limited and in most cases an already certified group of people consequentially contribute to this consequential writing, which was first defined as "classic(al)." The masses that constitute both the students and teachers in composition courses are excluded from this idealized group of authors and public figures; their constructed subjectivity derives from another image altogether. Established "universal" courses and large nonfaculty domains of teachers, both of which contain marginal readers and writers of canonical discourse, maintain not only the "importance" of American writing, but also the infinite postponement of its purported egalitarianism. Yet the irrepressible importance of American writing has nonetheless promoted the field of composition, a field that must (nonetheless) continually be denied its legitimacy if its actual and coherent structural "place" is to be maintained.

I have contained the regular patterns of conflict created by these agendas in the metaphoric carnival, in processes for marginalizing distinct social groups, and in sociological explanations of how "spoiled" and "normal" identities interact in response to their relational, not intrinsic, qualities. These explanations of important translations, displacements, and recreative functions of the carnival, and of the problematics of "change" in settings that were designed to preserve stigmatized identities, at least tell composition's story *as* a story, not merely as one inconsequential, peripheral incident after another.

But as I am well aware, this strategy has set a number of traps for the kind of conclusion that would traditionally be counted as offering positive alternatives, a completed "good story" about composition. A study that repeatedly places apparent "changes" or "new" developments under a superstructure whose purpose is adapting its first motives to new settings can hardly end with integrity if it proposes reform, as I have already pointed out. In addition, it is obvious that the interpretations I have made in the major portions of this study do not, by themselves, tell a "good story." Having once unveiled a role for composition studies in the larger society's symbolic domains, we instead turn up inferences quite similar to those that gender and social critics now draw about any marginalized group. These inferences are not, and by my reasoning could not be, sudden unmaskings of the illegitimate carnival as an unrecognized site of lost, or established, kingdoms. We might try to revive the spirit of historical rhetoric; we might try to construct a new, total, unified version of "English" led by elevated servants who would interpret its mysterious double messages. But neither "solution" will solve the logically contradictory situation of composition studies. The butler, the mother/maid, and a "father text" have not, in fact, "done it."

This conclusion can, therefore, only suggest some alternative images for composition studies, not reorganize its most immediate details into an intrinsically coherent, unified, and consistent, but closed and rationally self-justified, text. The work of storytelling, as Michael Ryan has said about "deracination" of any kind, "can never be complete, either *at one go or once and for all*. The work involved is constant and repetitive, like . . . keeping a house clean" (117).

This is not to say that no actual alternatives to the conditions I have described come immediately to mind. But alternatives are not different, or reformed, total actualities—model curricula or administrative plans—which would beg questions about the conditions in which they were formed. Changes in these immediate realities depend on considering new premises against which unexpected outcomes might occur. In concluding, then, I have speculated about what might count as alternative stances for those in composition studies to those outside, to their own self-identity, and to the treatment of students.

In Context: Liberalism, Separatism, and an Alternative

Professionals in composition studies are often preoccupied with their posture toward their "Others," for very good reasons. The intellectual project of retheorizing mechanistic composition teaching that composition historians and theorists have taken up in the last twenty years has, as Robert Connors says, an openly "propagandistic" agenda (quoted in North 87). This intellectual agenda has attempted to convert existing composition teaching by reforming its purposes to fit the copiousness of ancient rhetorical education, but this is a political agenda as well. Composition specialists in many substantial and polemical publications overtly refer to their political situations vis-à-vis literary studies, their institutions, and their public settings.

These published statements are echoed by anecdotal data, frequent comments that focus on the issue of alienation and acceptance. Many report how composition is "ignored," trivialized, unequal, and otherwise marginalized in comparison to more privileged departmental, collegiate, institutional, and social surroundings. The implicit desire expressed by this local political awareness is to *correct* this treatment. The implied outcome of correction would be mutuality, parity, and finally an end to self-consciousness about status. Put another way, the implied goal in these political complaints is to lift composition out of the context that voices the "call" to its seemingly trivialized, carnivalesque identity.

Composition specialists who want to persuade those around them to elevate their traditional or current "place" do not universally wish to remove themselves, their students, or their disciplinary field from its traditional academic home, although this alternative is frequently identified. But their political statements do persistently argue that surrounding communities perceive the field inaccurately. One of the most frequently suggested corrections has it that composition is *equal* to its sister studies and that this equality should be recognized in the field's rhetorical lineage, in the actual magnitude of its teaching responsibilities, and in mutuality of purpose among all language scholars and educators. By this argument—which often equates "reading and writing" with "literature and composition"— teaching and research in composition should no longer be perceived across a "gap" or "gulf" separating them from literary studies or from any other field that is "basic" in a larger discipline, as perhaps calculus is in mathematics. Great efforts go into explaining unrecognized intellectual (if not ideological) connections between composition and literature, which could become two parallel strains in one disciplinary home (see, e.g., Horner, *Composition and Literature: Bridging the Gap*).

A second approach, which the "process paradigm" and empirical research methods have highlighted, is fundamentally separatist, although it only rarely suggests actually removing composition from English departments, or from ancillary "centers" and "labs," to make it a separate but equal academic department and discipline. This approach to correcting the perceptions of others about composition has emphasized "scientific" grounds for understanding writing, has unified new theories in "paradigm shifts," and has pointedly defined composition as "interdisciplinary." The last defining move, for instance, emphasizes connections between composition studies and established social scientific research methods in cognitive psychology and ethnography and stresses links to research in established humanistic fields such as historical rhetoric and linguistics. Separatists have also taken steps to change the material surroundings in which composition is taught and studied and thus to force those outside it to reevaluate its traditional identity. They have in a few cases established semiautonomous college- or university-wide programs (e.g., at Michigan and UCLA), have organized groups to resign from the Modern Language Association, or have joined its activities as a parallel but separate-from-literature strain of English studies. Stephen North's *The Making of Knowl-*

edge in Composition also encourages this separatism to correct internal splits in the field. North believes that the "long-term survival" of composition as a knowledge-making enterprise depends on placing varieties of methods where they must depend on, not compete with, each other (369).

These two approaches to correcting perceptions of composition studies are mingled, not entirely discrete. In many settings, equality and integration find support from the energy of nontraditional research in composition; in many others, material separations have increased dialogue among those "outside" and "inside" composition. Both kinds of labor to partition, mark boundaries, and form identities have everything to do with perceived and actual inequalities. Nonetheless, neither movements to establish integrated equality nor those to separate and redefine composition apart from its traditional literary surroundings have achieved their desired outcomes, although these results are perceived to be slowly occurring at many institutions. Neither movement, moreover, can make a very strong claim to have reorganized traditional perceptions of composition, except to make it now a "force to be reckoned with," an entity that can achieve responses that would have been denied before.

This achievement itself is not insignificant. The improved conditions of many individuals who now pursue interests in composition studies in new undergraduate and graduate programs make this clear. But I qualify the results of both integrationist and separatist moves because neither has worked on the fundamental structure that necessitated them. Neither, that is, openly examines the system of privilege or separation that creates both alienation and the desires to overcome it. The hegemonic strategy in question here makes "low" status intrinsic to student writing and by extension demeans those who are deeply involved in its academic treatment. Both separatists and integrationists inadvertently reinforce their alienation by defending and maintaining the "studentness" of a particular kind of writing, precisely *as* the student's right. This strategy, which as we will see allows "movements" from composition to occur while student writing remains stably inside its regulated frameworks of inconsequentiality, is a strategy that persistently implicates composition in lower-status, initiative teaching. The field does not appear to have outcomes especially relevant to powerful writing or to the power of other equally new disciplines.

To follow the reasoning of Toril Moi in *Sexual/Textual Politics*, both approaches might be said to represent typical approaches to leadership in movements undertaken by other marginalized groups. Once such groups become aware of their unentitled status and look for ways to overcome their alienation from "central" cultures by changing the perceptions of others, they normally turn to these two solutions to their problems of status. Commonly, desires for rapprochement and integration, or for the symbolic status of a separate entity, are demands for "equal access to the symbolic order" (Moi 12).

In composition, the first desire represents a kind of liberal request to make the field a recognized partner in achieving the purposes for which literary study was first established as a national project. Separatism, which has parallels in feminist and other minority political movements over the last thirty years, would in this narrative be a later stage, often undertaken when a preliminary desire for integration appears to have failed. Separatists reject the established symbolic order and assert difference from it, as the heralds of the "process paradigm" and composition researchers certainly have undertaken to do. In this way, composition follows the lead of feminists and blacks who have emphasized their historical and biological differences from traditions in white, male, patriarchal systems. This desire is certainly evident in those who have encouraged members of the Conference on College Composition and Communication to resign from the Modern Language Association, as it is in programs that establish "special" (and ultimately nonprivileged) personnel ranks for those who teach composition, on the grounds that their "work" is not correctly rewarded or evaluated according to the established symbol systems that apply to faculty.

This last example, of course, suggests the difficulty with the separatist position, that its promotion of "separate but equal" status may result in entrenchments of existing inequities for those inside—a "new ghetto," but a ghetto nonetheless. It may also result in inverted prejudices against those outside the field, those who have been perceived to keep writing in its low place. However, the liberal, integrationist stance is even more troubling. Unless its proponents radically question "English" as a cultural phenomenon, this position argues for complicity in all the agendas that established composition to place the writing of the majority firmly under the gaze of bourgeois disapproval. To urge only intellectual, disciplinary integration with literary studies finally justifies the mechanistic, error-hunting emphases in early composition teaching, as well as continuing systems of discrimination that "place" students in courses and their teachers in the unentitled position of "hired help."

Each of these results of integration for the majority was entirely reasonable at the outset, when elitist reasoning made composition "equal" but initiative in the new university. But no intellectual work to point out the parallels between reading and literature or between writing-as-authorship and composition, or to "respect" research in composition, addresses logical and social problems that sharing privileged literary subjectivity creates for those who address contemporary writing. This shared social image, not equal intellectual endeavors, first united literary study and composition courses, with the political results we now try to undo. The traditionally passive subjectivity required by "composition and literature" in tandem exempts writers from analyzing writing processes or written products in terms of their material location in specific times, places, classes, and in interactive but discretely textual purposes. If an active "writing," not an extension of oral composing, is the subject (content) of composition studies, its equal partnership in traditional literary constructions of its students and their writing is logically insupportable.

The main issue here, of course, is that an alternative strategy for persuading those around composition, its "Others," to view it differently would depend first on bringing to light the precise nature of the existing "equality" of composition with literary studies, its shared place in the agendas of the now traditional new university. An alternative strategy would identify shared agendas that derive from and maintain outworn visions of the "individual." Were this articulation accomplished, the benefits of equal status might be open to question, for in its most classic form this equality has led both fields to accept traditional social hierarchies, winnowing devices, and cultural indoctrinations that do not fit contemporary culture. These instruments of the past have political results that are incongruent with a fluid society that cannot beneficially continue to privilege one "language" or one group of writers over another.

Such an alternative articulation does need elements of the second, separatist, strategy. Applying Toril Moi's point about feminism, we can argue that it is *"politically* essential" that composition be described *as* composition if it is to counteract the attitudes that demean it *as* itself (13). But an alternative approach to overcoming the alienation that those in composition studies experience would be to assert this separate, historically different identity of composition only while openly pointing out what has been at stake in dividing "levels" of writing, in defining canonical versus "vocational" or "instrumental" texts, in declaring repeated "new" literacy crises, and in other intellectual and administrative developments. These pointed explanations would elaborate on various reforms of the "mind" of the field. A genuine alternative would further require questions and answers about human results for both students and composition professionals in their divisions, definitions, and new intellectual movements.

The field might, that is, enjoy a different, if not a "new," identity, not by "combating" its situation with male-coded fortitude, but by precisely acknowledging how it is a culturally designated place for political action. Composition studies has always had the process available to transform its marginalized culture into a site where cultural superstructures and their privileging results are visibly put into question. An *actually* improved status depends on openly consolidating the field's internal, existing resistances to the cultural superstructure that first defined it.

This process of intellectual redefinition would re-represent the field as irrefutably counterhegemonic, not as a victim stuck in webs of unproductive compromise. For instance, composition was culturally designated to teach *all* students, not an elite group, and it is therefore already an encompassing site for empowering, not for repressing or "correcting," the discursive power of the majority. In addition, the status of the field's teachers and the constructed marginal identity of its always "new" students highlight enduring definitions of "composition" as the central site for colonizing and regulating otherwise questionable, nontraditional entrants to the academy.

Other characteristics of recent composition equally define it as an already designated place for counterhegemonic intellectual politics. In its current emphases on writing-in-progress, it verges on the claim that categories of "high" and "low" texts are social, not essential, categories. "Good" writing, as composition can most authoritatively define it, is the result of established cultural privileging mechanisms, not of pure "taste." The field might vividly demonstrate, in practice and in theory, that a mixture of ideas, timing, entitlements, and luck have designated some rather than others as "important" writers/thinkers. The field's most productive methods of evaluation also judge writing by situational rather than by universal standards and thus insist on the arbitrariness of evaluations and their relativity to particular power structures. Additionally, the field's research can open rather than close borders among established fields. It thereby argues that making new knowledge is a shared rather than an isolated process, a matter of cooperation and conflict in struggles among ideas and classes, but not of disciplined individual competition.

These often-stated but persistently unpoliticized practices and insights in the field have positioned it to transform its ancillary identity by engaging intellectual as well as practical political actions. As the institutional site designated as a passive enclosure for "unauthorized" discourse, composition has simultaneously been designated as a marginalizing power. But this enormous power to contain the discourse of the majority can be, if its professionals wish to claim it, the strength that re-represents the field's identity. Composition is *also,* that is, an active existing site for dismantling particularly troublesome versions of hegemonic discursive "common sense"— particularly exclusivity, humiliation, repression, and injustice hidden in the nineteenth-century bourgeois moralities.

We have frequently translated these counterhegemonic implications of the field's practices and intellectual positions into undifferentiated signs of its "vitality" or "energy." But this

abstract "energy" can be plugged into questions and intellectual actions that undo concrete political structures that have a
great deal at stake in negative images of composition teaching
and the writing of its students. Composition is not, that is, a
modern place to celebrate a liberal "healthy pluralism" that
will continue to re-form the system around it; rather, it is a
place for demonstrating an active, revolutionary rereading of
the counterhegemonic resistances that this negative cultural
situation has produced. Applying what Julia Kristeva has said
of resisting traditional definitions of females, we can transform
the field's image by understanding the implications of composition as "that which is marginalized by the patriarchal symbolic order" (quoted in Moi 166).

It is, of course, difficult to refute the traditions of those who
believe that the humanistic subjectivity promoted in traditional freshman English does the necessary work of "civilizing" (or finally of excluding) college freshmen. But refutation
is impossible if composition professionals remain unaware of
the political implications of these traditions and argue for
"change" only on grounds that naturally appear trendy, untheorized, and self-serving to those who disagree. Without
articulating the actual political lineaments of "civilization," no
reasoned argument, only a quarrel, can result.

The temptation to avoid this alternative critique is great.
Both pluralism and the new respectability of the field in many
of its larger contexts persuade us to stop by accepting
"changes" and reforms like those documented by Hartzog and
others. However, the American definition of the "public" is
at stake in bringing the politics of composition to consciousness and working to subvert the intellectual and material conditions that maintain it. Without agreeing with recent complaints about the results of higher education, complaints that
implicitly long for the situation in which nineteenth-century
students were taught, we can nonetheless accept that the
particular results of traditional dispositions of composition
have made clear the equation between power and discourse.
An alternative stance toward those outside composition could
at least motivate those within it to reconsider the effects of the
system that has placed them where they are, especially effects

on the influence, not the essentialist "quality," of particular groups of writers.

Alternative Subjectivities: Among Ourselves

It is, of course, only convenient to separate an alternative stance toward those "outside" composition from one that those in it might take to gather their resources around a new political model. I have already characterized the field as having moved aggressively to establish itself as a discipline with a model that simultaneously defined its past as "current-traditional" rhetoric and teaching and its present as an interest in "process." This simultaneous creation of terminology to label both an outworn history and its new energy has served the field quite well, as has similar language created by other marginalized or novice groups. This move has both unified and motivated composition professionals, giving them a readily perceptible sense of possible research emphases and of themselves as a group. This terminology has also been as politically important to composition studies as any subsequent movement or action its professionals might take as a group, for it allows the self-identification that is the benefit of separatism. Those who are marginalized outline the future as they form a discipline, in ways that those who maintain limits on them cannot.

Nonetheless, the status of composition and its stance in forming this self-identity remain highly problematic in political or any other terms, as Stephen North agrees in *The Making of Knowledge in Composition*. North has written the most ambitious extant taxonomy of "parts" of knowledge-making in composition. He distinguishes varieties of research and teaching practices in categories formed by *scholars*, who are "historians," "philosophers," and "critics," and by *researchers*, who are "experimentalists," "clinicians," "formalists," and "ethnographers." Without needlessly recounting the lineaments of these categories in this widely read account, we nonetheless need to pause for attention to North's assumptions and predictions in his conclusion, "Futures."

North distinguishes between a "field," which he says composition is, and a "discipline," which he says is a problematic label for composition because it "ordinarily implies preparation for *doing* something. . . . However, the modern version of the field is founded, really, on the subversion of the practical tradition" (364). In other words, to call composition a discipline is, he says, to affirm that it is moving away from its "practical traditions" in the teaching of his "Practitioners." Their claim on knowledge-making in composition is based on "lore"; their means of disseminating knowledge are informal, oral traditions in local, not written, communities (21–55).

North does not entirely cover over the political stratifications that his assessment relies on. In his predictions about the future, he claims that scholars and researchers in composition will want to imitate those in literary study who have distanced themselves from teaching (367) and that they will, in a mixed-methods department of composition, re-create the structures of privilege that organize the departments to which they now belong (370). But by choosing to dichotomize the interests of composition along "practical" and "knowledge" lines and then to suggest reunification, he does largely overlook the political situation in which the field-cum-discipline has been formed and the marginalized status of all its branches.

North assumes, for instance, that a new department of composition, "expected—and equipped—not only to disseminate knowledge, but to make and accumulate it in ways that would meet with academic approval" (370), would sort out "cross-methodological misunderstandings," establish "a spirit of methodological egalitarianism," and reestablish "practice as inquiry" (371). Developing this last expectation, North mentions the poor treatment of practitioners by others in the field, their "communal allegiance," and their "spoon-feeding" by scholars and researchers above them (372). To replace this situation, he offers the model of the National Writing Project, where Practitioners are treated with dignity and there is little "of the old top-down, theoretician to practitioner hierarchy" (373).

No one would object to North's egalitarianism, but his presentation of it suggests that "change" has to do with placing disembodied ideas and "lore" in a re-formed setting, where fundamental structures that now operate on composition are not treated as ground under the situations he wants to change. Granting his excellent intentions and even granting a provisional need for his imagined academic isolation of composition, we must still recognize the reiteration that his vision implies. He overlooks institutional and cultural contexts in which practitioners teach and the culturally passive nature of the writing and writers that scholars and researchers take on, assuming that academics appointed to facilitate student writing can rearrange their interrelations without reference to these clearly political contexts.

Without a redefinition of student writing and of the subjectivity of the student writer, accomplishing North's proposal might make no discernible difference. It would not alter institutional and social visions of composition as a punitive, or at least winnowing, device, nor would it focus composition studies on the empowerment of students that writing implies. But more important for relations within the field, North ignores matters like the magnitude of enrollments in writing courses and organizations of institutional budgets that have created the class of practitioners with whom he sympathizes. For instance, establishing his new department of composition in a university that supports research, but which also requires students to take writing courses, would not change the expectation that practitioners would be predominantly graduate students and the part-time, ad hoc, or nonfaculty instructors who have increasingly characterized and reinforced the status of composition courses and their students since their first definitions at Harvard. In this situation, the "top-down" dissemination of information from scholars and researchers, which he criticizes, would without doubt remain a fact of intellectual life. Only a few people with regularly budgeted salaries—the traditional but now relocated director of composition and the few additional faculty now hired in changing departments—would have access to the time to create and distribute knowledge.

Consequently, a genuine alternative to existing relations among those inside composition will be to acknowledge the economic and social status of the majority of composition teachers, not only their intellectual situations. The division between faculty and nonfaculty in any institutional setting, like the perceived difference between research and teaching, cannot be overcome by establishing new institutional units, whether they be programs, departments, or the centers and clinics that often house composition now. Nor is this difference, which depends finally on discrete budgets for these varying activities, likely to be overcome along social lines. Imagined camaraderie in an isolated composition studies "unit" should also be imagined as short-lived, for the intellectual work of North's Scholars and Researchers and Practitioners arises in actual people whose different professional situations determine, and are caused by, their complex self-identifications with differing professional roles.

As in the case of an alternative stance toward those outside composition studies, alternative relations within depend on subjecting political relations within the field (and within the discipline) to an open critique. This critique would systematically examine institutional practices toward each category of professionals in composition. But most importantly, it would reveal the agendas that have determined an acceptable subjectivity for composition teachers and that now foster a more privileged subjectivity for those who do "research." Composition professionals would, for instance, question the traditional image of teachers' "self-sacrifice," "dedication," and absorption in trivial details. The importance of these characterizations is held over from the burden of mechanistic, mechanical paper marking in earlier composition courses, just as the subjectivity of "women" has been held over from their first biological roles. But in light of the comparable time spent by those who conduct research and teach other subjects, it is unlikely that these personal attributes in composition teachers, whose classes are normally small in relation to their counterparts, are entirely needed. This is not to say that composition is not a great deal of "work," of all the kinds described here. But it is possible that placing those who teach composition in the role of hired mother/maid has a great deal to do with the presexual, preeconomic, prepolitical subjectivity imposed on composition *students* and with the initiative role of these courses for them. So long as these identities are maintained for composition students and their courses, it is unlikely that requirements on Practitioners of whatever rank will change. These expectations invite them to be irresponsible about making "knowledge" in the sense that scholars and researchers do, despite their possible commitments to "practice as inquiry."

Similarly, composition researchers and scholars have taken their self-identity from already established models in other disciplines, not from intrinsic elements in their object of study. Alternative relations among them will involve defining this object of study, writing, with a mind to allowing it, not established methods or precedent research, to focus their work. Under this rubric, scholars, researchers, *and* practitioners might collaborate in much the same way that scientists and technicians do. Technical groups do not focus on a free play of ideas that may lead to an ideal product, but use their foundational intellectual differences and multiple abilities to assign various parts of a well-defined project to specific people who have a specific goal in mind. Their separate expertise, not rank or position, determines their weight in decision-making processes. Like a group of scientists and technicians building a specific new biotechnology, composition specialists of many sorts might work together as ad hoc groups, without needing equal mastery of each element of their project. They might, that is, forego the "equality" that in traditional collaboration leads to enclosed debates, in favor of taking on the open struggle among ways of thinking and talking about a subject that can be tested only in terms of specific results.

To date, scholars' and researchers' desires to remove themselves from the status of practitioners have become confused with a desire, common enough in other fields, to remove its members from the defining activity of any sort of academic practitioner—teaching. But in new working groups, teaching or any immediate contact with a fully contextualized act of writing would become an essential part of a whole study whose theories might be more or less available to specific members. While it is necessary, if the status of composition is to be improved, that the field promote an academic language and show signs of status that other theorists and scholars can recognize, it does not follow that these two strategies can succeed only when attached to depoliticized, "pure" research, as North recognizes. They need not be divorced from problem solving in specific immediate contexts. Many active graduate student/faculty research groups in composition now pursue this model (e.g., at Carnegie-Mellon and the University of Pittsburgh), which could be enhanced by focusing on results that enable more fluent and effective writing, not on "pure" knowledge making.

It might appear that I am only restating North's desire to equalize interests among existing divisions of those in composition, but the issue here is more pointedly that composition studies (whether defined as a field or a discipline) has already taken actions and positions that could force it to re-form the situation from which it came, in a dubious move to imitate its "Others" and their establishments. Imitating the symbolic identities of those who spawn us expresses a normal desire to demonstrate our legitimate lineage and our claim on their perceived status. Doing so is almost inescapable, unless we openly criticize the workings of identity formation. But another alternative to this sort of re-formation, if an alternative is desired, is to reconceive the project that composition represents in political terms and define immediate goals that groups of variously qualified and knowledgeable people can aim to meet. These goals, as I have emphasized, can never exclude either the articulation of the politics of composition they most clearly involve or the actual consequences that solving particular problems will create.

The stakes in this reconceptualization are quite high. In one scenario, composition could become an autonomous department, with internal hierarchies that produce the same sorts of relative levels of status reported by survey respondents for fields within English departments. In another, autonomous composition might become a new ghetto, the isolated home of nonregular appointees guided by a few people in secure positions who take on the many relaying functions of current directors of composition in English departments, but in a new setting. But in the narrative I am proposing, either sort of isolation might or might not take place. The important alternative to each of these political/symbolic results would be a pointed and continuing awareness of processes that form ghettos, of hierarchical structures that maintain them, and especially of the fit, or lack of it, between their specialized interests and their culture's disposition of the writing it has identified as unfit for the bourgeois gaze of "reason."

This alternative involves open analyses not only of the "features" of particular discourses, but of their privileging mechanisms and discriminatory practices. This field's self-consciousness would be parallel to that of any new discipline defining itself in full consciousness of its politics rather than as an intellectual "body" of knowledge or set of methods. Its internal cooperation in curricular and professional matters would depend on agreeing that writing is an action toward its surroundings; it would not depend on simulating benign but finally static pluralism. Relations among insiders would take place under the rubric of active awareness that they never teach (or write) neutrally, but to maintain or undermine an establishment.

The field would thus be guided by metaphors that begin in the results of writing. Were we to assume that no discourse is inherently privileged over another and that any discourse produces ideas only as a result of actual struggles, we would not give priority to internally coherent theories that unify and legitimize a "discipline," but to the ways that we can together make it easier for any group of people to write successfully to reach particular goals. This model would not establish internal relations to praise pluralism, but to articulate the ways that various practices and research projects empower discourses. In this view, knowledge for its own sake is made and disseminated with an eye on the "knowledge for its own sake" discourse it represents. As in radical feminist studies, relations between "ideas" or theories and actual cultural dispositions of writing would not be suppressed, but would become substantial discussions of the student's (and the professional's) immediate position in relation to any act of writing.

Alternative Subjectivities: Revising the Student

I have been arguing throughout this chapter, and in this entire study, that powerful attitudes toward student writers and unprivileged writing inevitably control the status of composition studies, its relations to those outside it, and its self-images and ways of working out its new professionalization.

History, interpretive theories, and data from immediate reports all verify that the rubber hits this particular low road on a cultural plane. The horizons of our culture, however, are always disappearing, fading into deeply held but ambivalent convictions about how elitist claims on powerful discourse can coexist with egalitarian education.

Many sources support this connection between the status of student writing and the field assigned its study and pedagogy. We find, for instance, that composition professionals most often focus on issues in teaching when they describe their most-hoped-for "changes" in the field (Appendix) and that familial roles in relations to student writers have much to do with the wider status of teachers of composition (chapter 4). Additionally, as the prominent work of Mina Shaughnessy and of various process theorists like Linda Flower and David Bartholomae has demonstrated, the prospect of theorizing composition instruction in terms of student learning and actual student writing has persistently captured the imagination and respect of many who otherwise doubt the "intellectual content" of the field. Consequently, the identity of the student in teaching, research, and administrative practices offers a key to the politics of composition in every issue considered here.

As I have described them, students in those freshman courses taken to be at the center of composition studies are socially and politically imagined as children whose Victorian innocence retains a tainted need for "civilizing." Institutional practices toward them, individualistic "process" theories that finally treat them as emerging, or as failed, but never as actually responsible "authors," and blurred images of their teachers all contribute to their ongoing treatment as only tentative participants in consequential learning about writing. My major point about this status has been that students learn, in the most common versions of introductory courses, to write only intransitively—as, to, and about nothing in particular. The subjectivity of the composition student, his or her cultural "call," echoes a call to traditional literary subjectivity. But this way of imagining a writer logically contradicts the active nature of writing, which is never normally undertaken without reference to its results. This subjectivity, despite the limited consequences of "grades" or performance on tests, covers over the rewards (and punishments) that inevitably follow from greater and lesser acquaintance with how effective writers construct and maintain consequential textual worlds.

But students in more advanced courses in writing, those with historical precedents different from the freshman composition "program's" original agendas, are taken to have only "vocational" or practical aims. They are often treated as people who will be engaged in writing to record already fixed knowledge and interests, not as those who will generate them. Students in typical professional and technical writing courses, and in some degree those in "creative" writing, reverse the priority given to tainted innocence in freshman courses. They instead answer a call to be placed outside the intransitive subjectivity assigned to their younger counterparts, but not, in fact, to have moved "beyond" it. Defined precisely by their lack of passivity and by a "task" orientation, they are nonetheless implicated in the subjectivity generally assigned to composition. They are, that is, equally divorced from writing that includes social and economic consequences beyond conventionality and correctness. Nonetheless, this postlapsarian subjectivity often paradoxically intimidates teachers, who find it difficult to move from one to another image of the student despite the relative clarity, if not the formulas, in many materials designed for this "older" group.

Both images of student writers help sustain the belief that composition studies, its teachers, and its assignments are marginal to the politics of discourse. The business writing student, to take an easy example, may be taught to write generic letters, memos, and reports whose forms are standardized in specific companies, as though this student were going to become a company cipher, not a member of a collaborative group of people who shape public communications after struggling among themselves. Like the five-paragraph theme, formats that many advanced courses emphasize have little to do with the writing, and especially with the writing situations, that actual, influential people encounter.

To construct an alternative subjectivity for the student, these habits would have to be reversed. A new subjectivity for the student of composition would have to be identified and applied in pedagogy, theory, and administrative practice.

For instance, a new theory might redefine "process" and other pedagogical emphases in political terms by specifying some essential elements in any writing event. These include the Purpose or outcome intended in writing, its temporal and spatial Situations, its actual and imagined Participants, appropriate Evidence and Language, and conventional Form or Presentation (see Hoffman et al.). Given these actual constraints on acts of writing, including the amount of time a writer or a group actually has to accomplish the outcome intended, "processes" become variable realities actually defined by the material and social conditions for writing, including the availability of specific technologies. This theory of what an act of writing involves might be used in describing not only writing assignments, but written texts and many other pedagogical *topoi* that have led to specific research programs in composition studies. This theoretical articulation reconceives the student of writing as responsible, participatory, and at least potentially influential in specific writing situations.

Of course, without the additional commitments I have described—commitments to articulating many relations between discourse and power and to undertaking close analyses of the social implications of current and past writing pedagogies—these new practices could merely show formulaic and artificial concern about "relevance," a concern that typically projects the traditional, univocal individual onto imagined situations that he or she will control. The student would remain "motivated" in a self-contained, essentialist way, with no object in mind. What is needed additionally is the articulation and critique already suggested, disclosing connections between specific social and textual superstructures and highlighting how writing situations construct their participant writers before, during, and after they undertake any piece of writing. Without this additional reflexivity in pedagogical and theoretical accounts, the student's writing is left in its self-contained world of textual features, where its consequences are already limited to intransitive matters of "quality."

But with these commitments, students of writing might be imagined as actual people in actual writing situations. Such writers do not write without reference to the appropriateness of that action in a specific circumstance. They conceive of resistant written language as the actual form of their desires, not as a set of determinate "meanings" that they can singularly shape. Given responsibility to account for the place their writing will take among others in specific situations—its particularity and the responses it is designed to elicit—students could become aware of the window on full participation in discourse communities that their writing represents.

These assertions may appear idealized and beyond the ordinary interactions that go on in classrooms. But it is important to remember that they are meant to focus all the issues raised in this study, especially the political approach to textual analysis that reverses the traditional formalist priority of textual "meaning" over complex textual situations. To date, it is uncommon for either freshmen or advanced students to be asked to discover how much, what kind, and what quality of writing they are responsible for, either as students or as later professionals. It is equally uncommon to ask them to imagine the results they wish from a piece of writing or to give attention to the realities of deadlines and collaboration that writing situations impose on their individual processes. For instance, few people who write effectively are responsible alone for every element of a text's production. But the roles of the person or situation that creates an actual writing "assignment" or of the person or organization responsible for a text's publishable form are rarely enacted in composition courses, even in those that depend heavily on peer group and collaborative processes. Students are rarely asked to become either the "writing teachers" that successful writers actually must be for themselves or the teachers of reading they must be for others.

In each of these particularities, I am emphasizing how those in composition studies can analyze and historicize discourse, not the additional special expertise that various writing situations always demand. But in the "natural" development of composition studies over the last several years, neither transitive nor intransitive writing has been at the center of the field. With the exception of new studies by Linda Flower and her collaborators and by social process theorists like David Bartholomae, Shirley Brice Heath, and Patricia Bizzell, much of the prominent recent conversation about composition has been pointedly "about" it. Critiques of its theories, schools, and relations to status have temporarily superseded interpretive analyses of how students write, of what they write, or of how well they succeed in doing so depending on their specific instruction.

Beyond excellent descriptions of actions taken by writers, the emerging discipline of composition has not given direct attention to assuring that student writers will be empowered by writing. Few studies either address the multiple identities that successful students must assume or test instruction against its results. Although a great deal of research now in progress examines the cultural and social influences that constrain and enable any writer's writing, it is clear that the pedagogical urgency that reorganized composition studies in the 1970s has been replaced by other results of this reorganization. Much "research" explains writing as a field, but not as an action by student writers.

What I take to be a temporary gap in specific attention to successful writing has resulted from a newly successful, if unarticulated, form of hegemonic selection. This specific version does not locate "the" tradition, but establishes that "tradition" itself is relevant to composition studies. Institutions have easily cooperated with this particularly inviting way to re-create themselves, in positive actions toward a field of composition that distracts its members, in any role, from complex political implications of writing. New faculty positions in composition are, by virtue of anyone's common sense, taken to carry with them "pure" research emphases that divert their appointees from examining what and how successful student writers write. While some research programs now aim to describe "real world" writing in both academic and professional settings (e.g., Bazerman; Odell and Goswami), little research about college writers identifies a "student tradition." This tradition would include many research questions that take student writers to be active rather than passively defined citizens of discourse communities. Some possibilities for study are the patterns of writing development throughout early adulthood and beyond, how or whether students remember and use their introductory writing instruction, how successful student writers approach and complete assignments to write

in many fields, and particularly how those who perceive themselves as entitled to belong to powerful discourse communities
have developed this confidence, the quality that women and
minority writers have found it such a struggle to acquire. We
have a great deal of information about the amount of writing
that professionals must do and the relation of its quality to
their advancement, but we have little information about the
ways that specific practices in collegiate writing and reading
instruction influence those who write more or less fluently
in the future. In sum, there is little open analysis and little
pedagogical attention to various means that privilege or limit
the writing and the writers that composition takes to be its
province.

The intransitive student's subjectivity is thereby transferred
to the field of composition studies itself. It does not normally
account for the results of its work and so has little claim to its
"importance" beyond the introductory ideological agendas
that history gave it. New programs in composition and other
"new" institutional approaches to student writing do not automatically redefine it, or its writers, as something other than
the "problem" it was established (literally) to correct. The
politics of writing has been perceived to be beyond the interests of students and has been defined for them and their
teachers in ways that make this perception accurate. Composition studies has not taken the most obvious way toward translating the carnivalesque into an open commentary on the
status it wishes to change. Those who teach and conduct
research about limited, initiative writing are inevitably implicated in limited, initiative roles. But they also have alternatives
in rethinking their images of the students they teach.

Appendix · Works Cited · Index

Appendix

The Status of Composition: A Survey of How Its Professionals See It

This report of a national survey of professional composition specialists may appear to add a flavor of social scientific methodology and argument that undercuts the theoretical predispositions of this study, but it is intended, on the contrary, to reinforce my commitment to lifting quantifiable "facts" out of the flat interpretations they generally encourage. This survey was undertaken and is reported to test my interpretations against the experiences of many colleagues, as the placement of excerpts from it in the text has partially accomplished. But it was also formed and written in full awareness that observations and reports in this genre can easily distort the relation between fact and the symbolic political domain that creates and interprets it.

For instance, in their classic study *Social Stratification in Science*, Jonathan and Stephen Cole reported that they could not, on the basis of statistics about appointments or about frequency of prominence of publications, promotion, direct rewards, or other quantifiable circumstances, find any empirical evidence to support claims that "science actively discriminates against women and Jewish members of the scientific community" (159). Against this apparently outrageous surmise, these authors also noted that they "did not examine the attitudes of scientists toward women or minorities within their ranks" (123n). Their text and its subtext were, that is, kept entirely separate, so that "the consequences of these attitudes" (123n) were left to speculation. In the interests of an objectivity that characterizes "good science" but that generally covers over the point of making such a study at all, their report offers evidence that no politics of science need be explained.

My intention, as the following results show, has been to unite text and subtext. Although my survey method acknowledged received practices of gathering empirical information, both the request for participation and the instrument itself were open invitations for collaboration, not random or scrupulously factual in their orientation. The letter of invitation stated a working hypothesis: that composition is a marginalized entity in its established realizations and that its students, teachers, and courses have been associated with initiation rites before a later "real action" in textual education. The letter also referred to Carol Hartzog's *Composition and the Academy*, stating that "she makes it clear that things have changed in many places, and I hope to elicit answers that comment on this perception." The participants, who may be perceived as a cognoscenti, were selected by choosing every tenth person listed (in any role) on the 1987 program of the Conference on College Composition and Communication. Additionally, I solicited responses from committee members on NCTE standing committees related to composition and participants in the 1987 national Writing Program Administrators' conference. The total of 284 invitations elicited responses from 129 people (45 percent, or a response rate within the normal range for social scientific surveys). One hundred fourteen (40 percent) completed questionnaires, while 15 graduate students, highschool teachers, and others who judged themselves outside the intended pool responded with letters explaining their unwillingness to participate. In addition, 30 people from both groups enclosed notes of support, offering further help or supporting this project as "important for the profession," "really needed," or "a great service to us all."

I am not, therefore, claiming either statistical significance or scientific objectivity for this report. Its generalizations are claims made with the warrant of the research underlying the earlier part of this study and my own close reading of the text of responses—both quantifiable and discursive—that I received. I would not exclude this perspective, despite the strong qualification, because the report that follows is, however flat and textualized, a representation of many positive and negative human experiences. The participants' persisting sense of extraordinary professional tensions is the most persuasive evidence we have that language learning and participating in public discourse is never a politically neutral structure, even though it may be evidence of the sort that even its sources tend to explain away. Dismissing such evidence as "merely anecdotal" is the strategy of superstructural mainte- nance that covers over the legitimacy and power of all under- class groups, but the stakes in transforming the status of instruction for participation in public writing make me particu- larly unwilling to defer to that strategy here.

These data indicate that the status of composition is not simply understood. It is not "bad" or "low," nor is it "equal" or "high," at least not in the view of these participants in the field. The survey responses confirm my interpretive claim in the text that the identity of composition teachers, students, and administrators is blurred in the conjunction of actual and symbolic, perceived and official, situations they commonly encounter. Especially in the research universities where com- position courses were first made programmatic concerns, per- during, specific *affective* discriminations continue, whatever new administrative structures, curricula, and reward systems may be accessible. Institutional origins strongly color the am- bience around composition, confirming workings of locally selective hegemonic traditions that retain over time traces of the original conditions of an institution's establishment.

Survey

GENERAL DATA

Name (if you wish):
years since leaving graduate school:
Current rank:
Ph.D. field:
Type of institution (university, 4-yr college, other):
How would you define your relation to composition in your
   institution? (teach only, administer/teach, graduate faculty
   field, etc.):
Telephone # if you are willing to talk further:

I. Tenure

   1. Are you now tenured?
   2. If so, how many years after your first full-time appointment did you receive tenure?

3. If longer than seven years, please explain why:

4. If you are not tenured, what is your current relation to receiving tenure? (E.g., will come up in regular fashion, not in tenurable position):

5. Have you or any of your colleagues experienced evaluations for tenure made difficult by having composition as a field?

6. If yes, please explain the problem:

7. Have you seen changes in your department's attitude toward hiring and/or tenuring composition specialists?

8. If so, please explain:

II. Promotion

1. For how many years have you been in your rank?

2. As you currently assess your future, will your department promote you in a regular fashion?

3. If no, please explain:

4. If you are a full professor, how was your promotion evaluated? (Please rank the relative importance of each alternative, 1–6):

_____ Publication

_____ Teaching

_____ Service (specify) _____

_____ Countering an offer

_____ Promoted with a move

_____ Other (specify) _____

5. Have you or any of your colleagues judged that promotion is related to fields of specialization in your department?

6. If yes, please explain:

III. Research Awards

1. Are research awards (time, money) regularly available to your department?

2. If yes, have you applied in the last 5 years? In the 5 years prior to the last 5?

2.1 If yes, have you received awards?

2.2 If no, why have you not applied?

3. If you have applied and been turned down, please note

any reasons, stated or implied, that were related to the topic or method of research:

4. Frequency of applications and quality being equal, do you and colleagues in composition receive research awards as often as others in your institution?

5. If no, please explain:

6. Has your institution's support for research in composition increased since you arrived?

7. If yes, please explain:

IV. Departmental and Institutional Acknowledgments
of Composition

1. Are awards for composition teaching given on the same basis as awards for teaching other courses?

2. Are there special composition teaching awards?

3. If composition teaching is not rewarded as often as teaching in other fields, please explain why:

4. Have lecture series in your department and institution included composition/rhetoric specialists?

5. If no, please explain:

6. Have recognitions for research and/or publication in composition been equitably visible in your department/institution?

7. If no, please explain:

General

1. Please rank (1–9) the following fields as you perceive their status in your department:

_____ Literature

_____ Literary theory

_____ Linguistics

_____ Folklore

_____ Film

_____ Composition

_____ Rhetoric

_____ Feminist studies

_____ (Other—please specify)

2. Please identify as precisely as you can the sources of any

tensions associated with composition that you have experienced in your department:

3. Please assess the nature of any changes in composition's status in your department in the last 5 and 10 years:

4. If you could make one change in composition's relation to your department/institution, what would it be?

Institutional and Departmental Representation

The entire group of 114 who answered the survey questions represented universities (85 respondents in Ph.D.- or M.A.-granting institutions), four-year colleges/universities (23 respondents) and two-year community colleges or colleges attached to larger institutions (6 respondents). This distribution suggests that graduate degree–granting institutions encourage the sort of professional development that put respondents at the conferences from which most of this sample was chosen, and perhaps that university appointees are more supportive in spirit and have more time to respond to this sort of research.

Of those responding, 103 (90 percent) held positions in departments of English, which are tenurable *or* nontenurable. Two held nontenurable positions in an independent writing program, and 9 held appointments in writing centers or in departments of forestry, sociology, or education.

Descriptions of Responsibilities

Perhaps the only characteristic that would distinguish this group from one selected in the same way, but from conferences and committees in some other discipline, is its overwhelming choice of administration as at least one important professional responsibility. (See table A–1.)

As we begin to look at more particularized perceptions of self and institutional identities for composition teachers, it is important to keep in mind that respondents to this survey were also a weighted group who have professionally defined themselves as "in" composition, whatever their Ph.D. field may have been. They attend its conferences, serve its organizations, and define their responsibilities in their home institu-

Table A-1.   Responsibilities of Respondents

Kind of Work	Placement in Lists			
	Listed First		Listed Second	
	Number	%	Number	%
Administration	49	43	23	20
Undergraduate teaching	44	39	32	28
Graduate teaching and research	21	18	24	12
Total number / Percent of mentions of a ranked responsibility	114	100	79	60

tions as administrative, often after an administrative appointment has ended. In responding to the question about their responsibilities, many mentioned administrative appointments they no longer held, perhaps to give credibility to their judgments but also, certainly, to reveal broad concerns about teaching writing.

Field of Study, Tenure, and Tenurability, According to Years Since Entering the Profession

The first questions asked about respondents' perceptions of the status of composition concerned tenure and institutional attitudes toward those in various specializations who seek it. A respondent's own relationship to tenure and field of specialization naturally determined his or her answers, so I separated the respondents into groups according to their reported years since leaving graduate school. Within these groups, I further looked for varying fields of specialization defined by the respondents' fields of graduate study. The years in which respondents left graduate school and the numbers of respondents in each cohort were divided as follows: (1) from 1980 to 1987 (34), (2) from 1975 to 1979 (35), (3) from 1964 to 1975 (31), and (4) those who have been out of school for more than eighteen years (10), leaving before 1965. (Four

Table A-2. Respondents' Ranks

Ranks	Number	Percent
Full professors	34	30
Associate professors	37	33
Assistant professors	29	25
Instructors or unranked staff	14	12
TOTAL	114	100

respondents were still engaged in graduate study but were nonetheless employed full-time.)

The ranks of the entire group of 114 respondents are indicated in table A–2, and their reported fields of specialization are described in table A–3. As discussions of individual cohorts highlight, the Ph.D. in rhetoric/composition is a recently awarded degree.

The respondents were asked a series of questions about their tenure: (1) Are you now tenured? (2) How many years after your first full-time appointment did you receive tenure? (3) If longer than seven years, please explain why. (4) If you are not tenured, what is your current relation to receiving tenure? (5) Have you or any of your colleagues experienced evaluations for tenure made difficult by having composition as a field? (6) If yes, please explain the problem. (7) Have you seen changes in your department's attitude toward hiring and/

Table A-3. Respondents' Definitions of Their Fields of Specialization in Ph.D. Study

Field	Number	Percent
"English" (including special designations of fields in literature)	61	54
Rhetoric/composition	38	33
Education and others (including no reported Ph.D. field)	15	13
TOTAL	114	100

or tenuring composition specialists? (8) Please explain the change. Answers to the last two questions were collated as a whole that will be discussed later. Answers to questions regarding the respondents' own tenuring situation are included in descriptions of the cohorts according to years since leaving graduate school.

These respondents reported as a whole the following conditions around their tenure: 54 (47 percent) had no problems with tenure related to composition, 40 (35 percent) had problems related to composition work, 9 (8 percent) were unsure if the problems could be connected to the field of composition, and 12 (10 percent) either did not answer or were in untenurable positions. (Their judgments of general difficulties with tenure, however, stay within a range of ±9 percent in answers to later questions about general conditions for tenure in composition; see below.)

Newcomers: 1980–87

The 34 respondents who left graduate school in 1980 or after (including one instructor who is now in a forestry department where he also teaches writing) are described according to field of specialization and rank and tenure in table A–4. It is important to note that "assistant professor" does not imply tenurability in all of the cases listed in the table. Of the 18 in that rank, 3 did not hold tenure-accruing appointments, and 1 replied that it was "unlikely" that he would receive it because of the institution's practices toward composition as a field.

These respondents were, of course, more aware of current conditions for gaining tenure than those who already had it, although gaining tenure in composition remained a vivid moment for those in the other chronologically separate groups. Among these newcomers, 10 (29 percent) answered yes to the question about whether they perceived problems with tenure and composition; 15 (44 percent) answered no. Six (18 percent) were not in tenurable positions, which is notable considering that three of these six professionally active people held degrees directly related to composition teaching. The remaining 3 in this group faced the future with some trepidation; they answered "not yet" or "?"

Two patterns emerge from this group. First, of 34 people

Table A-4. Fields of Specialization and Tenure Status of Those Leaving Graduate School from 1980 to 1987 ($N = 34$)

1. Field of Specialization	Number	Percent
English (only)	3	9
Including:		
American Literature	2	6
American Studies	2	6
Romantic Literature	3	9
Literary Criticism	1	3
SUBTOTAL	11	32 (rounded)
Rhetoric/composition (as primary field or in addition to literature, linguistics)	17	50
Education	4	12
Forestry or no field	2	6
TOTAL	34	100

2. Tenure and Rank	Tenured	Untenured
Full professors (0)	——	——
Associate professors	5	——
Assistant professors	——	18[a]
Instructors	——	5
Unranked	1	5
TOTAL	6	28

[a]Three are in untenurable positions

in it, over half (21, or 62 percent) studied rhetoric, composition, or an education program related to the teaching in these fields. Second, this group ranged from the entirely secure (6) to the entirely insecure (13). The rest (15) were in positions that any academic in the first seven years of a career might hold.

Eight to Eleven Years: 1975–79

The 35 respondents who left graduate school from 1975 to 1979 are described in table A–5 according to graduate field, tenure status, and rank. To determine trends, if any, during these years, I further distinguished their fields of specialization according to years since leaving graduate school. Of the 7 who left school in 1979, 4 reported rhetoric or composition as their field of specialization; of the 5 in the 1978 group, 2 did; of the 11 in the 1977 group, 5 did; of the 3 in the 1976 group, 2 did; and of the 9 in the 1975 group, 1 did, for a total among them of 14 (40 percent) who held degrees in rhetoric and composition. Except in the earliest year (1975), when only 10 percent perceived rhetoric, composition, or a related field as their Ph.D. area, the percentages in each year remain fairly constant, ranging from approximately 40 percent to approximately 60 percent.

The entire group did not, however, appear to have perceived rhetoric and composition as a field within "English" so often as younger colleagues when they formed their profes-

Table A-5.   Fields of Specialization and Tenure Status of Those Leaving Graduate School from 1974 to 1979 (*N* = 35)

1. *Field of Specialization*	*Number*	*Percentage*
"English" or "English/Lit."	11	31
A literary specialization	10	29
Rhetoric/composition	14	40
TOTAL	35	100

2. *Rank and Tenure Status*	*Tenured*	*Untenured*
Full professors	8	——
Associate professors	18	——
Assistant professors	——	9
Others	——	——
TOTAL	26	9

sional identities in graduate school. This difference is certainly reasonable since a discipline of composition was usually unrecognized before the late 1970s. A total of 21 (60 percent), including leaders in the field of composition who are well known as its champions within MLA and CCCC and who are among its extremely productive scholars and researchers, did not perceive that they were trained in rhetoric and composition as Ph.D. candidates.

Of the 9 who were untenured at the time of the survey, 3 reported no problems with tenure in their departments in relation to composition; 1 reported that no one was receiving tenure in her institution because of budget restrictions; 5 reported problems associated with tenure for composition. In addition to these 5 who were untenured, 8 of the associate and full professors reported difficulties with tenure, for a total of 13 (37 percent) who perceived a difficulty with tenure related to field.

As a whole, 20 of these respondents reported no difficulty with tenure in composition, 13 reported overt negative departmental attitudes in tenure cases, and 2 reported that their institutions do not give tenure.

Twelve to Eighteen Years: 1965–74

Thirty-five respondents left graduate school in the ten years from 1965 to 1974, suggesting that the entire sample of program participants, committee members, and conferees to whom this survey was sent was weighted toward a slightly less experienced group who had been in the profession for fewer than twelve years. It may be instead that fewer of those who entered teaching before the members of the first groups considered the issues raised by this study compelling enough to answer, but it is also likely that fewer members of the profession who started between 1965 and 1974 have become active in composition.

If we look at this entire group in two cohorts separated by years of experience—those who entered teaching from 1970 to 1974 and those who entered from 1965 to 1969—these inferences are further supported. The first group produced 20 respondents, the second 15 (see table A–6). In the group of 20 who began their careers more recently, from 1970 to 1974,

Table A-6. Fields of Specialization and Tenure Status of Those Leaving Graduate School from 1965 to 1974 (*N* = 35)

Cohort 1 (1970–1974); N = 20	
1. Fields of Specialization	*Number*
"English" or "American"	6
A literary specialization	9
Rhetoric/composition or education	5
TOTAL	20

2. Ranks (All Tenured)	*Number*
Full professors	8
Associate professors	11
Assistant professors	1
Others	——
TOTAL	20

Cohort 2 (1970–1974); N = 15	
1. Fields of Specialization	*Number*
"English" or a specialization	7
Rhetoric/composition	1
Education	2
Sociology	1
No Ph.D.	4
TOTAL	15

2. Rank (All in Secure Positions)	*Number*
Full professors	8
Associate professors	3
Assistant professors	1
Instructors, lecturers, unranked	3
TOTAL	15

5 of the 20 listed Ph.D. fields as rhetoric, composition, or education; 6 identified themselves as in "English" or "American." Noticeably, the remaining 9 of these respondents particularized their graduate training by very specific designations—for example, "17th century," "romantic poetry," and "biography."

All of these 20 are now tenured. The briefest time reported to tenure was three years (2); the longest was thirteen years (1); the average time to tenure for this group was six years.

In the group of 15 who entered the profession in the earlier five years, the same patterns appear (see table A–6). This group, like those who began in the five years after them, were divided in their perception of their difficulty in receiving tenure. Seven said there was no problem. Among the remaining 8, 4 reported problems, 2 replied with "no, but," and 2 responded with a question mark.

If we combine the data from both groups, we can infer that of these 35 respondents, 8 (23 percent) formed professional identities in graduate school that are connected to composition as a field. The majority received training in literary specializations (22 or 63 percent), and 5 (14 percent) held no Ph.D. or a Ph.D. in an entirely different field.

Among these 35, 15 (43 percent) reported no trouble connected to tenure for composition. Trouble was unquestionably identified in the responses of a lesser number (12, or 34 percent). But in addition to these and 3 who did not answer, 3 replied "no, but" or "not yet," and 2 answered with an indecisive "?" In sum, 57 percent of this group who began their careers from 1965 to 1974 (16) thought that the question of tenure was at least associated with composition as a field.

More Than Eighteen Years: Those Who Began before 1965

Only 10 respondents of 114 entered the profession before 1965, which may indicate not only that composition is a young field but that active participation in any professional group may trail off after twenty to thirty years. Many of these respondents are, however, household words in composition and the profession at large. Their contributions include widely recognized textbooks, monographs, and administrative contributions that have had influence and presence beyond their home institutions.

All of these 10 respondents were full professors whose fields of specialization are described in table A–7. They received tenure in 3 to 10 years, in an average time of 6 years, although 4 had it within four or fewer years. Their responses to the question concerning their difficulties with tenure were more positive than those in the group who entered the profession from 1965 to 1974. Seven (70 percent) perceived no problem; 2 (20 percent) perceived problems; 1 (10 percent) answered with a question mark.

Problems with Tenure and the Field of Composition

The 110 respondents who answered the questions "Have you or any of your colleagues experienced evaluations for tenure made difficult by having composition as a field?" and "If yes, please explain the problem" were more positive about the future for their colleagues than they were about the tenor of their particular experiences. That is, the group included 34 (30 percent) who replied yes to the first question, 5 (5 percent) who answered yes or no (including 4 who said that their and colleagues' tenure had been for work in literature that had allowed them to beg this question), 66 (60 percent) who responded no, and 7 (6 percent) who gave no answer but added

Table A-7.   Fields of Specialization of Those Leaving Graduate School before 1965 ($N = 10$)

Field of Specialization	Number
English literature	6
Rhetoric/composition	——
Education	2
No Ph.D.	2
TOTAL	10

an explanation of why they had not. These numbers and percentages are not statistically significant, but there is at least a slightly more positive cast of mind about the future of tenuring in relation to departments' evaluations of work in composition.

Among the 34 who answered that they had perceived problems with tenure related to composition as a field, only 1 attributed the difficulty to problems with the quality of a particular person's work. The disposition of these responses is shown in table A–8. Specific comments on many of the categories reported in the table show that the composition research on which tenure evaluations are based is not considered to be "theoretical" or that it "has no content."

Among responses classified in table A–8, 12 respondents explained specific instances of difficulties that they perceived as related to having composition as a field. Very difficult personal situations were revealed: 2 were promoted before tenure, then suffered from second thoughts of colleagues about actually tenuring people in composition; 2 people reported results from an institution that, they say, "routinely passes over people who spend too much time on composition"; 1 reported that she "made changes in the program," then left her position after warnings about receiving tenure; 3 reported similar difficulties when appointments to administer composi-

Table A-8. Respondents' Characterizations of Problems with Tenure in Composition (among 34 Identifying Problems)

Type of Problem	Number of Mentions	Percent[a]
1. Respectability of field	12	35
2. Composition is pedagogy, not research	7	21
3. Rejection above departmental level	6	18
4. "Exclusivity"	3	9
5. Specific difficulties	12	35
Total number of problems identified	40	[117]

[a]Based on percentage of group of 34; total percentage exceeds 100 because of multiple identification of problems.

tion were later not "counted" for tenure; 1 said that she had, in an unprecedented departmental action, been put up for review two years after the beginning of her appointment; 2 other less specific cases involved releasing all of the people in composition, or some of them, while retaining others in literature. One person was told at hiring that he would never be promoted or allowed to serve on committees because he had been hired to teach writing courses. But he witnessed changes from this situation in his department to active hiring in composition. Nonetheless, he reported that a more junior colleague in composition had been reviewed first by the usual three outside reviewers, then by three more because the first group was perceived as "too complimentary."

Were it not that these 12 specific accounts are embedded among 34 identifications of composition as a field with problems in receiving tenure, it would be reasonable to assume that these individuals are reporting just that, individual cases that should not be weighted heavily in any view of composition. No one who has voted on a tenure decision of any kind can accept one or another side of reports about individual tenure decisions without caution. But considering the context for this 32 percent of the responses, and persuasive evidence that composition was not established within English to produce tenure, it is unlikely that these reports or others like them have been invented out of whole cloth.

Changes in Departmental Attitudes toward Hiring and Tenuring in Composition

Of the 114 respondents, 61 (53 percent) said that they had witnessed changes in departmental or college attitudes toward hiring and tenuring composition specialists. Three (3 percent) answered that they were unsure (yes and no). Forty-four (39 percent) answered no when asked if they had perceived such change, and 7 (6 percent) did not answer. (Four of these said they were not in English departments but other units established to conduct composition teaching, and 1 replied that her position, "academic professional," had been established before she took it but that she would rather be in a tenurable position.) Perceptions of change or of stasis were, therefore, mixed; no generally significant answer was given.

In addition, yes and no in these allocations do not indicate that yes, departments are integrating composition professionals and their field into their "central" traditions, or no, they are not. Taken together, respondents in each of these categories painted a complex portrait of varieties of change. Among the 53 percent who answered yes or "unsure" to this question about change, those who commented further with explanations fell into various groups who described a fairly standard pattern of changing responses to composition in departmental histories. The majority defined "change" in relation to various stages of hiring, as the questions suggested (see table A–9).

Forty-one of these responses show that changed attitudes toward composition as a field of specialization appear in various stages: interest in such a search, actual hiring at junior levels, and tenuring people in the field. Hiring has, however, also produced new negative responses to composition in the departments represented here.

Table A-9.   Changes in Attitudes toward Hiring and Tenuring in Composition Reported by Those Perceiving Change or Unsure about It ($N = 64$)

	Number of Respondents	
Type of Change	*Sure of Change*	*Unsure*
1. Greater interest in hiring	12	—
2. Active searches underway	3	1
3. Administrative pressure to hire	2	—
4. First person hired	6	1
5. Now include composition specialists when hiring	15	—
6. Have hired one full professor	1	—
7. Positive attitude engendered by a search	2	—
8. Negative attitude engendered by a search	3	1
9. Other specific explanations	17	—
TOTAL	61	3

Other perceptions of changed attitudes were defined as follows: Seven said that composition is now defined as a legitimate field of interest as it was not in the past. One older respondent reported a long tradition of recognition for composition that had begun decades ago; 5 others attributed significant change to administrative leadership on the part of a dean or department chair. Two respondents perceived change in relation to a new institutional structure—increased writing requirements and a new graduate program. But both of these respondents saw these as only cosmetic changes in regard to attitudes. Composition is, they said, still "second class." As yet another put it, change is "from major antagonism to resigned tolerance." Finally, 1 respondent reported that M.A.-qualified composition specialists (along with all other appointees at the institution) are "no longer eligible for tenure."

Those who answered "yes and no" or "unsure" to this question are also included in table A–9. Their explanatory comments give us a way to characterize these yes answers as well as the "no change" perceptions from an almost equally large group. Individuals said, "I'm the first [composition specialist] in eight years"; that the department had said it would hire in the field but had not in the end done so; and that "we'll find out next year when they look." In other words, some departments appear to approach composition specialists gingerly. One appointment may or may not lead to others, depending on the department's budget and its perception of the first appointee. One search may have negative or positive results, leading to taking the plunge (as departments perceived to have "long traditions" have done), or it may result in what appears to be overexposure, a feeling of having been burned in illuminations of what specialists in composition actually do.

Those who answered that no change had occurred in attitudes toward hiring and tenuring composition specialists in their departments confirmed the existence of this pattern. These 34 respondents (39 percent of the entire group) either gave no explanation or answered as indicated in table A–10.

Five respondents who might be grouped as the "absolutely not's" included 2 who said their departments "would never do it" (that is, hire or tenure in composition); 1 who said "they

Table A-10. Reports of No Change toward Hiring and Tenuring in Composition among Those Answering "No Change"

Reasons	Number
1. Long positive tradition	7
2. Will never change	5
3. "Everyone" teaches composition	3
4. Stable staff	2
5. Other specified explanations	6
Total statements of reasons	23

still hate doing it"; 1 who said that hiring in composition is a "negative priority"; and 1 who reported that a composition specialist was tenured because this person "would have sued us back into the Stone Age."

"No change" responses were also explained in more qualified ways. One person left a department for an appointment "where I would be valued." One noted that "it's mixed, some for, some nervous about it [hiring in composition]." One mentioned that while her department is unchanged in its attitudes, a writing workshop director has been employed by the college, and 2 said that their departments do more frequently turn to them for advice now. Echoing the few who responded that change was only cosmetic, 1 said, "We do more, but attitudes haven't changed."

Consequently, we would have to infer that these 104 respondents include, in both yes and no answers about change, only 24 (23 percent) who said that composition as a field represented by its specialists is in a *stable* relation to their departments. Eight of these reported a stable and positive tradition of honoring composition as a field. Seven reported a stable and negative attitude toward hiring and tenuring in the field, whatever actions may occur. The remaining 9 were in departments they characterized as neutral, holding to long-established dispositions of teaching among graduate students and literature faculty that in all but one case (with one composition specialist among 48 faculty) included no composition specialists.

The remaining 80 (77 percent) reported some sort of changes in relation to hiring and tenuring composition specialists, but these have by no means always been positive changes. Linking attitudes to actions, departments become interested in hiring composition specialists (12 responses in both yes and no categories) either when they perceive composition to be a field or when administrative "leadership" and "pressure" create this interest (13 additional responses). They may conduct searches (3 responses), they may waffle ("some are for, some are nervous about it"), they may make composition hiring "a negative priority." When they do search, departments are changed by the process of the search itself (5 responses). They may evolve a pattern of hiring composition specialists (23 additional responses), with as yet undetermined results for departmental attitudes. Or they may hire one person with tenure and rank (1 response) or hire a person who is tenured later only under duress. Alternatively, the process of the search may solidify, or even produce, negative attitudes toward hiring in composition, with the result that the department hires someone else who is in literature (1 response) or changes search priorities (3 responses).

Other changes now occurring, apparently as results of searches, hiring, and deciding tenure cases, include new writing requirements, new graduate rhetoric/composition programs, and minor shifts in departmental attitudes that lead colleagues to turn to those in composition for advice more often or lead them to "resigned tolerance." We might infer that the self-perception of those in composition in regard to changed attitudes toward tenuring and hiring is that the field is now more active than it was in the past. Increased hiring, newly articulated positive and negative positions toward this hiring from leaders and departments, and vivid tenure cases all contribute to a current self-consciousness on the part of those in composition.

This self-consciousness is often negatively defined, in the sort of response interpreted earlier as a result of stigma for individuals who choose various defenses to endure and combat it. But this attitude is obviously also a transitional state across the profession, whose general future direction remains unknown. We have some fairly solid evidence from the experience of other minorities who are in new situations, as composition specialists are, that integration works positively up to a point (for women, up to about 15 percent in formerly closed professional ranks), but that after a certain number are admitted, a backlash effect encloses these people in static roles in relation to their established surroundings.

Such a pattern would account for a perception of "change" when one composition specialist is hired in a department, as it would for difficulties in maintaining groups in composition within departments that perceive them to be taking on critical mass in relation to other specializations. In addition, using a model from minorities and their experience of integration would help us understand why searches may produce negative change in attitudes toward hiring. The actual "difference" of those in composition, as their history and research interests define them, may be much greater than a department intending to be "liberal" can comfortably assimilate. Thus, finally hiring someone trained in literature after conducting a search for someone in composition, or tenuring on the basis of literary publications in addition to composition research or textbooks (see chapter 5), may indicate a smaller ability to accommodate difference within a departmental identity than hiring and tenuring the pure "composition specialist" actually imply.

Promotion

Promotion was clearly perceived by these respondents as an issue separate from hiring, and even from tenure. As one put it, "Now that I'm tenured, I'll be assessed like everyone else." But, this person added, "It took *forever* to get tenure."

The survey asked how many years respondents had been in rank; whether they expected promotion (to any possible higher rank) to occur in regular fashion for themselves; what importance they judged publication, teaching, service, countering an offer, or having moved to have had in their promotion, if any, to full professor; and whether they believed that their departments related field of specialization to judgments about promotion.

Years in Rank

Most responses to this question (107) indicate that a large group of those surveyed had been in their ranks for only one to three years. The disposition of years in rank is described in table A–11.

Five of the entire group of respondents (1 from each rank, including full professor) stated that they were not in tenurable positions, so we can infer from their longevity and this information that a total of 12 respondents (8 who answered these questions plus 4 who said these questions were not applicable to them) were not subject to consideration for promotion.

Promotion in Regular Fashion

Sixty-seven respondents reported on their expectations for promotion. The largest group expected promotion, either certainly or "probably," bringing the total of definitely positive responses to 49, or 73 percent. An additional 8 people responded that they were unsure about promotion for a variety of reasons that will be detailed later. Their inclusion would bring the positive totals to 56, or 84 percent.

Among the 11 (16 percent) who did not expect promotion, 3 were on contracts that will end at a definite time, 1 responded that "none of us will be around in a few years," and 2 reported

Table A-11.   Respondents' Reported Years in Rank (*N* = 107)

Rank Years in Rank	Number of Respondents				
	1–3	4–6	7–10	11–15	16+
1. Full professors	10	6	6	1	7
2. Associate professors	20	11	3	3	——
3. Assistant professors	15	7	2	2	——
4. Instructors, lecturers, or unranked	2	3	2	6	1
TOTAL	47	27	13	12	8
	(44%)	(25%)	(12%)	(11%)	(7%)[a]

[a] Percentages do not equal 100 because of rounding.

that their publications or a cap on all promotions was the
issue.

Evaluation for Full Professor

   Reported perceptions of the weighting of various activities
in promotion decisions came from the 29 full professors and
7 additional people who had been promoted to associate professor or to another status that they perceived as higher (table
A–12). Publication was the first priority, and as might be
expected, teaching was the factor ranked second by most of
the respondents who had been promoted. But on the whole,
service was perceived as second in importance. That is, although teaching was ranked second by 17 of these respondents, service was ranked as the number one consideration
by 3, as the number two consideration by 14, and as the
number three consideration by only 11. These usually second-
and third-place considerations were, for this group, held
about equal in considerations of their promotions, suggesting
that their field is perceived to produce, appropriately, support
for others.

Possibility of Promotion

   Those who were unsure about the possibility of promotion
gave reasons that elaborated on these weightings of teaching
and service. They also open up a perspective on answers to
the question about whether departments relate promotion
decisions to a field of specialization.
   Among the 7 who were unsure about their promotions,

Table A-12.   Importance of Activities in Promotion Considerations

Ranked Activities	Rankings				Number of Mentions
	1st	2nd	3rd	4th	
Publications	23	8	5	——	36
Teaching	5	17	5	2	29
Service	3	14	11	——	28
A move	4	——	1	1	6
Countering an offer	——	1	——	——	1

explanations included "not until I have time to write a book" (this person gives workshops and writes pedagogical and administrative documents that are used internally); "the University is debating because I have published a popular composition textbook"; and 3 respondents who indicated that they had been kept in their departments without Ph.D.s and would probably not be promoted unless they met "normal" expectations.

Relation of Promotion to Field of Specialization

When asked if promotion is related to field of specialization in their departments, 62 (71 percent of the 87 who answered this question) replied no. One qualified by stating that "it is, I believe, related to sex." (Four did not answer; 7 were unsure.) The 14 respondents who replied yes (22 percent) included 2 who stated that composition appears to create a privilege for promotion. Three described their departments as accustomed to differentially evaluating work in "the many mansions" of scholarship; 1 said that "the department must promote to full professor in five years, no matter what"; and 1 echoed responses to questions about tenure difficulties with "no, not yet." Four others, however, spoke of various kinds of normal and extraordinary field-related prejudices:

> 1. Yes, partially due to relative new entry of composition; we have no full professor in composition.
> 2. Some departments will never change their negative attitude toward composition as a specialty. . . . They [people in composition] have grudgingly been afforded a certain status. The central administration is very aware of our strength in the composition/rhetoric area and is extremely supportive.
> 3. The Chair debated the authenticity of a national award that a . . . book . . . had won (but not the award won by a poetry book of a colleague). Thus, he denied my promotion but supported that of my colleague.
> 4. While work in composition is worthwhile, literature is better.

We might infer, then, that perceptions of prejudices against composition lessen greatly after its teachers and researchers are firmly ensconced in their departmental processes. In addition, composition professionals appear to devote much of their energy to "service," and they perceive that this effort is recognized by their departments as comparable to successful teaching. The picture we have of these individuals in departments appears to be quite similar to one we might paint of those in any field, with this exception for "service" and for additional field-specific prejudices. Especially in light of the distinct hiring process portrayed by this group, these prejudices are probably of a different quality than normal or projected anxieties from other perspectives.

Support for Research

If composition professionals perceive conditions for their promotion to be more equitable than conditions for hiring and tenure, they are even more positive in their perceptions of research support from institutions and departments. The questions asked about support for research addressed its availability, respondents' frequency of success in applications, equity in awards among fields, and perceived changes in support for composition research. Respondents had many definitions of "research" and of support for it, ranging from the large grants they say only or most often go to scientists and social scientists, to released time, summer grants, "expenses," professional development workshops, and money for computers (not, it should be noted, for computing in their own research). Five respondents did not reply to any of the questions; many others answered only some of them.

Respondents overwhelmingly reported that their institutions and/or departments regularly provide one or another sort of support for research. Of 106 responding to the first questions, 85 (80 percent) answered yes or "occasionally"; 2 responded that support comes only from outside the institution. Thirteen respondents (12 percent) were in institutions where research support is unavailable.

The frequency of applications and success of the 89 who answered all three parts of the question about their own applications for research support show that 93 applications for research (not all to investigate problems defined as composition topics) had been made by this group in the previous ten years. One additional person indicated that she had "outside funding." Some respondents had applied and been turned down before later success; some had received more than one award. Although no control group from English or another humanistic department was used to measure this level of activity and 4 of these respondents defined themselves as "in" literature or as receiving grants toward research in it, a two-thirds (66 percent) rate of awards among this group defines them as aware of funding opportunities, active in pursuing them, and capable of competing successfully when they do.

In addition, those responding to these questions appear to believe that research awards in composition are made as often as in other fields (see table A–13). Among each of these groups, 3 said, "We see ourselves, and others see us, as teachers/practitioners, not researchers." Nine commented that "we [those in composition] get *more*." On the other hand, 2 said that composition research is less well supported than science or social science research, and 2 said that in their institutions, composition *and* English are not seen as "new and impressive."

The discursive responses to questions asking for explanations of attitudes toward research in composition fell into no numerically significant groups, but these comments do further elaborate on answers about availability of support, frequency and success of applications, and perceptions of change that were addressed later. For instance, those explaining the reasons why they had not applied in the last ten years (22 people) included 4 who said they had received money for literary research (1 after three rejections for a composition project)

Table A-13.   Equity in Research Awards for Composition
           (N = 91)

	Number	Percentage
1. Composition receives equal consideration	58	64
2. I know of no inequity	19	21
3. Inequity perceived	14	15
TOTAL	91	100

and 1 additional newcomer who said that he would apply in literature, believing that such an application would be most credible. Five additional respondents said the methods and problems of their research were "too basic" or unacceptable on other grounds, including its collaborative nature. Two others said they "cannot compete" with their peers, and 1 said that the institution wants to fund only scientific projects.

Some were more neutral, including 1 who noted that only a few awards of any sort are available, 1 who did not apply but was "given" leave by his department, and 1 who saw "no need for it yet." Two reported that they had no time to apply, 1 that she "gets all [the released time] I need," and 1 who indicated that "I don't do research . . . at least not the kind that requires outside funding." Thus the definition of "research" in composition as a fundable project was reinforced, as was a significant self-perception that people in composition are defined as busy teachers or administrators who do not require research awards. (Two others answered with question marks.)

This same pattern reappeared in explanations from those who said that they perceived inequality. That is, of the 17 reporting no applications, 4 said that self- and institutionally defined identities precluded applying, at times because of nonfaculty status, large teaching loads, or isolation. Competition with those in literature, with older colleagues, or with all outside "liberal arts" were also perceived to limit awards in composition. But this group also included 9 who saw composition research as having a *greater* chance of funding in their institutions and 1 who saw the process of applying over five years as finally educational for the committee making awards.

Finally, in 48 responses explaining causes for institutional changes toward recognizing composition research, the respondents portrayed the same patterns they perceived in conditions around tenure, but did so with a more positive cast of mind. The sources of change, for instance, include many of the sources for hiring. New faculty, once hired, generate support for research. Sixteen respondents attributed positive change to new faculty. An additional 11 mentioned administrative encouragement from deans or vice-presidents, sometimes as the result of a grant that motivated this support. New undergraduate or graduate programs were mentioned as a source of increased research support by 9.

Results from generalized "change" vary. Other respondents referred to money, some to research assistants, some to released time, some to a travel budget. One mentioned "one whole secretary." While a few who noticed no change explained with "status quo," "it's equitable," or "no time to apply," 5 noted that there is "more knowledge and interest in composition now," indicating that a process of education, like that accomplished by job searches and hiring, has changed their institution's willingness to support composition as a research field, not only an area of teaching.

Perceptions of the Relative Status of Fields in English

The survey asked respondents to rank, on a scale of one to nine, eight fields (literature, literary theory, composition, rhetoric, linguistics, feminist studies, film, and folklore) and an open category ("other") according to their perceptions of these fields' relative status in their departments. The question was intended to discover the lineaments of status among both traditional and changing conceptions of "English" as a whole. The respondents uncovered both predictable and surprising judgments of status within English.

Those responding to this question included 90 who ranked both composition and literature along with most of the other categories, although some fields were not mentioned when they were not represented in the respondents' departments. An additional 15 said this question was "not applicable" to their departments, either because they were not in English departments, or because they perceived all of these categories as equal in their academic settings. An additional 3 answered with dualistic ranking systems that I will discuss at the end of this section.

Because those ranking these fields also used the same rank number across categories to indicate ties in their judgments of status, I sorted out responses according to the number and percentage of times a particular field was placed at a one to nine rank (see table A–14). Taking into account fields unrepresented in departments and others that were given the same numerical ranking in judgments of ties, the total number of mentions in one of the nine categories for ranking may be greater or smaller than the total number of respondents (90) who mentioned both composition and literature. (For example, 102 placed various fields "first" or "second" in status; 91 placed various fields in third place; only 76 placed a field in fourth place; only 29 mentioned a field in ninth place.)

The respondents clearly perceived literature to have the highest status in their departments. They most often placed literary theory in second place, and they placed composition or rhetoric (or the two combined) in third place, where it (or they) received 31 mentions (34 percent of 90 ranking these fields). Linguistics was a close contender for third place, but literary theory and composition/rhetoric appeared again as the fields that were ranked fourth. Each of these options received 23 percent of mentions for fourth place. Linguistics was ranked fifth among the nine rankings. Composition and rhetoric also held sixth place in these rankings. The seventh rank went to film studies, which was placed at that level 12 times. Folklore held eighth place, receiving 13 mentions (23 percent), and ninth place was held by "other."

Evaluated this way, data from these respondents suggest the following levels of status among fields:

1. Literature
2. Literary theory
3. Composition/rhetoric
4. Literary theory and composition/rhetoric
5. Linguistics
6. Composition/rhetoric
7. Film
8. Folklore
9. Other

That is, below the clear leader (literature), literary theory and composition/rhetoric appear to be vying for position in many settings, but composition/rhetoric has relatively low status (in sixth place) in many others.

Table A-14. The Relative Status of Fields within English[a]

Status	Literature	Literary theory	Composition and rhetoric[b]	Composition	Rhetoric	Linguistics	Feminist studies	Film	Folklore	Other
1st	61 (68%)[c]	15 (18%)	19 (21%)	16 (22%)	2 (3%)	2 (3%)	0 (—%)	0 (—%)	0 (—%)	3 (10%)
2d	18 (20%)	30 (36%)	14 (16%)	13 (18%)	11 (17%)	6 (9%)	7 (10%)	2 (4%)	5 (9%)	9 (29%)
3d	5 (5%)	8 (9%)	19 (21%)	11 (15%)	12 (18%)	17 (27%)	11 (15%)	12 (21%)	5 (9%)	3 (10%)
4th	3 (3%)	19 (23%)	13 (14%)	10 (14%)	8 (12%)	12 (19%)	11 (15%)	0 (—%)	6 (11%)	4 (13%)
5th	2 (2%)	5 (6%)	6 (7%)	5 (7%)	6 (9%)	15 (23%)	10 (14%)	9 (16%)	8 (14%)	2 (6%)
6th	0 (—%)	3 (4%)	10 (11%)	9 (13%)	9 (14%)	8 (12%)	10 (14%)	11 (20%)	4 (7%)	1 (3%)
7th	0 (—%)	4 (4%)	5 (6%)	5 (7%)	8 (12%)	3 (5%)	8 (11%)	12 (21%)	10 (18%)	1 (3%)
8th	0 (—%)	0 (—%)	3 (3%)	2 (3%)	10 (15%)	1 (2%)	10 (14%)	6 (11%)	13 (23%)	3 (10%)
9th	1 (1%)	0 (—%)	1 (1%)	1 (1%)	0 (—%)	0 (—%)	4 (6%)	4 (7%)	5 (9%)	5 (16%)
TOTAL	90 (99%)[c]	84 (100%)	90 (100%)	72 (100%)	66 (100%)	64 (100%)	71 (99%)[c]	56 (100%)	56 (100%)	31 (100%)

[a] Example: 90 respondents mention a rank in relative status for literature. Of these, 61 (68%) rank it first in status; 18 (20%) rank it second. Fourteen respondents did not answer.

[b] Combined.

[c] Total percentage does not equal 100 because of rounding.

But mentions of feminist studies must also be explained because this subfield received the fourth largest number of mentions (literature = 90; composition/rhetoric = 90; literary theory = 84; feminist studies = 71), ahead of linguistics (64) and film and folklore (56 each). Given its recent definition as a field, its prominence among more established possibilities for ranking indicates that it will assume at least sixth place (where it received 10 mentions) or eighth (where it also received 10 mentions, or 14 percent), to compete for status with fields now ranked above it. Had feminist studies been combined with literary theory in these data, the two together would clearly reorder rankings in third and fifth place. Nonetheless, 2 respondents noted that they "still fight to get approval for womens' studies courses."

We can infer that these respondents recognized composition/rhetoric as a field as often as they did literature and that they appeared to be aware of recent elevations in its status. Rankings from 3 respondents were excluded from these data because they provided dualistic, past and future, rankings; these rankings commented directly on the changes perceived by the other respondents. One only noted, "I perceive Rhetoric and Composition highly. The Literature people don't." The second differentiated two lists for "older" and "younger" faculty. Combining the three lists shows the following orders for "old" and "new" status:

Old	New
1. Literature	1. Literary Theory
2. Linguistics	2. Rhetoric
3. Film	3. Literature
4. Folklore	4. Film, Composition,
5. Literary Theory	and Feminist Studies
6. Composition and	5. Linguistics
Feminist Studies	6. Folklore
7. Rhetoric	

Obviously, 3 respondents cannot characterize tradition or predict trends. But these lists follow the general disposition of status imagined by most, apart from its reduction of literature's rank.

Those Who Rank Composition First

Those 17 people who ranked composition first in status in their departments usually come from four-year colleges (see table A–15). Although this entire cohort of respondents who were predominantly from four- and two-year institutions is proportionately too small to generalize from, it does make sense that the atmosphere in such institutions would be less competitive in regard to any field and that composition would have been a dominant traditional enterprise of all department members at least until recent designations as research institutions came to some of them. We can at least infer that institutional affiliations account for almost all placements of composition as *first* among possible fields.

Departmental and Institutional Recognitions of Composition

To determine whether composition's perceived status is verified in actual support and recognition, I included three questions about awards for teaching, inclusion of composition specialists in lecture series, and the relative "visibility" of accomplishments in publication and research.

Table A-15.   Institutional Affiliations of Those Who Rank Composition First ($N = 17$)

Affiliation	Number
1. Four-year college/university	8
2. Two-year college	4
3. Research universities	2[a]
4. Graduate degree given only in composition/rhetoric	2
5. Respondent not in an English department	1
TOTAL	17

[a] One respondent was a dean in the field of composition; the other was a longtime department chair in the field.

Teaching Awards

One hundred twelve respondents answered three questions about awards for composition teaching, questions that I took to be crucial in revealing whether the traditional association of composition studies with "teaching" rather than with substantial research is entrenched by, or is meliorated by, special recognitions for excellence in composition teaching. Answers to the questions "Are awards for composition teaching given on the same basis as awards for teaching other courses?" and "Are there special awards for composition teaching?" are tabulated in table A–16.

In response to my invitation to explain any inequities, 12 people gave explanations or qualifications of positive answers. Three who might be called neutral said that there simply are not many awards available for any teaching or that since graduate students do this teaching, they are not eligible for awards. Four who explained on the positive side included 3 who said that composition teaching is rewarded *more* than teaching in other fields, with an additional respondent explaining that awards are given to student writers, not to teachers. The remaining 5 explained negative attitudes toward composition teaching: it "is not esteemed as much"; it has "less prestige"; it is "used as a way to get an education and money, not as a way to give them"; the award given "isn't really for teaching"; and "lip service is paid to teaching writing, but we are 'service' and second class in a research university."

Negative explanations were rare, but the small number who

Table A-16.   Composition and Teaching Awards

	Yes	N/A[a]	Unsure	No
1. Awards given on same basis as others? (N = 112)	73 (65%)	19 (17%)	10 (9%)	10 (9%)
2. Awards for composition teaching? (N = 96)	16 (17%)	1 (1%)	— —	79 (82%)

[a] No teaching awards given.

indicated that there are no special awards for composition teaching does imply that it is not privileged in any way, despite the traditional definition of "teaching" as its mission. Nonetheless, teaching composition does appear to be recognized as often as other kinds of teaching in the departments represented. Almost as many privilege it over other kinds of teaching as appear to stigmatize it when making teaching awards.

Guest Lecturers

One hundred ten respondents answered the question "Have lecture series in your department/institution included composition/rhetoric specialists?" Again, this question was asked to discover whether perceptions of discrimination match departmental or institutional actions, for actual and scarce money is required to invite lecturers. Eighty-three respondents (75 percent) answered yes to this question; 20 (19 percent) answered no, and 7 (6 percent) said it did not apply to them.

To the prompt "if not, please explain," 17 people answered with what might be categorized as neutral and negative information. One said there are no lecturers from any field; 2 said that only creative writers are invited; 2 said that there are only a few invited from any field; and 3 said that internal workshops are conducted. Among those who clearly intended to demonstrate a negative perception, many referred to budget decisions. One said, "Yes, but there is less money for them"; another said that "only if there is money left and I push." One other said that invitations to composition/rhetoric specialists had ceased because of a change in leadership, while 1 responded that "I haven't promoted it, yet." The remaining 4 indicated that "there is no interest in it" (2 respondents), that lectures are "always related to literature," and that composition is "not seen as important."

At least by this measure, composition/rhetoric is seen to be an active and intellectually equitable field in 75 percent of the respondents' departments. This figure indicates that curiosity about it, if not its complete acceptance, has been stimulated across the country.

Recognition of Publications and Research

Of the 105 respondents who answered "Have recognitions for research and/or publication in composition been equitably visible in your department?" 75 (71 percent) answered yes, 13 (12 percent) answered no, and 17 (17 percent) judged the question not applicable. The 13 who explained either yes or no answers might again be separated into "neutral" and "negative" groups. Those 9 who were neutral included 3 who said, "We are recognized without regard to field," 1 who mentioned two people who had written well-known textbooks, 3 who said that no one does research or publishes at their institutions, 1 who said there are few recognitions of any kind, and 1 who answered (predictably, by now) "not yet." Among those 5 who answered negatively, 1 said that while recognition comes, research is done "on our own time." The remaining 4 comments were "writing is not considered a discipline"; "publications in composition don't have the same status"; recognition "is based on traditional literature"; and a summarizing "research in composition still lags behind in significance and acceptance."

Summary of Responses about Supports for Teaching, Lectures, and Achievements

In each of these areas—teaching, invitations to lecture series, and recognitions for achievement—the departments represented are perceived to treat composition professionals and the field equitably. Consistently small percentages of the respondents reported inequity (9 percent in teaching, 19 percent in lecture invitations, and 13 percent in recognition of research achievements).

These data suggest, as I have argued throughout this study, that there are important differences between *actual* conditions and felt perceptions in regard to composition. Few fields comparing themselves to other areas of specialization (e.g., literature faculty comparing itself to rewards and recognition for achievements in physics) would report better dispositions of resources for their teaching or toward recognition of their intellectual research lives.

Tensions, Patterns of Change, and Desires

Assuming that the data resulting from my first questions would reveal unstable mixtures of positive and negative perceptions of the status of composition, I asked additional questions designed to act as further glosses on earlier answers. These included three questions about sources of tension, about perceptions of change over the last five to ten years, and about the respondents' personal wishes for change.

Sources of Tension

The first of these questions was meant to elicit a summarizing and reflexive comment on the experience of the respondent: "Please identify as precisely as you can the sources of any tensions associated with composition that you have experienced in your department."

Since this question was phrased to elicit entirely open-ended answers and no suggestions were made about possible sources of tension, I read its 129 different answers to identify recurring themes. A "tension," of course, implies two forces or concepts that are perceived to be in opposition, so I looked in each response for terms of conflict. For instance, the statement that "composition is not a respectable field" could be opposed by one that says that it is credible, but it might also (as was the case in a number of respondents' answers) be opposed by what one called the "hard fact that it is where the action is," or opposed by others' statements that its lack of respectability creates difficulties about methods of teaching composition. These oppositions are more complex than a vote for and against a proposition; they show a negative symbolic judgment opposing apparent "realities."

In addition, these oppositions urge us to consider whether composition might be "a field" for those who hold degrees in it, publish research about it, share professional affiliations with others they meet because of these interests, and teach it, but nonetheless might *not* be "a field," but only a kind of teaching, in the experienced professional lives of some colleagues. As I identified this and other sources of tension, I consequently remained aware that the respondents were discussing perceptual incongruities along with what they and others took to be *actual* differences that also produce tensions—for instance, differences in student demand for certain kinds of courses.

Tensions Perceived by Those Who Rank Composition First

Answers from the respondents who had placed composition first in their ranking of the status of various fields were distinguished because these respondents might be imagined to be grinding the smallest axes among the whole group. These 17 referred to 18 separate reasons for tensions. Six of these replied that there were no tensions or left the answer blank. The answers of the rest identified all of the areas but one that the other respondents were to mention. That is, among those who believed that composition's status is the highest in their departments, 7 described sources from "within composition teaching." Two identified sources of tension from "ranks"; 2 described sources of tension resulting from "change"; and 2 identified sources of tension resulting from perceptions of composition as a "field." (The comments made on these categories are included in the discussion of all responses below, which takes up these categories in this order, according to their frequency of mentions among the whole. The entire group of responses is tabulated in table A–17.)

Tensions Perceived by the Entire Group of Respondents

I used these views from those who had ranked composition first in status and the remaining 98 responses to categorize

Table A-17.   Perceived Sources of Tension around Composition (N = 129)

Sources	Number	Percent
1. Within the actual teaching of composition	40	31
2. Faculty ranks and power relations	23	18
3. Perceptions of composition as a field	20	16
4. Change	16	12
5. Distribution of resources	12	9
6. No tension	18	14

answers that another reader might have wished to group differently. A fifth category, not mentioned by those who placed composition first in status in their departments, was "distribution of resources," which was mentioned directly by 12 of those who ranked the field lower in status and who cannot be identified by their institutional affiliations with primarily undergraduate or two-year institutions. This absence of references to resources by those from two- and four-year schools might be explained by noting that in these institutions, appointments are usually made to those who appear qualified for a variety of teaching responsibilities that include composition, but not to candidates whose research interests are distinct and require special support.

The five sources of tension related to composition and their distribution among 111 respondents are described in table A–18. As is true of the answers to all of the questions in this survey, these categories for sources of tension might appear among any group asked about any entity or group characterized as "new" in its surroundings. What is distinct here is that composition is in no way "new" in departments of English, but a course and a potential professional affiliation that came into being with American academic departments of English.

Tensions from the Teaching of Composition

The largest number of responses describing sources of tension came from "within" composition teaching, although only

Table A-18.   Perceptions of the Nature of Changes in the Status of Composition ($N = 159$)

Kinds of Change	Number	Percent
1. Changes related to its actual teaching	48	30
2. Changes in its academic legitimacy	45	28
3. Changes related to hiring and tenure	26	16
4. New structures in departments/colleges	21	13
5. Miscellaneous summaries	4	3
6. N/A or unsure	15	10
TOTAL	159	100

a relative few of these (4 among 40) referred to conflicts about getting the teaching itself done—disagreements about the relative merits of exit exams, placement systems, word processing, sequences of assignments, or approaches to minority students. Two others mentioned problems about office assignments and work loads for teaching assistants or a conflict between composition and nonfiction writing.

But 15 respondents identified problems between factions in literature and composition that result when composition is taught by everyone or by some literature specialists. Five mentioned that the high work load and relatively great amount of time required to teach composition are too demanding for those in literature; 4 additional people generalized that composition teaching is "barely tolerable" for literature professionals. Two others simply said that "most people don't like to teach writing" or that it is "onerous." Two mentioned that literature specialists "really teach literature" when they teach composition; 1 mentioned that the freshman curriculum is perceived as "intellectually threadbare" and not central to the mission of English; the remaining person in this group reported that his department chair had said that "composition should be taught in context" and that the composition specialists (unfortunately) manufacture artificial contexts for it.

Another large group among these 40 reported that actually teaching composition creates tensions among those who want to stress grammar and correctness and those who emphasize "process" or revisions in their teaching (9 responses), those who emphasize research-based teaching (2 responses), and those who are perceived to be simply "subversive" (1 response). These 12 respondents, that is, indicate that new methods in composition are a major source of tension when they conflict with traditional ways of teaching derived from conceiving of it as a corrective enterprise, one related to propriety, manners, and passive students. Those who teach composition in ways that do not obviously enact these assumptions create disagreements or a sense of discomfort. This tension is quite unspecific in comparison to disagreements about placement or an approach to minority students, but it is nonetheless quite specific in an ideological sense.

Among this group of 40 responses, 7 mentioned this conflict

in other terms, using the words "older," "traditional," or "senior" to indicate that teaching composition is perceived differently by those who formed images of its purposes and methods before their younger colleagues came on the scene.

If these responses are read together with those similar to them in the category of "change" below, it becomes clear that a primary source of tension from composition as a "new" field is that it disturbs an established ideological framework and its applications in teaching, the framework described in the first part of this study. Colleagues react especially to composition as a "specialization" or a "field" that they consider has "always" been their province, but not as a completing site that housed lower orders of writing, of students, and inevitably of teaching responsibilities. New assertions about teaching composition appear to be outlandish criticisms of long-held beliefs about the nature of success in its teaching. They require self-examination and reevaluation of professional identities that were described and internalized long ago. The opposing refusal in recent composition studies to accept stigmatized status for its teachers or students, combined with further assertions that composition has a "theory," would naturally create tensions among those who have had a great deal at stake in assuming that "among ourselves" the low status of composition and its mechanistic teaching are acceptable, and in fact ideologically privileged, ways of enacting its mission.

Faculty Ranks and Power

A large group of responses (23) connected tensions around composition to discriminations among various ranks of personnel, ranks that take specific privileged or underprivileged relations to composition teaching. Fourteen people mentioned tensions resulting from the place of tenured faculty over either part-timers and nonfaculty or over untenured faculty. In one case, evaluations by those with tenure over unranked nonfaculty were mentioned; in another, resentment of a tenure-track specialist director from untenured M.A.-qualified faculty was the issue. Two mentioned the unhappiness of part-timers about job insecurity, and 3 mentioned "remarks" by full professors that denigrated part-timers or others who teach composition (as the full professors in these cases did not). One pointed to the "guilt and resulting resentment" that stimulate these remarks. The 4 respondents in this group who mentioned tensions between tenured and nontenured faculty included 1 who said that her D.A. degree made her "suspect" and 2 who said that composition evaluations were "not on the same footing" as others and that they were made by "tenured faculty who have not taught composition in recorded history." The remaining response in this group was from a new faculty member who said he needed research projects that would be perceived as "scholarly" by those who do not think composition is a scholarly field. His "tension" was around how to maintain his interest in his field while pleasing those who evaluated him.

Three respondents identified another set of tensions resulting from power relations in departments. One of these said that problems arose because of the productivity of those in composition as against the nonproductivity of some senior faculty members. Two reported other versions of the same perception, with 1 specifying "envy of the young, often female faculty who tend to out-publish many of the old guard."

The remaining 6 respondents who reported the source of tensions in their departments in terms of rank and power included 1 who mentioned quarrels about class size and class loads; 1 who mentioned that while everyone in her department is theoretically assigned to composition, only one-third end up teaching it; and 2 who mentioned a problem resulting when composition people are allowed to teach literature courses. The other 2 mentioned a triangular power relationship that had been alluded to in other respondents' comments on support and recognition of their research. That is, these respondents specifically identified a three-way tension between young composition professionals, administrative support and recognition of their programs and their grants and publications, and older faculty members' nonrecognition of their achievements. Insofar as grants, college-wide writing programs and requirements, and prominent hirings are matters considered in evaluations of deans or department chairs by those above them, we can understand administrative alliances with active composition specialists who nonetheless unsettle their older colleagues. Additionally, of course, deans and department chairs hold their positions because they are perceived to be educational leaders who desire that their units accept change and value high achievement.

Perceptions of Composition as a Field

Fewer responses than we might imagine on the basis of answers about difficulties with tenure, 20 (15 percent), specifically pointed to the identity of composition as a field as a major source of tensions in their departments. The largest group among these, 15 people, explained this tension as a question about the authority of the field as against their untenured status, as against resentments of their achievements in composition, and as against a perception that "anyone can teach composition." Four people in this group further specified that this tension is between their own belief that composition is an equal academic field and their colleagues' perception that composition is "worthwhile" teaching, but not a field. "They see us," one said, "as the rude proletariat."

These 15 did not differ markedly from the remaining 5, whom I grouped together as simply describing "prejudice." One mentioned treatment as a "lesser colleague"; 1 mentioned "slighting remarks"; 2 mentioned worry about "power, turf, and the 'proper' mission of English" and "encroachments" of composition.

The remaining comment about prejudice offers an interesting twist on the denigration of composition specialists perceived as the "rude proletariat." To what appears to be a theoretical contrary, this respondent said his department's "greatest tension is from the hot shot Marxist theorists. . . . They are new, have little time for day-to-day work of the department, carry all the prejudices of their corrupt elders, and speak to graduate students about composition and teaching in tones that say 'if you put your fingers in that shit, they will never come clean again.' They have no way of speaking about what we do." This rich comment reflects on the respondents' earlier rankings of status among fields. Where literary theory is now perceived to be in competition for status with an earlier version of literary studies that presented itself as methodologically monolithic but authorized, new literary theorists may well feel themselves in direct competition with composition specialists. They would thus have "no way to speak" of composition as a natural brother, equally engaged in demystifying written texts and their production. Few Marxist theorists have perceived the teaching of writing as a premier example of inequities that they describe in other terms.

Change

As 1 respondent pointed out, change is always a source of tension. The 16 responses that specifically referred to "change" identified particular kinds of change that do, however, give us ways to understand this specific source of problems related to composition. Eleven referred to changes in enrollment patterns, with 7 mentioning new undergraduate requirements or programs in writing and 4 mentioning changed configurations of enrollment at the graduate level.

Two additional respondents mentioned changed personnel assignments to composition teaching as the source of tension in their departments, and 2 indicated that the field of composition had become too aggressive. As 1 of these said, certainly speaking for a number of people whom this survey did not reach, the disruptive change has been "hiring people who say they 'specialize' in something others have built careers on." This perception that composition is now in some respects an uppity newcomer also appears in other comments on tensions from within actual composition teaching situations, as we have seen.

But 1 respondent described what must be a more common, if rarely stated, tension: "The old problem: there are those who are wistful about the loss of the old-fashioned 'literature-based' English department. They resent the energy and popularity of composition, creative writing, professional writing, and writing across the curriculum. But they also *like* the health these courses bring to the English Department enrollments."

Resources

Those who did not place composition first in status in their departments made 12 explicit references (9 percent) to the distribution of departmental and institutional resources to composition. By "resources" I mean not only funds for hiring, but the resource of already hired faculty members who may be, as one respondent thought, the "wrong" people to assign to composition teaching—people who are resentful about last-minute assignments to composition classes after their originally scheduled classes do not receive sufficient enrollments. Another said that these sources of tension are faculty members from other departments who are now "redundant" and are assigned to composition because "anyone can teach it."

The remaining 9 responses in this category indicated that decisions about actual funds create tension for and about composition. In 5 cases, respondents mentioned that arguments about whether to allocate departmental positions to composition were underway (cf. "Tenure and Hiring," above). Three responses mentioned beliefs that "composition is getting all the gravy." Generalized "gravy" included, we can infer from earlier responses, positions, salaries, and funds that release time for research. An additional person mentioned resentment about high salaries for newly hired composition professionals in tenured ranks. One response mentioned a tenure quota requiring that one of three composition faculty members be released, and the remaining 2 responses mentioned the tensions associated with allocating resources to part-time positions and paying very little to those in these positions.

Of course, people in any field in any department may perceive conflicts caused by resources it does or does not receive, especially if it is new as a field and looked on with caution by its established neighbors. Nonetheless, these responses do reinforce the other views among these composition professionals who identify tensions around composition as results of change, as results of assertions that composition is a field, and especially as results from questioning the established tradition that composition has always been part of English, as the lower transgressive kind of "part" that this study describes.

Perceptions of Changed Status in the Last Five and Ten Years

The second reflexive question asked respondents to step back and assess composition's status: "Please assess the nature of any changes in composition's status in your department in the last five and ten years." The respondents answered with 159 different explanations of their perceptions of change, which are classified in table A–18. Ninety percent of their perceptions fell into five categories:

1. Changes related to the actual teaching of composition
2. Changes in the academic legitimacy of composition
3. Changes related to hiring and tenure
4. New structures in departments and colleges
5. A small "miscellaneous" category

The word "status" in the question obviously prompted responses identifying changes in the academic legitimacy of composition, although the respondents' answers fell into positive, neutral, and negative subgroups in regard to this change. Earlier survey questions about hiring and tenure also may account for answers identifying a change in status as a result of hiring and tenuring composition specialists. But the majority of responses—those about teaching, about new structures, and the others described here—were not directly prompted by survey questions.

With the exception of 15 views of change that saw it as change for the worse or what might be called negatively neutral (it was bad, it is bad), these responses report improvements in the status, teaching, and staffing of courses. This improvement is not insignificant in any of the possible senses of the word: these composition professionals appear to be participants in both substantial and symbolic elevations of composition and its teaching.

Changes in Teaching Composition

Two categories dominated in these 48 definitions of change in relation to teaching: 11 mentioned new writing across the curriculum programs, and 8 mentioned methods and emphases that oppose "current-traditional" teaching. Among these were comments specifying "inquiry-based learning," "collaboration," "the erosion of the five-paragraph theme formalism," "process," and institution of an exit exam. An additional 4 mentioned computer-assisted instruction; 3 mentioned new writing centers; and 1 mentioned "better organization and planning of courses." One mention each was made of emphasizing seniors' research and modeling literature courses after composition process methods. A large number of respondents (27) identified change in educational, not political, terms.

Fifteen other responses among these 48 focused on related changes in curriculum and staff, mentioning varieties of curriculum management. Six mentioned additions of courses or requirements in composition; 3 mentioned adding composition as a possible track in their departments' majors; 1 mentioned decreased class size; 1 mentioned changed course evaluation forms that now focus on the student; 1 mentioned new computerized registration for classes; 1 mentioned that his composition curriculum had gone from two required courses, to none plus an exit exam, to reinstating one course.

The remaining 6 responses referred to changes worked among those who teach composition: 3 mentions were made of staff development programs; 2 said, "We talk more now about composition and rhetoric"; and 1 said that in his department an earlier emphasis on teaching composition had moved to an emphasis on research about it.

No one responding to this question mentioned changes in the teaching of composition that were perceived to be regressive or to entrench practices they did not approve of.

Changes in the Academic Legitimacy of Composition

The next largest number of perceptions of change (45) mentioned varieties of change in the status of composition as a field. Among these, 27 (60 percent) described its elevation, 11 (24 percent) reported no change, and 7 (16 percent) reported negative changes.

The group who perceived *positive* changes in the status of composition explained those changes in three basic ways. Those who were quite general (12) mentioned that composition is now "politically more powerful," that it is seen to be "with us to stay," that its status is "improved but not ideal," or that there is "greater recognition that composition is a specialization, not just teaching"; some said only "onward and upward." Eight others who specified the visibility of the field of composition said that it is more "entrenched," "active," "recognized as a field," or "made visible by Computer Assisted instruction and Writing Across the Curriculum." The third group (6) mentioned specific improvements from specific sources of support for higher status—the administration, graduate students, or student demand for courses. One of these said that a subgroup of those in composition and others outside the department of English now recognize and value composition as a field.

The 11 responses that indicated *no change* in the status of composition in their departments included 3 who said that its status was always good in their settings. Three qualified their perceptions by saying that composition remains as it was, "but now we have a director," "but now we have more courses and faculty," or "basic writing is now supported as a program although its teachers are still discriminated against." Four others modified their perceptions of the status quo with negative explanations: "it is still second class"; "it is still seen as remedial; it *is* remedial in a research institution"; "the Ph.D. in composition is seen as inferior"; and "we have hired a director and now we cannot change anything." The remaining response said only, "No *perceived* change."

The 7 who saw the status of composition moving in a *negative* direction included 2 who had seen administration and faculty outside their departments reduce their support. The remaining 5 mentioned difficulties including "we are all new and unwanted," "we have now hired 35 part-timers in 10 years," "composition was put outside the department and now it is ignored by English," "they are more scared of it," and "its status was higher in '75–'83, then it went down."

These answers indicate, we might infer, that changes in the other categories—in hiring, in additions of courses, or in administrative structures—can also bring with them new problems for the status of composition. "Change" never automatically indicates improvement, for it may include the possibility of instituting new discriminations. Nonetheless, we must conclude that the status of composition as a legitimate academic field has been elevated in the eyes of more than half the respondents.

Changes Related to Hiring and Tenure

The 26 responses that identified change in terms of hiring and tenuring in composition emphasize how important these matters are for changes in a peer group's identification of its "insiders." Six people mentioned tenuring composition specialists as enormously significant, noting that this means that "it is less them and us" or that "these people now serve on personnel committees and can educate the rest of the department, so we are fast achieving parity." Six mentions were made of additions to the department, with specifications of 2, 5, 8, and 10 new members who were "in" composition. An additional 4 mentioned that a director had been hired who had made composition into a "program," and 2 said that "100% of our hires have been in composition in the last [five and ten] years." The remaining 8 who specified hiring and tenuring as the changes in their departments reported resulting changes as "expertise," "the most productive scholars are in composition," "putting the director (WAC coordinator) outside the department," and "grudging acknowledgment" after hiring in composition.

Changes in Status of Institutional or Departmental Programs

The 21 responses that identified changes in their departmental or institutional structures point toward how organizational patterns around any field determine its status, for good and for ill. Fifteen responses mentioned new graduate programs in composition either at the M.A. or Ph.D. level, so it is clear that many equate status with the creation of programs, especially for graduate work in the field. Three people identified improved status with having the "major share of the market" for students. One said only that "we have grown enormously." The remaining 3 responses mentioned that their department's status is either down or improved because of a new definition of the status of their institution or that a new composition research center had been established.

Miscellaneous Summaries

The remaining 4 responses addressing the changed status of composition elaborate on and qualify the nature of change and the common tendency to equate it with improvement. For example, 2 comments in this group might be taken as cautionary tales in miniature. One pointed out that changes related to adding and giving equality to certain personnel may be undone when those people move on to other places. "The future of rhetoric," this person said of his department, "is up for grabs." When a formerly closed environment recognizes and accepts certain people only as token signs of change, not because it has changed its basic metaphors for its self-identity, the loss of these people may leave the institutional setting as it was before they came and may even further entrench its earlier closed identity. This event can create an additional belief that the lost faculty were unfaithful to the department that took them in and that others like them may be similarly exploitive.

Another response specified that new faculty in composition indicate administrative support, but also create control over formerly self-determined matters of teaching and curriculum. The new faculty may also, this respondent said, "give the appearance of strength in a program which is very weak." The importance of this comment is apparent from the many responses to this survey that indicated that only one person in composition had been hired in recent years, sometimes as the result of administrative pressure. An appearance of changed philosophies of composition can substitute for actual change in the texture of composition teaching, its self-identifications, and its perceived status.

Desires

A final question in this group of three invited respondents to summarize and reflect on their perceptions of the status of composition in their departments: "If you could make one change in composition's relation to your department/institution, what would it be?" I asked this open-ended question about the wishes of the respondents to identify the issues that they think of as most important and to prompt them to imagine an ideal future.

Most of those who responded to this question wanted to maintain composition in much the same basic configuration that it now takes in departments of English and their surroundings. Of the 107 responses to this question, 9 explicitly wanted no changes, 4 said they were unsure of their wishes, and 7 did not answer. These 20 (and 1 additional person who said "I would take over") represent happiness with things as they are.

The 87 remaining answers invite more than one classification system. Among them, most people wanted to maintain composition in its current shape but wanted to *correct* specific problems, generally to *improve* what is now done, or to make changes that would *expand* composition staff, courses, or commitments to it of other sorts.

But it is clear that these responses aim toward one focal point: the human issue of alienation, or difference, revealed in answers to other survey questions. In revealing the importance of this affective discomfort, many made comments indicating desires to *integrate* composition better with its surroundings. But an almost equal number indicated desires to *separate* composition curricula, personnel, and research from their traditionally defined roles and the place of these roles in English. For instance, we might take desires to start writing across the curriculum programs as at least implicitly favoring separatism, although this desire is often presented as a way to "help" the English department beyond introductory-level composition courses. The respondents also expressed wishes to redefine the composition curriculum, to distinguish it from the initiating and essentially remedial set of courses that composition was established to be within English. It also appears from the responses that this agenda, in whatever form it is expressed, is distinct from another, which wishes for more upper-level writing courses within English curricula.

Issues of maintenance and of alienation become apparent in comments on the question, which I have grouped for description in yet a third way. Using the language of the respondents to establish categories, I classified these responses according to desires for *changes in teaching composition,* for more and different *resources,* for an *ideal status,* and for variations on *research* (see table A–19).

Changes in Teaching Composition

The major portion of the answers to this question identified the respondents' wishes for composition as issues of teaching. Forty-nine responses (43 percent) expressed desires about the

Table A-19. Respondents' Desires to Make "One Change" in the Relation of Composition to Their Departments ($N = 87$)

Suggestion	Number of Respondents
1. Teaching ($N = 49$, or 56%)[a]	
a. Curriculum	
Expand it	18
Separate it from English	4
Put it in English	1
Varieties of movement	4
SUBTOTAL	27
b. Staff and staffing	11
c. Teaching conditions	
Assignments	2
Course management	6
"Improvements"	3
SUBTOTAL	22
TOTAL	49
2. Resource Allocation ($N = 21$, or 24%)	
a. Increase positions	15
b. Increase money and time	5
c. Equalize part-timers in composition and literature	1
TOTAL	21
3. Achieve Ideal Status ($N = 14$, or 16%)	
a. Eliminate privileging of literature	9
b. Change perception of composition	2
c. Better relations outside English	3
TOTAL	14
4. Change Research Direction ($N = 3$, or 3%)	
a. Greater commitment	1
b. Work with other departments	1
c. Investigate "real world"	1
TOTAL	3

[a] Total percentage does not equal 100 because of rounding.

composition curriculum, teaching conditions, and changes in the staff and staffing of composition courses. The first group (27, or 56 percent of these 49) explicitly mentioned changes in the curriculum that would expand it and/or would either better integrate it with or separate it from English curricula. That is, 18 mentioned additions—of writing across the curriculum (9), of upper-level courses in English or departmental majors (6), of graduate courses related to composition (2), or of remediation and assessment programs (1). Four separatists wanted to "take composition out of English" altogether, while 1 integrationist wanted to place it *in* English. The remaining 4 responses mentioned better integrating either the undergraduate, advanced, and graduate curricula (1), sequencing courses at freshman and junior years (1), or integrating the literature and composition curriculum with a "discourse-centered" model (2).

These responses indicate that many desire to expand the composition curriculum and that within that expansion roughly equal groups would like to integrate it into the English curriculum better or to emphasize its difference from literary studies by establishing pointedly cross-curricular or non-English programs. It is possible, of course, that many who want additional courses across disciplines see this expansion as "help" for English-based introductory writing courses and do not in any way perceive themselves as wishing to emphasize new differences with traditions about composition in English.

The 11 responses that mentioned changing teachers or staffing patterns in courses included 7 who wanted to rearrange the teaching of senior tenure-track or tenured faculty. Six of these wanted senior faculty to be assigned to composition teaching, with 1 mentioning that the result would be to eliminate the part-time staff. The remaining response was, to the contrary, a suggestion that some faculty members should be exempt from teaching composition. Again, we see evidence of desires to integrate and to separate, here with the majority wishing to integrate teaching assignments but with all alluding to the discomfort of alienations and differences.

The third group (11) whose desires have to do with teaching itself wished for changes in the conditions for teaching composition. Only 1 mentioned a change in the content of the course,

opportunities to "vary the five-paragraph theme." Six mentioned changes in course management: 2 wanted reduced class
sizes, 3 wanted reduced loads in composition, and 1 wanted
to raise the number of credit hours awarded for taking composition. Three additional responses called for staff to be guided
by "expertise," to take composition "seriously as a field," and
for the appointment of a director.

We can perhaps safely infer from these answers that most
respondents, when asked to imagine composition in an ideal
aspect, desired to accomplish a change that Carol Hartzog
found to be relatively difficult to make, a change in the curriculum (*Composition and the Academy* 58). Mentions of this desire
may derive from disappointments about changing composition teaching in the past, although they surely also arise from
visions of expansions and improvements of already successful
courses.

Resources

The next largest group of wishes (21) had to do with allocating resources to composition. This group expressed the most
frequently identified desire in any of these categories of
wishes—increasing the number of positions allocated to composition teaching (15 mentions). Ten responses mentioned
adding positions for composition specialists; 5 mentioned simply "more positions." Increases of many sorts were the theme
among this group. Other respondents (5) wanted more pay,
secure funding for TA lines, more released time for composition teachers, upgrading of positions to tenure-track status,
and "more funding for travel, fellowships and postdoctoral
positions in composition, and a journal." The remaining suggestion in this category was that the ratio of full- to part-time
teaching in literature be equalized with that ratio in composition teaching.

It would be reasonable to argue that any group, given the
choice of one change to make in its field's relation to its department, would wish for increased resources. The relatively recent allocation of tenurable positions to composition specialists and the desire to hire more of them indicate that the
identification of composition teachers with only "hired help"
is changing among the departments represented here.

Ideal Status

Only 14 respondents mentioned an idealized status for composition, and 9 of these put their ideal in terms of "eliminat[ing] the privileging of literature." Specifying this desire, some responses mentioned changing the perception that publishing in literature is "the kind of work I really should be doing," changing the makeup of a department over a long period of attenuation, highlighting classroom research to make it equal to textual analysis, and admitting that composition is not of a lower status "even if the full professors won't teach it."

The remaining 5 responses in this category included 2 that might be said to elaborate on these wishes for an improved relation to literary study. One person specified that in her ideal department composition/rhetoric would be thought of as "an intellectual enterprise, not a 'science,' " and another wished that it would be considered "a liberal arts methodology, not a skill." One person said, "I wish some members of the department would not have the 'hydraulic' notion that if a writing program is healthy, then the literature program must necessarily be threatened."

The 3 other responses were also desires to better integrate composition, but with neighbors outside English. Two mentioned bettering relations with departments in education, and 1 wished for rhetoric and English to be reunited.

Research

Few respondents located their most important changes for composition in its research methods or subjects, probably because the question pointed toward departmental, not intellectual, issues. The 3 answering in terms of research mentioned both a generalized "greater commitment" to research and 2 implicitly separatist wishes for working with other departments and for investigating writing in the "real world."

Taken together, answers in all three categories of desire suggest that if we take the respondents to this survey as a microcosm, those who will guide the future of composition want to see the writing curriculum and its staff changed. Whether expressing separatist or integrationist desires, the respondents also indicated that they did not think that their current departmental situations were ideal for actually teaching college students to create their own discourse and that to be effective in this teaching, teachers need other conditions and information that they do not now have.

Conclusions

I have detailed answers to this survey's questions because they were solicited to elaborate on and test my own analyses and especially because recorded comments allow many people to describe the politics of composition. The inferences to be drawn from these answers would include agreement that composition is now perceived to be in a changing relation to its original carnivalesque status: it has become a "field" that produces specialized scholarship, and it is active in the ways that academic professions describe as achievement. But more pointedly, these answers reveal a number of persistent blurrings of identity and status. For instance, while actual rewards and recognition for achievements in composition are perceived to be equitable, these answers also clearly identify a symbolic issue of alienation, an unsettled and uncomfortable sense of dislocation in a time of defining the respondents' field. The comments and wishes for change offer no unified view of how to reduce or eliminate this discomfort, which is felt in relation to hiring, tenuring, teaching practices, and the perduring issue of relative acceptance that stigmatized groups face.

The comments also suggest that composition professionals are now engaged in a reflective process. They are examining new curricula, criticizing the infrastructure of power relations that constrain their interactions, and perhaps mistakenly associating additions of faculty members with necessary change in the structures that have kept composition teaching and students in their ancillary place. In sum, they perceive their field to be increasing its actual distance from its surroundings in, and by virtue of, an affectively unstable situation. Composition is not the formerly accepted lower-class enterprise completing a higher mission within English, but it is not yet something else.

Works Cited

Adams, Hazard. "How Departments Commit Suicide." *Profession '83*. New York: MLA, 1983.

Althusser, Louis. *Lenin and Philosophy and Other Essays*. Trans. Ben Brewster. London: New Left Books, 1971.

Altick, Richard. *The English Common Reader: A Social History of the Mass Reading Public, 1800–1900*. Chicago: U of Chicago P, 1957.

Apple, Michael. "On Analyzing Hegemony." *Curriculum and Instruction*. Ed. Henry A. Giroux, Anthony N. Penna, and William F. Pinar. Berkeley, CA: McCutchan, 1981. 109–23.

Applebee, Arthur. *Tradition and Reform in the Teaching of English: A History*. Urbana, IL: NCTE, 1974.

Bakhtin, Mikhail. *Rabelais and His World*. Trans. Helen Iswolsky. Cambridge: MIT P, 1968.

Bartholomae, David. "Inventing the University." *When a Writer Can't Write*. Ed. Mike Rose. NY: Guilford, 1985. 134–65.

Bartholomae, David, and Anthony Petrosky. *Facts, Artifacts, and Counterfacts: Theory and Method for a Reading and Writing Course*. Upper Montclair, NJ: Boynton/Cook, 1986.

Batsleer, Janet, Tony Davies, Rebecca O'Rourke, and Chris Weadon. *Rewriting English: Cultural Politics of Gender and Class*. London: Methuen, 1985.

Bazerman, Charles. "Physicists Reading Physics: Schema-Laden Purposes and Purpose-Laden Schema." *Written Communication* 2 (1985): 3–23.

Berlin, James. *Rhetoric and Reality: Writing Instruction in American Colleges, 1900–1985*. Carbondale: Southern Illinois UP, 1987.

——. *Writing Instruction in Nineteenth-Century American Colleges*. Carbondale: Southern Illinois UP, 1984.

Bizzell, Patricia. "Cognition, Convention, and Certainty: What We Need to Know about Writing." *Pre/Text* 3 (1982): 213–43.

Blair, Catherine Pastore. "Only One of the Voices: Dialogic Writing across the Curriculum." *College English* 50 (1988): 383–89.

Brooke, Robert. "Underlife and Writing Instruction." *College Composition and Communication* 38 (1987): 141–53.

Bruffee, Kenneth A. "Social Construction, Language, and the Authority of Knowledge: A Bibliographical Essay." *College English* 48 (1986): 773–90.

Cain, William E. *The Crisis in Criticism: Theory, Literature, and Reform in English Studies.* Baltimore: Johns Hopkins UP, 1984.

Channing, Edward T. *Lectures Read to the Seniors at Harvard College.* Ed. Dorothy I. Anderson and Waldo W. Broden. Carbondale: Southern Illinois UP, 1968.

Chapman, David W. "Conflict and Consensus: How Composition Scholars View Their Discipline." *ADE Bulletin* 87 (Fall 1987): 1–3.

Chapman, David W., and Gary Tate. "A Survey of Doctoral Programs in Rhetoric and Composition." *Rhetoric Review* 5 (1987): 124–89.

Cole, Jonathan R., and Stephen Cole. *Social Stratification in Science.* Chicago: U of Chicago P, 1973.

Connolly, Paul, and Teresa Vilardi. *New Methods in College Writing Programs: Theories in Practice.* New York: MLA, 1986.

Connors, Robert J. "Composition Studies and Science." *College English* 45 (1983): 1–20.

———. "Historical Inquiry in Composition Studies." Paper delivered at CCCC, 1984. Qtd. in North 72–90 passim.

———. "Mechanical Correctness as a Focus in Composition Instruction." *College Composition and Communication* 35 (1985): 61–72.

———. "The Rhetoric of Mechanical Correctness." Newkirk 27–58.

———. "The Rise and Fall of the Modes of Discourse." *College Composition and Communication* 32 (1981): 444–63.

———. "Static Abstractions and Composition." *Freshman English News* 12 (1983): 1–12.

Connors, Robert J., Lisa Ede, and Andrea Lunsford, eds. *Essays on Classical Rhetoric and Modern Discourse.* Carbondale: Southern Illinois UP, 1984.

Corbett, Edward P. J. *Classical Rhetoric for the Modern Student.* New York: Oxford UP, 1971.

———. "The Cornell School of Rhetoric." *Rhetoric Review* 4 (1985): 4–14.

———. "John Locke's Contributions to Rhetoric." *College Composition and Communication* 32 (1981): 423–33.

Crowley, Sharon. "The Evolution of Invention in Current-Traditional Rhetoric: 1850–1970." *Rhetoric Review* 3 (1985): 146–64.

———. "Response to Robert J. Connors, 'The Rise and Fall of the Modes of Discourse'. . . ." *College Composition and Communication* 35 (1984): 88–91.

Culler, Jonathan. *On Deconstruction.* Ithaca: Cornell UP, 1982.

D'Angelo, Frank. "Nineteenth-Century Forms/Modes of Discourse: A Critical Inquiry." *College Composition and Communication* 35 (1984): 31–42.

Douglas, Wallace. "Rhetoric for the Meritocracy." Ohmann, *English in America* 97–132.

Doyle, Brian. "The Hidden History of English Studies." *Re-reading English.* Ed. Peter Widdowson. New York and London: Methuen, 1982. 17–31.

Eagleton, Terry. *Literary Theory: An Introduction.* Minneapolis: U of Minnesota P, 1983.

———. "The Subject of Literature." *Cultural Critique* 2 (1985–86): 95–104.

Ede, Lisa, and Andrea Lunsford. "On Distinctions between Classical and Modern Rhetoric." Connors, Ede, and Lunsford. 37–50.

Emig, Janet. *The Composing Processes of Twelfth Graders.* Research Report No. 13. Urbana, IL: NCTE, 1971.

Faigley, Lester. "Competing Theories of Process: A Critique and a Proposal." *College English* 48 (1986): 527–42.

Farmer, Marjorie, ed. *Consensus and Dissent: Teaching English Past, Present, and Future.* Urbana, IL: NCTE, 1986.

Foucault, Michel. *Discipline and Punish.* Trans. Alan Sheridan. New York: Random-Vintage, 1977.

Franklin, Phyllis. Address, ADE conference. Jackson Hole, WY, 20 June 1985.

Fulkerson, Richard. "Four Philosophies of Composition." *College Composition and Communication* 30 (1979): 343–48.

———. "On Theories of Rhetoric as Epistemic: A Bi-Disciplinary Point of View." *Oldspeak/Newspeak: Rhetorical Transformations.* Ed. Charles W. Kneupper. Arlington, TX: Rhetoric Society of America, 1985. 195–207.

Fussell, Paul. *Class.* 1981. New York: Ballantine, 1984.

Goffman, Erving. *Frame Analysis.* New York: Harper-Colophon, 1974.

———. *Stigma: Notes on the Management of Spoiled Identity.* Englewood Cliffs, NJ: Prentice-Hall, 1963.

Graff, Gerald. *Professing Literature: An Institutional History.* Chicago: U of Chicago P, 1987.

Graff, Harvey J. *The Legacies of Literacy: Continuity and Contradictions in Western Culture and Society.* Bloomington: Indiana UP, 1987.

Gray, Donald. "New Ideas about English and Departments of English." *English Education* 18.3 (1986): 147–52.

Green, Mary. Personal interview, Arizona State University. Phoenix, 10 September 1987.

Hairston, Maxine. "The Winds of Change: Thomas Kuhn and the Revolution in the Teaching of Writing." *College Composition and Communication* 33 (1982): 76–88.

Hall, Stuart. "The Toad in the Garden: Thatcherism among the Theorists." *Marxism and the Interpretation of Culture.* Ed. Cary Nelson and Lawrence Grossberg. Urbana and Chicago: U of Illinois P, 1988. 35–57.

Halloran, S. Michael. "On the End of Rhetoric, Classical and Modern." *College English* 36 (1975): 621–31.

———. "Rhetoric in the American College Curriculum: The Decline of Public Discourse." *Pre/Text* 3 (1982): 245–69.

Hartzog, Carol. *Composition and the Academy: A Study of Writing Program Administration.* New York: MLA, 1987.

———. Personal interview, UCLA. Los Angeles, 8 May 1987.

Heath, Shirley Brice. "Toward an Ethnohistory of Writing in American Education." *Writing: The Nature, Development and Teaching of Written Communication.* Vol. 1 of *Variation in Writing: Functional and Linguistic-Cultural Differences.* Ed. Marcia Farr Whiteman. Hillsdale, NJ: Lawrence Erlbaum, 1981. 25–46.

Hillocks, George, Jr. *Research on Written Composition: New Directions for Teaching.* Urbana, IL: NCTE/ERIC, 1986.

Hoffman, Nicole, Jo Miller, Regina Oost, Dean Rehberger, and Susan Staker. "Empowering Student Writers." Panel addresses at Wyoming Conference on Freshman and Sophomore English. Laramie, WY, 16 June 1987.

Holbrook, Sue Ellen. "Women's Work: The Feminizing of Composition." Presentation, CCCC. St. Louis, March 1988.

Horner, Winifred, ed. *Composition and Literature: Bridging the Gap.* Chicago: U of Chicago P, 1983.

Howell, Wilbur Samuel. *Eighteenth-Century British Logic and Rhetoric.* Princeton: Princeton UP, 1971.

Hoyles, Martin. "The History and Politics of Literacy." *The Politics of Literacy.* Ed. Martin Hoyles. London: Writers and Readers, 1977. 14–32.

Huber, Bettina J., and Art Young. "The 1983–84 Survey of English Sample." *ADE Bulletin* 84 (1986): 40–61.

Hudson, Hoyt. "The Field of Rhetoric." *Quarterly Journal of Speech Education* 9 (1923): 167–80.

Kernan, Alvin. *Printing Technology, Letters & Samuel Johnson.* Princeton: Princeton UP, 1987.

Kitzhaber, Albert. "Rhetoric in American Colleges, 1850–1900." Diss. U of Washington, 1953.

————. *Themes, Theories, and Therapy: The Teaching of Writing in College.* New York: McGraw, 1963.

Knoblauch, Cy, and Lil Brannon. *Rhetorical Traditions and the Teaching of Writing.* Montclair, NJ: Boynton/Cook, 1983.

Lachmann, Renate. "Bahktin and Carnival: Culture as Counter-Culture." *Cultural Critique* 11 (1988–89): 115–54.

Larsen, Elizabeth K. "The Effect of Technology on the Composing Process." *Rhetoric Society Quarterly* 16.1–2 (1985): 43–58.

————. "A History of the Composing Process." Diss. U of Wisconsin–Milwaukee, 1983.

Larson, Richard. Letter to the author (describing Ford-sponsored study of actual practices in composition instruction). 23 July 1987.

Lerner, Gerda. *The Creation of Patriarchy.* New York and Oxford: Oxford UP, 1986.

Lunsford, Andrea. "Essay Writing and Teachers' Responses in Nineteenth-Century Scottish Universities." *College Composition and Communication* 32 (1981): 434–43.

Lyotard, Jean-François, and Jean-Loup Thébaud. *Just Gaming.* Trans. Wlad Godzich. Theory and History of Literature 20. Minneapolis: U of Minnesota P, 1979.

Macdonel, Diane. *Theories of Discourse.* Oxford: Basil Blackwell, 1985.

McGann, Jerome J. *A Critique of Modern Textual Criticism.* Chicago: U of Chicago P, 1983.

McLuhan, Marshall. *The Gutenberg Galaxy: The Making of Typographic Man.* Toronto: U of Toronto P, 1962.

Marius, Richard. Letter to the author. 15 May 1985.

Mead, W. E. "Report of the Pedagogical Section: Graduate Study of Rhetoric." *Papers of the MLA* 9 (1901): xix–xxxii.

Meers, G. Eunice. "Specific Aims in the Literature Course." *English Journal* (1919): 488–95.

Miller, Susan. "Is There a Text in This Class?" *Freshman English News* 11 (1982): 22–33.

————. *Rescuing the Subject: A Critical Introduction to Rhetoric and the Writer.* Carbondale: Southern Illinois UP, 1989.

Moglen, Helene, and James Slevin. "Report of the MLA Commission on Composition and Literature." New York: MLA, 1986.

Moi, Toril. *Sexual/Textual Politics: Feminist Literary Theory.* New York and London: Methuen, 1985.

Monroe, Debra. "Fact and Fiction: Distinctions between Composition and Creative Writing." M.A. thesis. U of Kansas, 1985.

Murphy, James, ed. *The Rhetorical Tradition and Modern Writing.* New York: MLA, 1982.

Myers, Greg. "Texts as Knowledge Claims: The Social Construction of Two Biologists' Articles." *Social Studies of Science* 15 (1985): 593–630.

NCTE Commission on Composition. "Teaching Composition: A Position Statement." *College English* 36 (1974): 219–20.

Neel, Jasper, ed. *Options for the Teaching of English: Freshman Composition.* New York: MLA, 1978.

Newkirk, Thomas, ed. *Only Connect: Uniting Reading and Writing.* Upper Montclair, NJ: Boynton/Cook, 1986.

North, Stephen M. *The Making of Knowledge in Composition: Portrait of an Emerging Discipline.* Upper Montclair, NJ: Boynton/Cook, 1987.

Odell, Lee, and Dixie Goswami, eds. *Writing in Nonacademic Settings.* New York and London: Guilford, 1985.

Ohmann, Richard. *English in America.* New York: Oxford UP, 1976.

———. *The Politics of Letters.* Middleton, CT: Wesleyan UP, 1987.

———. "Reading and Writing, Work and Leisure." Newkirk 11–26.

Ong, Walter. *Fighting for Life: Contest, Sexuality, and Consciousness.* Ithaca: Cornell UP, 1981.

———. *Rhetoric, Romance, and Technology.* Ithaca: Cornell UP, 1971.

Parker, William Riley. "Where Do English Departments Come From?" *College English* 28 (1967): 339–51.

Quintilian. *Institutes.* Trans. H. E. Butler. Loeb Classical Library. Cambridge: Harvard UP, 1920.

Reid, Ronald F. "The Boylston Professorship of Rhetoric and Oratory, 1806–1904: A Case Study in Changing Concepts of Rhetoric and Pedagogy." *Quarterly Journal of Speech* 65 (1959): 239–57.

Richardson, Malcolm. "Henry V, the English Chancery, and Chancery English." *Speculum* 53 (1980): 726–50.

Rohman, D. Gordon, and Albert Wlecke. *Pre-Writing: The Construction and Application of Models for Concept Formation in Writing.* U.S. Office of Education Cooperative Research Project No. 2174. East Lansing: Michigan State U, 1964.

Rosenfield, Lawrence W. "An Autopsy of the Rhetorical Tradition." *The Prospect of Rhetoric.* Ed. Lloyd Bitzer and Edward Black. Englewood Cliffs, NJ: Prentice-Hall, 1971. 64–77.

Ryan, Michael. *Marxism and Deconstruction.* Baltimore: Johns Hopkins UP, 1982.

Scholes, Robert. *Textual Power.* New Haven: Yale UP, 1985.

Schweickart, Patriocino. "Comment on Jehlen." *Signs* 8.1: 170–76.

Shaughnessy, Mina. *Errors and Expectations: A Guide for the Teacher of Basic Writing.* New York: Oxford UP, 1977.

Slevin, James. "A Note on the Wyoming Resolution and ADE." *ADE Bulletin* 87 (1987): 50.

Smith, Barbara Herrnstein. "Masters and Servants: Theory in the Literary Academy." Lecture delivered at Ohio State University. 20 May 1987.

Spivak, Gayatri Chakravorty. *In Other Worlds: Essays in Cultural Politics*. New York and London: Methuen, 1987.

Stallybrass, Peter, and Allon White. *The Politics and Poetics of Transgression*. Ithaca: Cornell UP, 1986.

Stewart, Donald C. "NCTE's First President and the Movement for Language Reform." *College English* 48 (1986): 444–56.

———. "The Status of Composition and Rhetoric in American Colleges, 1880–1902: An MLA Perspective." *College English* 47 (1985): 734–46.

Tchudi, Stephen N. *Explorations in the Teaching of Secondary English: A Sourcebook for Experimental Teaching*. New York: Dodd, Mead, 1975.

Tompkins, Jane P. "The Reader in History." *Reader-Response Criticism*. Ed. Jane P. Tompkins. Baltimore: Johns Hopkins UP, 1980. 201–32.

Trimbur, John. "Literacy and the Discourse of Crisis." Unpublished manuscript.

Tuman, Myron. "From Astor Place to Kenyon Road: The NCTE and Origins of English Studies." *College English* 48 (1986): 339–49.

Weber, Samuel. *Institution and Interpretation*. Theory and History of Literature 31. Minneapolis: U of Minnesota P, 1987.

Welch, Kathleen E. "Ideology and Freshman Textbook Production: The Place of Theory in Writing Pedagogy." *College Composition and Communication* 38 (1987): 269–82.

Wellek, René and Austin Warren. *Theory of Literature*. 3d ed. New York: Harcourt, 1956.

Widdowson, Peter, ed. *Re-reading English*. New York and London: Methuen, 1982.

Williams, Raymond. "Base and Superstructure in Marxist Cultural Theory." *Schooling and Capitalism: A Sociological Reader*. Ed. R. Dale et al. London: Routledge & Kegan Paul, 1976.

Winterowd, W. Ross. "The Purification of Literature and Rhetoric." *College English* 49 (1987): 261–73.

Woods, William B. "The Reform Tradition in Nineteenth-Century Composition Teaching." *Written Communication* 2 (1985): 377–90.

Zoellner, Robert. "Talk-Write: A Behavioral Pedagogy for Composition." *College English* 30 (1969): 267–320.

Index

SUSAN MILLER is the author of *Writing: Process and Product*, *The Written World: Reading and Writing in Social Contexts*, *Rescuing the Subject: A Critical Introduction to Rhetoric and the Writer*, and numerous historical and theoretical articles about composition, rhetoric, and academic culture. She has directed composition at Ohio State University, the University of Wisconsin-Milwaukee, and the University of Utah, where she is Professor of English and a faculty member in the University Writing Program and in Educational Studies.